God at the Center

GOD
AT THE
CENTER

Meditations on Jewish Spirituality

David R. Blumenthal

1817

Harper & Row, Publishers, San Francisco

Cambridge, Hagerstown, New York, Philadelphia, Washington
London, Mexico City, São Paulo, Singapore, Sydney

I wish to acknowledge with gratitude the following persons and institutions for permission to reprint quotations:

Rabbi Samuel Dresner for permission to reprint several stories about Levi Yitzḥak from his *The World of a Hasidic Master: Levi Yitzḥak of Berditchev,* 2nd ed. (New York: Shapolskky, 1986). Charles Scribner's Sons, for permission to reprint material from *Contemporary Jewish Religious Thought,* ed. A. Cohen and P. Mendes-Flohr, copyright © 1987.

Library of Congress Cataloging-in-Publication Data

Blumenthal, David R.
  God at the center.

  Bibliography: p.
  Includes indexes.
    1. Bible. O.T. Pentateuch—Meditations.
2. Fasts and feasts—Judaism—Meditations. 3. Spiritual
life—Judaism. 4. Levi Isaac ben Meir, of Berdichev,
1740–1809—Teachings. 5. Hasidism. I. Title.
BS1225.4.B58 1987   296.7   87-45686
ISBN 0-06-254839-5

88 89 90 91 92 HC 10 9 8 7 6 5 4 3 2 1

For Philippe, Jonathan, and Benjamin

Your sons will be as olive saplings around your table. (Psalm 128:3)

Rabbi Joshua ben Levi said, "Why is Israel compared to an olive tree? To teach us that, just as the leaves of an olive tree never fall either in the season of heat or in the season of rain, so the Jewish people will not be cut off forever either in this world or in the next." (Talmud, Menaḥot 53b)

Just as the olive tree does not have leaves which fall all the days of the year, rather its leaves are always green, so here "Your sons shall be as olive saplings around your table." (Zohar I:115b)

Contents

The Holidays

Introduction

THE SETTING

The years between 1740 and 1810 were crucial to the formation of the spirit of modernity. It was during those years that some of the crucial texts which were to form political and cultural life for the next two centuries were written and lived.

These were the years of the emancipation. The Declaration of Independence and the Declaration of the Rights of Man were written. These texts embodied an idea that had been developing for a century—that the common man was entitled to liberty and to self-determination. The texts, in turn, expressed and gave form to two revolutions which became the models for all subsequent assertions of the right to political enfranchisement.

The process these ideas set in motion was not completed with their ratification, however, nor even with the constitutions they subsequently engendered. Neither the Declaration of Independence nor the Declaration of the Rights of Man extended liberty to women or to slaves, and the latter did not include Jews among the newly emancipated. But the text had set the ideal. Modern political history, indeed, can be seen as the history of the continuing enfranchisement of the disenfranchised: Jews, women, slaves, the working class, the poor, the colonized, and so forth. In a certain sense, one can say that the process of emancipation which was set in motion in the years between 1740 and 1810 is still not complete; the texts are still unrealized.

The emancipation, in its turn, rested upon the enlightenment, the belief in the quintessential goodness and rationality of humankind. "Le siècle des lumières" began with Montesquieu and Voltaire and included Diderot, Rousseau, and others. The parallel "Age of Reason" included Berkeley and Hume, while it rested on Hobbes and Locke. Kant and the Germans, too, were a part of it. The enlightenment was rooted in an empirical study of humanity and aimed at freeing humanity from superstition and rooting society in reasoned relations. Critical thinking, education, and human cooperation were seen as the key to achieving humankind's potential. The texts of these thinkers set the ideal. Modern intellectual history, indeed, can be seen as the struggle for freedom of the mind (and later the heart) from the tyrannies of authority, tradition, superstition, fear, social constraints, and even its own darkest side. In a certain sense, one can say that the process of enlightenment is still not complete; the texts are still unrealized.

The years between 1740 and 1810 also saw the development of the Reign of Terror and the Napoleonic state. These political forms were rooted in the authority of the masses, yet they continued to accept the state as ultimate. The emancipation thus produced the adumbration of the modern totalitarian state. Representing the good of the masses, the modern state could turn ruthlessly against minorities in its midst without fear of revolution. The tracts of this period are seeds. They are every bit as much texts of modernity as the tracts of the emancipation and the enlightenment. They too may be seen as the basic texts of modern history. Are they too only partly realized?

Finally, the years between 1740 and 1810 encompassed evangelicalism, that is, the revival of Christian piety. Rooted in parallel movements in Germany, England, and the New World, the "Great Awakening" included such figures as John Wesley, the Moravians, and Jonathan Edwards. It taught a return to personal awareness of God and to transforming religious experience (conversion). It found its roots in the personal reading of Scripture, its authority in the individual layperson, and its expression in the enthusiastic worship of God and in the mission to preach the word of God to others. In the face of rationalism, these texts called for inner illumination. They appropriated the emancipation of the individual for religion. Modern religious history, indeed, can be seen as a see-saw battle for authority between the church/state and the individual's own awareness of God. Here too the texts are crucial, for they set the ideal. Here too they must be seen as only partially fulfilled.

Jewish history in the period from 1740 to 1810 is as varied and as seminal as secular history. The organized Jewish community of the Middle Ages, the *kehilla,* which had its own courts, taxes, schools, and hospitals, died a slow death under the demands of the modern citizen-state. In its place voluntaristic communities and institutions sprang up. This period also saw the preliminary models for the liberal Jewish religious forms of the nineteenth century. Hasidism, of which Levi Yitzhak was an integral part, was born and had its initial growth. Only Zionism had not yet made its appearance during this time period.[1]

Modernity, then, was composed partly of the motifs of emancipation, enlightenment, statism, and personal piety. It worked itself out against the background of tradition and individual human lives. It is still with us, however, as we watch the struggle for a humanistic way of life compete with rising statism, and as we see liberalism compete with fundamentalism. It is still with us as we wrestle with the holocaust, nuclear war, the scarcity of resources, and the sexual revolution. The roots of modernity, however, were all contemporary with Levi Yitzhak of Berditchev.

Historicism, which also has its early roots in the period between 1740 and 1810, taught us to see life as the story of the social embodiment of ideas or motives. Modernity became the ordering of the story of humankind. Sometimes this ordering was seen as bearing meaning, and hence a teleology was derived from it. The spokesmen for the "hermeneutics of suspicion," however, have alerted us to the fact that the telling of the story itself is an act of subjectivity, of choice of motif and language. History itself cannot be a guide; where then does one look?

Life is a series of texts superimposed one upon the other. There are the texts of tradition, the texts of modernity, and the text which is the very fabric of our own lives. Living itself is a story that is told, in which we play a willing (and sometimes not-so-willing) part. Life is the interaction of these texts upon one another. We cannot know the absolute truths of medieval theology or early modern historicism. But we can know what we read and we can know how we relate to what we read. Life is the intertextuality of what we receive and who we, the receivers, are. The "hermeneutics of retrieval" is the art of reading the various texts of our culture and of our lives anew. This book is an intertextual retrieval of one of the texts of early modernity, the Torah-meditations of the hasidic rabbi Levi Yitzhak of Berditchev.

LEVI YITZḤAK: A BIOGRAPHICAL SKETCH

Levi Yitzḥak* was born in 1740 in southern Poland into a family of rabbis.[2] He received a traditional rabbinic education, and by seventeen had acquired a reputation as a scholar. He married into a wealthy and scholarly family but soon left the security of his home to study with the Maggid of Mezeritch, the head of the hasidic movement. In the circle of the Maggid, Levi Yitzḥak discovered fervor in prayer— shouting, jumping around, joyous song, and trembling. He also discovered an intense messianism and a deep mysticism rooted in the difficult literary sources of that stream of Jewish tradition. At one point his family lost its money and Levi Yitzḥak had to seek employment as a rabbi. He served several communities but it was not easy; hasidism was just beginning and the opponents were very strong. He was forced to move from place to place, even taking a job in the north where the opponents were particularly strong.

Everywhere he went Levi Yitzḥak followed the precepts of hasidism: Judaism does not demand that one study all day and night if one has to earn a living to support one's family; study is for all. So Levi Yitzḥak organized study groups for the common people—for the tailors, the bakers, and so on. Judaism does not demand that one practice severe asceticism; God is available to all. So Levi Yitzḥak taught simplicity, sincerity, and joy in prayer. He himself taught a class in the recitation of Psalms for those who could not study. One story among very many:[3]

Several weeks before Rosh ha-Shana, when he was rabbi in Berditchev, Levi Yitzḥak let it be known that he needed someone to blow the shofar in his synagogue. [The ram's horn is sounded on the Jewish New Year to invoke God's mercy in judgment.] At once there descended upon him all manner of shofar-blowers from the city and even beyond, each anxious to sound the shofar in the synagogue of the Rav.

---

*Levi Yitzḥak (pronounced "Lay'-vee Yits'-chak," with the "ch" as in the German and Scottish "Loch") is one name. Jews did not receive family names in eastern Europe until later in the nineteenth century. It is therefore inaccurate to refer to him as "Rabbi Levi" or "Rabbi Yitzḥak." As a matter of fact, Levi Yitzḥak is usually known as "Levi Yitzḥak, the son of Sarah."

formal teaching and preaching. Like other hasidic rabbis, Levi Yitzḥak used the occasion of a Torah commentary to expound his thought. It is not systematic, but it contains depth of spiritual insight. It is the *Kedushat Levi* that serves as the source text for this book.

Levi Yitzḥak's life in Berditchev was not easy. Apparently, during the year spanning 1793 and 1794, he had a nervous breakdown; but he recovered from it. On October 10, 1810, Levi Yitzḥak died. Although he had children and although other hasidic rabbis built family dynasties, no one succeeded Levi Yitzḥak as leader of his followers. Only his work and the stories of his deeds are left to us.

THE THEOLOGICAL BACKGROUND

Jewish theological insight centers about a strange paradox: God is wholly other; He is completely different from us, not to be grasped by our modes of thought and consciousness. Yet God also makes Himself known; He allows Himself to be grasped by our minds and our deepest spiritual experience. Thus the Bible teaches: "To whom shall you compare Me so that I be similar, says the Holy One?" and yet it says: "By this shall he who wishes to be proud vaunt himself: by grasping and knowing Me." The medieval liturgist phrases it this way: "I tell of Your glory, though I have not seen You; I make metaphors for You and depict You, though I do not know You." Maimonides, the philosopher, formulates it according to his own method: "Know that the description of God, may He be cherished and exalted, by means of negations is the correct description" and yet he teaches: "It is the foundation of foundations and the pillar of all the sciences to know that there exists a First Existent." Jewish mysticism also encompasses this great paradox: "One who worships God out of deep devotion is in the realm of the Nothing" and "Then, the male is united with the female."[6] The paradox is the text; the rest is commentary.

As Jews puzzled over the paradox of God being unknowable yet revealed, they devised a series of intermediary worlds to bridge the gap between His incognoscibility and His concrete acts in nature, history, and life.[7] The early thinkers envisioned seven heavens with angels and archangels. Later tradition developed intellectualist hypostases. Still later tradition devised even more complicated structures. Much of medieval Jewish philosophy and mysticism was an attempt to fill in the gap between the unknowable God and His acts as we perceive them.

Jewish mysticism, which is a subset of Jewish spirituality, has many streams.[8] The two within which Levi Yitzhak wrote are the zoharic-Lurianic and the hasidic. The Zohar,[9] a thirteenth-century text, taught that in addition to the layers of angels and intellectual hypostases there was a certain development internal to God. God's "personality," while always whole and perfect, unfolded within itself even before He created the world and revealed Himself. These internal aspects or characteristics are called *sefirot* (singular, *sefira*). There are ten of them (see diagram, page xix) and they evolve from God's utter unknowability *(Keter* or *Ein Sof)* to His quality of wisdom *(Hokhma),* to understanding *(Bina),* to grace *(Hesed),* to power or judgment *(Gevura),* to royalty *(Tiferet),* to lower grace and lower power *(Nesah* and *Hod),* to righteousness *(Yesod),* and finally to the aspect of God that is actively engaged with the universe and its governance *(Malkhut).* God, as the Zohar understands Him, has levels of consciousness, aspects of being. Furthermore, these characteristics are interactive; God is not a stable state somewhere in the heavens but an ongoing dynamic process. This was very heretical, especially in the world of static medieval hypostases which was the milieu of the Zohar.

The role of humankind, according to the Zohar, is twofold: to receive the divine energy which emanates down through the sefirot, the intellectualist hypostases, and the angels *and* to return meditatively that energy to God. This meditation is accomplished through *kavvana,* [10] that is, the proper control of one's consciousness during all the natural acts of living. Thus one should meditate when one eats, studies, does good deeds, has sexual relations, and so forth. Thinking of the flow of divine energy and intending to return it to its source while performing the usual acts of living is the essence of zoharic piety. Sin, according to the Zohar, is improper return of the divine energy. It has as its consequence an upsetting of the dynamic flow from the divine to the universe and back. Sin disrupts the spiritual equilibrium of God and of reality. Levi Yitzhak accepted this worldview and many of his meditations are based upon it.

The Sefirotic Tree

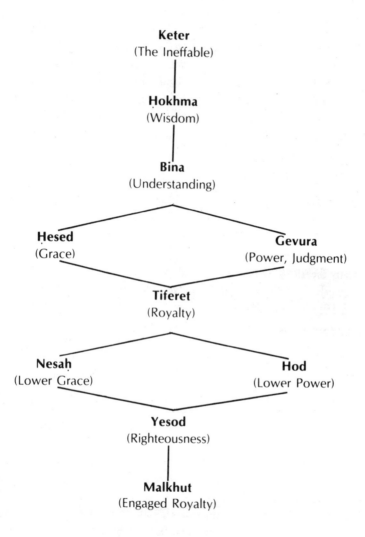

Keter
(The Ineffable)

Hokhma
(Wisdom)

Bina
(Understanding)

Hesed
(Grace)

Gevura
(Power, Judgment)

Tiferet
(Royalty)

Nesah
(Lower Grace)

Hod
(Lower Power)

Yesod
(Righteousness)

Malkhut
(Engaged Royalty)

Almost three hundred years after the Zohar Rabbi Isaac Luria, writing in the city of Safed in the holy land, modified the zoharic worldview and taught that, even before the sefirot developed, there must have been a stage which formed a bridge between God's incognoscibility and His creation-revelation.[11] Luria taught that, in the beginning, there was only undifferentiated God. In order to make room for His differentiated self and for the creation that was to evolve from that, God had to contract part of His being *(tsimtsum)*. Into the void thus created He radiated light. That light struggled to take on form but the light was too strong for the forms and so they shattered *(shevira)*. The fragments of the forms and of the light scattered into the void. These remnants are the shells *(kelipot)* and sparks *(nitsotsot)*. Long after the second and successful act of emanation and creation, the shells and sparks persist as a background to reality.

The souls of the righteous, according to Lurianic doctrine, can sense these sparks which need to be redeemed and returned to God. The task of humankind is to locate and meditatively rehabilitate *(tikkun)* the spark-fragments of the original emanatory act. Sin is an entanglement with the shells which, because they touched the divine at its most powerful stage, have a terrible power. Here too Levi Yitzhak accepted the Lurianic worldview and many of his meditations are based upon it. The zoharic-Lurianic worldview is known as *kabbala,* and it is one current in the mystical stream of the even broader river of Jewish spirituality. In this sense Levi Yitzhak is a kabbalist.

Almost two hundred years after Rabbi Isaac Luria, Rabbi Israel Baal Shem Tov founded the hasidic movement.[12] Theologically, hasidism made some modifications in the details of the zoharic-Lurianic worldview. Two of these need our attention. First, hasidism concentrated Lurianic redemptive action in the figure of the saint or righteous man *(zaddik* or *rebbe)*. This created a new form of holy man in Jewish tradition, one who possesses enormous responsibility and power. Second, drawing on zoharic-Lurianic doctrine but without using the detailed structure of intermediate worlds and forces, hasidism taught that God is everywhere—in people, in acts, in things, in moments. One need only look for Him to find Him. And, in the very finding of Him, one discovers and redeems a lost spark. This allowed a shift in emphasis in hasidism from the scholarly ascetic model of piety to the ideal of the humble God-aware person. And this, in turn, enabled hasidism to reach out to the common people and to become the first mass mystical movement in Jewish history.

Another spiritual contribution of hasidism to the development of Jewish mystical theology was the assertion that it is possible for any person to completely annihilate himself in God *(bittul)*. According to this teaching, meditation on God can lead to complete loss of self-consciousness and self-identity, to a total absorption into God's consciousness, though this lasts only for a few moments. This mode of spirituality is known in other mystical traditions; it was quite new to Judaism.

Levi Yitzhak wrote very much within this hasidic milieu. In fact, he helped shape it. He accepted the designation of the zaddik as the holy man par excellence. He expounded with great vigor the idea that God could be found everywhere and that, in the finding of Him, one redeemed those lost fragments of His divinity that reside in creation. And he advocated annihilation as a mode of worship accessible to all.

In entering into conversation with Levi Yitzhak, modern people will find some of these concepts strange. The zoharic notion that God has a personality which has good and bad sides (grace and stern judgment) contradicts the common idea that God is immutable and perfect. The understanding that God's personality has varying degrees of stability (depending upon the way in which divine energy is returned to it) seems almost heretical, for it subjects God to the vagaries of human spirituality. The notion of the control of one's spiritual consciousness as one performs the acts of everyday life is strange. The Lurianic theology of contraction, shattering, and rehabilitation may seem attractive to the mythic sense of modern people; but the real existence of shells and sparks, both with divine power, challenges the modern definition of reality. Contemporary religious persons will reject the absolute authority of the hasidic rebbe. The idea that God can be found everywhere is appealing; but the corollary—that there is a difference between the social-contextual and the spiritual-transcendental meaning of our acts—will be puzzling. Annihilation will find an echo among mystics, but it is a demanding and new form of spirituality for most modern people. Levi Yitzhak's strong convenantal theology, which asserts the chosenness of the Jew and denies chosenness to the non-Jew, will offend some Jews and non-Jews.

The strangeness of these theological constructs should not, however, preclude dialogue. A conversation, after all, is most interesting and productive when it is between people of differing worldviews. This book attempts to seek the contemporary spiritual insights into humankind and God that can be gained from such a mystical theology.

AUTOBIOGRAPHICAL PROLOGUE

When I was young Abraham our father was my spiritual ideal—the man alone, conscious of God, recognizing the futility of the civilization he had left behind, having property but not being affected by it, and, most important, stolidly pursuing God wherever the search might take him. Even the asked-for sacrifice of Isaac made sense, for God's demands were real even if irrational.

As I grew older Jonah became the figure who most closely resembled the way I saw myself spiritually—the man pursued by God, trying to flee the demand of the Presence yet unable to do so. Even the prophet's annoyance at the success of his mission made sense, for fulfilling God's will does not always bring inner satisfaction or personal recognition.

Since the death of my father and my teachers, I find myself much older. My search for a model within biblical and rabbinic culture continues; indeed it has become more difficult. I have nothing in common with Job, for I have known no suffering. I have no bond with Joseph, for I have neither been specially loved or hated, nor blessed with royal power. I have little attachment to the rabbinic heroes, for they were (and are) vigorous enforcers of God's will. And I have no such political instincts or skills, nor do I believe in political coercion to God's will. I do not have much in common with Maimonides, who has occupied a great deal of my professional life, for he was a rigorous aggressive intellect and I have no abiding faith in the ultimate usefulness of the mind; it can be as crooked as the heart. Finally, I do not have a strong sense of identity with the great hasidic figures of the recent past, for they were (and are) uncompromisingly authoritarian and halakhic (having to do with Jewish law). And I have no blind trust in instantiated authority.

As for models within western culture, I am suspicious of many modern Jewish thinkers as being detached from their roots, of many modern scholars as being engaged in intellectual archaeology, of Zionists as often being unprophetically nationalist, and of self-proclaimed Jewish mystics as being simply deluded. Furthermore, my belief in my ability to change the world has weakened from a desire to spiritually and morally reform all humankind, to a hope that I might influence a few intimates, to general doubt and puzzlement. Can anyone write a theology? Can anyone speak of, and for, God? How much can one person really do for another, spiritually and personally?

Over the years, however, and in spite of the doubt and puzzlement, the Presence has stuck with me. When I have been deeply angry over the fact that the path I chose was not completely my own, the Presence has drawn me to its bosom, quietly, in prayer. When I have studied the holocaust and been horrified, the Presence has embraced me, in moments of quiet reflection. When I have despaired of achieving the purposes I owe the Presence, it has come and been with me, in quiet companionship. In a world that was, and is, ruthless, the Presence has been gentle, if insistent. Always the Presence has been available to me through a personal observance of Jewish tradition. It has not come in the rough and tumble of professional life, nor in the confrontations of communal life, nor in the conflicts of family life, nor in the anguish of my own inner psychological life. Rather, it has come in the privacy of personal religious life and in spiritual moments of deep interpersonal encounter. As such, I have found the experience largely incommunicable. Viktor Frankl has noted that people will talk shamelessly of their innermost sexual life and fantasy, but that they are resistant to sharing religious experience. It is too personal; it is ineffable. I find this true.

In the tension between the Presence, my spiritual models, and my life, I have sinned and have worshiped three idols: my self, my parents, and my community.

My worship of my self, in its simplest form, has been the pursuit of pleasure. In its more complicated form, it has been the imposing of my will and ego on my surroundings. And in its most complex form, it has been my glorying in doubt. "I do what I do because I really want to do it, as an expression of my self"—has been one form of idolatry. "Shouldn't I have taught more, spoken more, insisted more? Shouldn't I have learned more, been more active? How can I make legitimate claims to spirituality when I have failed in so many ways?"—has been another form of idolatry. And yet, deep down, I have realized that neither success in self-fulfillment nor accomplishment in communication and action is the measure of spiritual achievement. Rather, perseverance on the path of the Presence, attachment to the Presence in the face of inner and outer worlds indifferent and hostile to spirituality, constitutes true worship.

My worship of my father and mother, in its simplest form, has been to preserve family traditions because they are family traditions. In its more complicated form, it has been to cling to certain ideas and values held by my parents, particularly many that were unexpressed. And in its most complex form, it has been to shape the personhood of God in the image of my parents. We are all guilty of all these forms of idolatry. As Freud has taught, what we believe and do, our deepest instincts, are molded by a desire and need to worship our fathers and mothers. And yet, deep down, I have realized that it is neither conformity to, nor rebellion against, the patterns, ideals, values, and image of my parents that is the measure of spiritual achievement. Rather, perseverance on the path of the Presence, attachment and loyalty to the Presence, constitutes true worship.

My worship of my community, in its simplest form, has been a defense of "my country and my people right or wrong," a prophetically blind loyalty. In its more complicated form, it has been my unquestioning service to my community's social and political concerns. And in its most complex form, it has been my devotion to the symbols of the community: the flag, the Torah, the unity, the enemy, even the ritual. How often have I seen service, not piety, rewarded? How often have I witnessed the worship of Torah and not God? How often have I too been drawn into this idolatry? Yet these are not the measure of spirituality. True, a Jew must live, breathe, eat, study, and practice within a Jewish framework. But true worship is the dogged return to the Presence, the living therein, and the evoking of that Presence in all aspects of life.

I have been embarrassed by my sins, indeed depressed by the depth of their rootedness in my being. Yet, I have been comforted, again and again, by the haunting Presence that turns me ever anew to face the reality and the basic truth of life lived in God's presence. In response to, and against, my deepest wishes, the Presence has returned me, again and again, to the profundity of the spiritual way.

Which other figures can serve as models for this spiritual way? Who can be an ideal? Three figures in addition to Abraham and Jonah come to mind. The first is the figure of Hanania in Agnon's story, *In the Heart of Seas*.[13] Hanania ("God has been gracious") is a wanderer, detached from civilization and life, without a past, with only a fleeting present, and always moving toward a messianic future. He travels around the world trying, in a small way, to put things back together: polishing old candlesticks, repairing old menorahs, and so on. He "picks up the pieces," as the American metaphor would have it. He is the remnant of the great Lurianic messiah, the modest hidden redeemer.

The second figure is Abraham Joshua Heschel, struggling to integrate his hasidic background, his German scholarly training, and his American experience into a spiritual whole. Traditionally observant yet spiritually alert, Heschel strove to teach and to act in a way compatible with the ineffable living Presence that haunted his life.[14]

A third figure has become important to me in recent years—Rabbi Levi Yitzhak of Berditchev. He is the man who always tried to see life from God's point of view, given God's abiding love for, and promise to, His chosen people, the Jews. Levi Yitzhak is the man joyfully infused with God yet haunted by His presence, swept off his feet by God yet struggling to be with Him. This is not the archaeological Levi Yitzhak, but it is the voice that speaks to me as I grow older.

This book is at once an exposition of that voice and a response from the depths of doubt, puzzlement, and attachment. It is a statement and an echo. In reviewing André Neher's *The Exile of the Word*[15] which is his rereading of the Book of Job, I commented that each person must read the great classic sources three times: once as a child for the plot, once as a young person for the various levels of accumulated tradition, and once as an adult to measure the sources against life as one has come to know it. That is the intent of this book—to take the measure of faith and of the Presence, of life and of spirituality, in the crucible of conflicting ideas and insights. If I have succeeded in conveying a sense of tenacious preoccupation with God and His word in a context of doubt, puzzlement, and attachment, then I have set forth the teaching as I understand it.

ON WRITING A CONSTRUCTIVE JEWISH THEOLOGY

When colleagues in the field of Christian thought write constructive theology, they frame their work in one of three ways. Some participate in a very elegant discussion of the nature of religion or religious language in the contemporary setting. This field includes sophisticated discussions about the hermeneutics of language, learned discourse on the implications of Freudian insight for religion, informed argument on the philosophical warrants for belief and practice, and scholarly debate on anthropological, cognitive, and experiential models for understanding and teaching religious traditions.[16] Reading such books, one feels as if one has dropped into the the middle of an ongoing high-level discussion in philosophical theology with citations and arguments on all sides.

Others participate in a very elegant effort to state clearly the nature of Christian spirituality, faith, and life. This field includes very beautiful presentations of the experiences that underlie baptism, communion, intercessory prayer, and the like; powerful essays on the love of God as it manifests itself in the lives of believers; and moving accounts of mystical or other deep Christian religious experience.[17] Such books are an "explication d'un texte vivant."

Still others participate in a very pressing attempt to derive a program of social justice for the oppressed from religious teaching. This field includes works in liberation theology for Latin Americans, peoples of the Third World, blacks, women, and so on.[18] Such books resonate for Jews because they echo the spirit of the biblical prophets.

Regardless of the content of this constructive theology, Christian colleagues most often write in the form of an argument—that is, they aspire to an orderly presentation of ideas, each chapter dealing with a separate concept or symbol. Books in this area are attempts to be systematic, to make a sustained argument, to present a case.

Insight, however, is not an orderly process; it comes in fits and spurts. Spiritual insight is no exception; it too is irregular as Maimonides, the greatest Jewish thinker of the Middle Ages, especially noted in his *Guide of the Perplexed*.[19] We see clearly for an instant and then our vision clouds over. We sense the Presence intensely for few fleeting moments and then we are back in our normal relational mode with it. It is also true that insight can be contradictory. One's reflection on God's love at one moment may contradict one's meditation on the same motif at another. One's perception of the fear of God at one time may differ greatly from one's experience of it at another. I think, then, that one cannot systematize spiritual insight, that one cannot really write a systematic spiritual theology.

The genre of the book of Jewish theology, even systematic theology, however, has existed since the ninth or tenth century. It is one of the characteristics of Jewish thought in the Middle Ages.[20] But, alongside it, there is an even vaster genre of commentation, of books written as commentary and super-commentary to sacred, and even to simply important, texts. These are, by their structure and nature, not systematic, though they contain profound thought. A Jewish theology, therefore, need not be a sustained argument. It may just as well be a text which is a response to another text. As Michael Wyschogrod has written: "Thought [as opposed to a philosophy] does not have to create a system . . . It does not interrupt its obedience to explore the rationality of the command. Thought probes here and there, always presupposing a living organism that does not suspend its life for the sake of the probes. The results of thought will always be partial, incomplete, even fragmentary."[21]

The purpose of this book, then, is to set forth a series of unsystematized insights into the nature of Jewish spirituality. They center around such motifs as the love of God, the fear of God, saintliness, sex, parenting, communal leadership, mystical experience, chosenness, knowledge of God, and so on. They have as their common core a way of seeing the world such that God and His holiness are at the center of our vision. These are meditations or reflections on life and sacred text as seen from within Jewish spirituality. In the After-thoughts, pages 221–28, I shall try to draw some conclusions.

The form of this book is that of a commentary. It is a response to a prior text. Each meditation, therefore, contains an explication of the source text and my response to it. Sometimes I agree with this partner in dialogue; sometimes I disagree. The reader will have to judge between us. This work, then, exists on three levels—the source text, my response, and the reader's understanding. When I teach this book, I encourage the listeners to respond on behalf of themselves, to participate in what rapidly becomes a give-and-take among the source, my response, and the participants. Insight shared is deepened.

This book, therefore, is not an entry in the ring of philosophic theology. Nor is it a formal explication of Jewish spirituality. It is a series of intuitive understandings, not a sustained argument. It is a palace with many doors, each of which comes from a radiant central room.

There are two ways to read this book. One can begin at the beginning, but one can also begin anywhere. The Table of Contents and the Thematic Index (pages vii and 241) will help the reader find the motifs she or he is interested in. The Glossary and the section on theological background in this Introduction will help the reader understand some of the technical concepts and terms used in the book. Suggestions for further reading are provided on pages 234–35.

In pondering this book, the reader should bear in mind the following questions: Did I understand the source text? What did I not understand? Did I understand the response? If one gets lost, ask the questions: Where is the kernel of holiness in this insight? How does this look from God's point of view? This will always reorient the reader in the right direction. Finally, the reader should not hesitate to be in touch with me. I enjoy hearing from concerned companions who also struggle on the path.

ON MATTERS OF STYLE AND PREFERENCE

In Hebrew, these short pericopae are not called meditations but *divre Torah,* that is, "words of Torah" or "Torah teaching." They are thus not prayerful meditations in the sense that Christians use that term, but short expositions of the spiritual teaching of Torah.

I have been asked how I chose the divre Torah of Levi Yitzhak for explication and response. The answer is complex. Some were chosen because they have a sense of the numinous about them; they touch on the holy as it relates to us. Some were chosen because I am interested in the issues: war, miracles, chosenness, sex, marriage, community leadership, charity, prayer, fear, love, the holocaust, the State of Israel, blessing, and so forth. Here, the point is to illustrate the primacy of the spiritual even in improbable situations as well as to offer a gentle spiritual critique of modernity and contemporary religious forms. Some were chosen to give a sense of the depth and complexity of the zoharic-Lurianic motif of hasidic spirituality. And some were chosen to illustrate the literary complexity of hasidic theology, the interpretation within an interpretation. All these reflections are intended to convey spiritual insight into the condition of modern humankind.

By contrast, I have purposely avoided those divre Torah of Levi Yitzhak which are misogynist, which are steeped in the tradition of play on letters and numbers (Hebrew, *gematria*), which simply are not clear, or which require too great an erudition in the classic Jewish sources for the intelligent lay reader. In these instances technical difficulties or ideological problems limited my choice. Levi Yitzhak is far more complex than this book allows me to demonstrate. But that is not the purpose of this book; it is, rather, to create a base from which I and the reader can respond and engage the process of spiritual reflection.

The language we use about God is like paint; we do not reproduce exactly, we create an impression with it. There is no absolutely right color and there are no absolutely right words for God. There is only the color or the language that feels right when measured against our internal vision and our need to communicate. Language, especially about God, is allusive; it hints; it teaches indirectly. Accordingly, I follow the biblical, rabbinic, mystical, and hasidic tradition of speaking about God anthropopathically, that is, as if He had human feelings and human consciousness. Perhaps He does; perhaps He does not. We speak about Him this way nonetheless for two reasons. First, He reveals Himself in this language, in the image of passion and concern. And second, the model of the human personality is the most powerful analytic tool available to us. It is much more complex than any computer program. It is much richer than any mechanical, intellectual, or biological model. Humanness is of the divine image and Jewish theology uses that language to help us understand God and humanity.

As we, at the end of the twentieth century, ponder humanness in its divine context, we must confront the claim that the language of Western culture, Jewish civilization included, is largely male-dominated. I, for one, think this is true; and, in an attempt to restore the universal human meaning of the divine in religious teaching, I have chosen to use egalitarian language throughout this book. Purists in style may object, but the aesthetic should never take precedence over the spiritual; that itself is part of Jewish theology. The result is that the archaeological Levi Yitzhak is distorted at those points where I include Jewish women in the forms of Jewish spiritual practice. Not that Levi Yitzhak believed that women were devoid of spirituality. He certainly would affirm that they, as fellow Jews, do have such potential. However, he did live in a preenlightenment society in which women had a place that excluded their equal participation in the forms of Jewish spirituality. My choice of egalitarian language is therefore within his spirit, though he, in his milieu, would never have used it or even thought that way.

There is one exception to my choice of the egalitarian mode of expression: pronouns referring to God. Here, I have chosen always to use the traditional masculine form. I have several reasons. God uses that language of Himself according to the tradition. The connotation attached to the use of female pronouns is one of idolatry (to call God "Queen" or "mother" is to defy the strictures of the prophets against worship of goddesses [Jeremiah 44]). It is not just the strangeness of it. And perhaps there is a remnant sexism in me; I feel better with the male pronouns when talking about God. I encourage women colleagues, however, to take similar texts and to write their own explication-response in their own style and with their own issues. Theology grows through serious discussion.

Every author has to choose an audience. I have consciously chosen the educated, spiritually sensitive person who is not an expert in the field of Jewish mystical theology. This includes colleagues in Christian and Jewish theology, fellow clergy, and informed laypeople, Jewish and Christian. Advanced reading in Jewish theology will help—the suggestions for further reading provide such guidance—but it is not necessary. Throughout, I have addressed this audience—which at times includes myself—as "we moderns" or as "modern people." I may have overgeneralized from time to time, but I have tried to catch as clearly as I can the contrast between Jewish spirituality and the common understanding of life shared by modern people.

In preparing a text, an author-editor has to make decisions about punctuation, capitalization, and the like. These may seem to be outside the spiritual but, as Levi Yitzhak teaches, nothing is outside the scope of the divine Presence. I had been capitalizing many words when I stumbled upon "the Golden Calf." The absurdity struck me. How can one capitalize the very embodiment of idolatry? And yet I had done it. But, if one does not capitalize idols, what does one capitalize? That is, to what does one give capital status? I have decided that, as a matter of spiritual principle, only the following shall be capitalized: God, pronouns referring to Him, and words which are substitutes for Him such as the Presence, Name, Glory, Infinite, King, Ayin, Nothing, and so on. Everything else is not He and does not deserve to be capitalized even though one usually does so in English—for example, holocaust, messiah, temple, and so forth.[22] I have, however, retained the usual English usage of capitalizing names of books, places, and holidays. This has been an interesting exercise in finding and redeeming a divine spark in the mechanics of English grammar.

All translations of the Bible and of Levi Yitzhak are my own. I have purposely mixed "Sabbath" and "Shabbat", and "zaddik," "saint," and "righteous person" because these are synonyms. I have tried to avoid technical terms and have provided a Glossary and Hebrew where it might be useful for the informed reader. I have chosen not to italicize foreign words except when they occur for the first time or unless they have special meaning. In the latter category I include only *kavvana* (directing one's spiritual consciousness) because of its centrality to Jewish spiritual thought and practice. All other Hebrew words are in normal type to indicate that they are a part of the normal speech of Jewish spirituality. The Hebrew letter *tsade* is transliterated "ts," "tz," or "z"; and the letters *kaf* and *qof* are both transliterated "k."

It is my hope that this book will be closely read. It is best understood when reading is followed by discussion. It is my hope, too, that it will stimulate spiritual reflection on the biblical source, on Levi Yitzhak, but most of all on our lives. All of us, even clergy and theologians, get caught up in doing the tasks of everyday life and we lose our spiritual bearings. It is my prayer that this book will act as the compass needle for some of those who seek the way.

It is my great joy to thank my students who, over the years, have read parts of this book and responded to it with sympathy and with criticism. Without them, I would never have reached the degree of clarity that the text now has nor would I have had the courage to persevere. It is a special honor for me to acknowledge here my three sons, Philippe, Jonathan, and Benjamin. They have loved me quietly and patiently. They have received my love into themselves. And they have supported me in my work even when they did not understand it. To them, this book is dedicated in love and with the prayer that they will read and meditate upon it, now and later.

Atlanta, Georgia
erev Yom Kippur
the anniversary of the death of
my father-in-law
and my teacher
may their memories be a blessing
5748

GENESIS

Mystical Creation

In the beginning, there was only God. And He filled all space and all time. There was nothing else. No place was devoid of Him; no moment was not occupied by Him. There was only His radiant light, everywhere. Then, from deep inside Him and for reasons known only to Him, He desired to create. So He made room inside Himself. He contracted and cleared a space for His universe. And He said, "Let there be light in the space." And there came forth from His all-encompassing all-filling presence a ray of His radiant light. The ray took on boundedness and there was limit and vessel. But the ray was too powerful for its limit and the vessel broke. And the pieces of boundedness and the fragments of His light mixed in the space and there was chaos.

So He said, "Let there be an attenuated light in the space." And it was so. The attenuated light flowed into the vessels and they did not break. And it flowed from vessel to vessel, being more attenuated with each movement. And there were heavenly worlds of angels, of chariots, and of fiery holy beings. The light continued to flow and it became more and more attenuated while the vessels became more and more bounded. And then there were physical worlds of space and time, of stars and galaxies, and of mountains and storm clouds. God spoke again and there were living things: plants and animals of all species and kinds.

Then God formed humankind, man and woman, and He made them in His image. He commanded them to be fruitful and multiply, and to explore and dominate His creation. And He gave them the power to sense and to focus His radiant light. Each one was given the ability to become aware of and to attenuate His presence according to his or her will. Some could transform the light into wisdom, others into life. Some could turn it into God-fearingness, others into love, and some into the goods of this world. Each human being, having been created in His image, was of His all-encompassing all-filling light. Each could know Him and each could attract and direct that light.

God saw everything that had flowed forth from His radiant light and He knew it was deeply good. And there was morning and there was evening, and there was Sabbath for humankind and for God.

The narrative of the creation story has held untold generations of minds and hearts in thrall with its majesty, its power, and its holy mystery. The narrative as related above reflects the teachings of Levi Yitzhak of Berditchev. It is a beautiful and powerful story. There is, to be sure, much more; but the basic elements are contained in the narrative as presented.

There are two poles to Levi Yitzhak's story: God and humankind. God is not the naively anthropopathic God of the Bible and rabbinic *midrash*. Nor is He the abstract God of the philosophers. Rather, He is the God of mystic all-ness, Who must make room for creation, Who acts by radiating His presence, and Who must do so twice because the first time He overestimates the capacity of reality to absorb Him. He is also a God Who yields control of His creative energies to humankind, Who incorporates human beings into the creative process. Humankind, the other pole, is the respondent, receiving and redirecting God's own energy. Human beings are not political animals or savages. Humankind is, rather, the child who responds, who feels and who acts upon its perceptions.

Between the poles is relatedness and purpose. God gives us insight; we reflect upon it. God enlightens us; we act upon that enlightenment. His purpose is to sustain us and our universe; our purpose is to recognize Him. His purpose is to renew creation at every moment; ours is to know Him and to be always in His presence. There is nothing else. The rest is structure, form. There is only God, humankind, and what is between them. The rest is games we play with one another. The core of existence, its true reality, hangs upon—and indeed, is—the story we tell of creation.

Four Types of Saint

The Bible says clearly that Noaḥ was a thoroughly righteous man (Genesis 6:9). Yet the rabbis of the tradition saw him as a man with faults, as an imperfect saint. There are many explanations; Levi Yitzḥak offered two of his own.

There are two types of saints, Levi Yitzḥak teaches. There is the saint who serves God with great enthusiasm and devotion but does not bring the wicked closer to God, and there is the saint who serves God with great devotion but who also reaches out to bring the wicked closer to the Creator. Abraham is an example of the latter for, in his sojourn in Ḥaran, he "made souls"—he made converts to the worship of the true God. Indeed, the rabbis teach that he who teaches Torah to the son of his fellow Jew is considered as if he had given birth to the child. Noaḥ, on the other hand, is an example of the former type of saint; for he, though he lived in a very corrupt generation, did not rebuke them and bring them closer to God. Noaḥ did not stand up and criticize in the name of God. He did not preach; he was no prophet. And the reason for it, says Levi Yitzḥak, is that "Noaḥ walked with God" (Genesis 6:9)—he walked only with God, content in his own personal spirituality, and he did not walk with his fellow human beings in their remoteness from God.

What a wonderfully strong warning to those who think of themselves as spiritual: do not be proud of your holy reservedness, do not be sure of the propriety of your remoteness from sin and error. Get out with the masses, with the suffering ones, even with the wicked. There can be no saintliness which is limited to the cloister.

Levi Yitzḥak's other explanation of Noaḥ's fault revolves around a principle in the Talmud which became central to hasidism: that God decrees the fate of humankind, but that the saint can actually reverse God's decree. According to this teaching the saint can compel God, so to speak, to reverse a decree of punishment for humankind.

Using this teaching as a basis, Levi Yitzhak asks, Why did Noah not pray to God to reverse His decree? Why did Noah not force God's hand and reverse the decree of the flood? Levi Yitzhak, drawing on the medieval commentator Rashi who says that Noah was "of those of insufficient faith," teaches that there are two types of saints. There is the saint who recognizes his own saintliness and power to reverse God's decree, and there is the saint who does not recognize his saintliness and hence does not reverse God's decrees. Noah, says Levi Yitzhak, was of the latter type. He said to himself, "I am too insignificant to be a saint. Who am I that I should pray to God to reverse His decree?" And Noah also said, "I am no more righteous than my generation. I am no better than they. If I am to be saved, surely they too will be saved." He therefore did not pray to avert the decree of punishment. He was, as Rashi teaches, "a man of insufficient faith." He was too modest, too meek. He was as nothing in his own eyes; so much so that he could not see the plain evil before him for lack of faith in his own piety. Noah, Levi Yitzhak teaches, didn't believe enough in his own saintliness; he was an incomplete saint.

Again, what a strong warning to those who would flee the unpleasantness of spiritual responsibility under the guise of modesty and meekness. To have faith is to recognize spiritual truth for what it is, and to recognize its distortion for what it is. To have faith is to develop and to exercise the power of saintliness. To have faith is to see and to assume the responsibilities of spirituality.

Being and Nothing in Spirituality

This reading opens with God's command to Abraham, "Get yourself out of your land, your birthplace, and your father's house to the land which I shall show you" (Genesis 12:1). The earliest rabbis noticed that the words "Get yourself" (Hebrew, *lekh lekha*) repeat themselves needlessly. Of course, Abraham was to take himself and his household and go. Why the repetition? The famous medieval commentator, Rashi, answers that the repetition teaches that Abraham was told to go "for your own benefit and good." In many years of study, I have heard many interpretations of what constituted Abraham's "benefit and good." Levi Yitzhak also had one.

"The rule is," Levi Yitzhak teaches,

that there are two types of worshipers of God: one who worships God out of deep devotion [Hebrew, *mesirut nefesh*] and one who worships Him out of deeds [mitsvot and other good deeds]. The difference between them is that the one who worships God out of deep devotion is in the realm of the Nothing [Hebrew, *Ayin*] while the one who worships Him out of good deeds is in the realm of being [Hebrew, *yesh*]. Because of this the former, being nothing in the realm of the Nothing, cannot call down upon himself the flow of God's blessings while the latter, being rooted in the realm of concrete being and action, can indeed call down upon himself God's blessings.

In these few sentences Levi Yitzhak has opened up for us one of his stunning typologies of Jewish mystical piety. There are some people, he tells us, who worship God by sheer intensity of emotion. They call up before themselves His Presence and keep it before them. They hold Him in their minds and hearts at all times and try to live their lives accordingly. Ritual, study, ethics, and the rest of Jewish life become a means to the end. There are others, though, who worship God by

observing His commands and doing His deeds. They loyally do what
He has asked in business and in personal life, in ritual and in study. For
them, the means is the end. Both truly worship God; there are two types
of worship.

Having set forth his initial typology, Levi Yitzhak goes on to follow
the logic of each position. Those who worship God out of deep
devotion are, by the very intensity of their way, absorbed in Him. They
are nothing in themselves. They are only outreaches of the great
Ineffable (Nothing) which is God. Hence they have no need of the
fullness of God's concrete blessings and, indeed, are not even capable
of calling it down upon themselves and those around them. Those who
worship God out of deeds, on the other hand, are rooted in the
concreteness of being. They are something, in a realm of commanded
acts. They are agents in a world of real expectations. Hence they need
the fullness of God's blessing and, with piety, are capable of calling it
down upon themselves and others.

Actually, Levi Yitzhak explains, the latter group—those who worship God through deeds—also participate in the realm of Nothing, but
only insofar as they do what they do for the sole purpose of giving
joy to God. They approach Nothingness asymtotically, through deeds.

What is the status of Abraham? As long as Abraham was outside the
land of Israel, Levi Yitzhak teaches, he was not able to worship God
fully for there are many commandments that pertain only in the holy
land. In the exile, then, Abraham was able to worship God only
through deep devotion. Now, however, the time has come for him to
uproot himself and to move to the land of Israel where he will be able
to worship God in full concreteness. The land will draw him from
Nothing to being, from intense emotional reality to concrete physical
reality. There Abraham will be able to worship God through deeds. For
this reason it is, as Rashi says, "for his benefit and good" that Abraham
must "get himself" out of the land of his fathers to the land God will
show him. Only there will he have need of, and hence be capable of
drawing down upon himself, the fullness of God's blessing—including
the child and progeny which are, literally, to embody God's promise
in the holy seed.

It is a strange thought to moderns that emotional intensity is not the ultimate in piety, that deeds and concrete needs are somehow more basic to religiosity than inner feelings. But creation, Levi Yitzhak teaches, is concrete, and spirituality must be so too in order to be true to His work.

The First Step

At the beginning of this reading, Abraham is visited by three men, who are really angels. He—in spite of the fact that he is still recovering from his circumcision—invites them into his tent, prepares food for them, and serves them. After they have eaten, they proceed with their business, which is to announce the birth of Isaac and effect the destruction of Sodom and the saving of Lot therefrom (Genesis 18–19). The midrash intervenes, however, between the meal and the fulfilling of the mission to say that, after they had eaten, Abraham—who for the purposes of the midrash is not aware of the fact that these are angels—invites his guests to give thanks to God for the food they had eaten. This, the midrash says, was Abraham's custom: to extend hospitality to strangers and to draw them, through service and discussion, into a recognition of God.

Levi Yitzhak, ever alert to the text in its concretely Jewish setting, asks the question: why did Abraham not invite his guests to pray before the meal (not only after it) as is the Jewish custom? His answer is that, before the meal, they were still pagans. After the meal, however, because they had afforded Abraham the opportunity to perform the mitsva of welcoming strangers, they were able to accept the yoke of heaven and to do a mitsva themselves, that is to thank God for the food they had eaten.

This is a very profound thought—that no one is eligible to accept the presence of God unless she or he has enabled someone else to do a mitsva first; that no one can even give thanks to God until he or she has first helped someone else to fulfill one of God's commandments.

Moderns would be inclined to think that piety starts with the self: do a good deed yourself and others will follow you; start with yourself and set the example for others. How very modern; how very capitalistic. No, says Levi Yitzhak: enable someone else to do a mitsva first, then you will be worthy to do one yourself; help a fellow human being to serve God first and then you will be eligible and able to serve Him too.

Modern people, even religious persons, would also be inclined to think that to be pious one must simply jump in and start doing good deeds, or that one must simply start observing religious rituals and then only keep up the pace, perhaps adding new observances or new good deeds to one's record. No, says Levi Yitzhak: think less of what you are doing for yourself religiously and think more of what you are doing to enable someone else to be religious. Think less of the good you are doing and more of the opportunities for service to God you are creating for others.

Now that Levi Yitzhak has raised the question, what *did* I do this week to help someone *else* serve God? What did I do this week to enable someone else to be closer to Him? I know what I did for myself, but what did I do for someone else? Will this coming week be better? If Levi Yitzhak is right, only by enabling the other to serve God will I be worthy of the smallest service to Him; only after helping someone else be closer to Him can I even give thanks to Him. This may seem condescending, it may even sound as if one must convert the other; but it is not. It is, Levi Yitzhak teaches, the path to true piety.

On Choosing a Mate

In this reading the aging Abraham must gamble everything on finding a wife for his only true heir, Isaac. So he sends his faithful servant back to his family with the oath that he find a wife for Isaac there and, if not there, then nowhere. Abraham's faith has already been tested and he is sure God will provide. But how is the servant to know who is the right woman for Isaac, for the bearer of God's promise of holy seed? The Bible tells us that the servant, upon his arrival, prays to God and sets up a sign: the women of the area will come to water their sheep, he will ask for water for his camels, and the one to give him water is the one who shall be God's chosen for Isaac. What is the meaning of this sign? Why is the woman's kindness to a stranger to be the decisive factor?

Levi Yitzhak read the medieval commentator, Rashi, who says that the sign was authoritative "because he [the servant] was certain of the merit of Abraham our father." But what does that mean? What merit? Here Levi Yitzhak offers a solution of his own.

There are two kinds of divine energy which God invests in the world: the first is measured, regular, and natural; the second is infinite, unending because it flows directly from God. Up until Abraham, the world—including human society—was guided by God's measured energy. Everything flowed within the bounds of nature and history. Abraham, however, discovered God's special energy, His grace. Abraham could reach out and touch the very well-springs of divine bounty, and he could draw this divine energy into the world, letting it spill over onto others. This is the meaning of the verse, "all the peoples of the world shall be blessed through you" (Genesis 12:3). Also, because of this presence of God's grace, Abraham led a life of good deeds and prayer.

The servant knew all this because Abraham had taught it to him and so, when he came to Ḥaran, he said, "I know the people of this place are evil and cruel, as is the custom among the nations. If, however, one of the women should come and show kindness to a stranger, it would be a sign that the root of her soul is in the blessing that pours forth from Abraham into the world." And so he set up the test for Rebecca with God. Her act of kindness is not simply a good deed. It is a witness to her soul; it is a testimony to God's grace in her life. Note, says Levi Yitzḥak that, when the text refers to Rebecca's lineage the first time (Genesis 24:15), it says "Rebecca who was born to Bethuel," not "Rebecca the daughter of Bethuel," because the root of her soul was in the blessing of Abraham and not in her father. Note too that, when Rebecca performed her kind deed, the servant immediately gave her the presents—before he asked about her family—because he wanted to acknowledge immediately the presence of Abraham's blessing of God's grace in her life.

In these days of computerized dating and live-in relationships, this is a very powerful insight. The person one should marry is the one whose soul is rooted in the blessing of Abraham, whose person is invested with the energy of God's grace—and sometimes a simple act of kindness which reflects that blessing and grace is the only way to tell, for such acts are not socially useful or professionally functional; rather they flow from an inner blessedness.

I know someone who had been seeing a young woman for some time and had been contemplating marriage. While he was still hesitating, the two went to pay a call on his great uncle who was a holocaust survivor. The great uncle was a diminutive man, hunched over, with a number on his arm, who had survived by making belts for the German army in one of the underground factories. He had never learned English and the young man had never learned German. In those days American Jewish families tended to ignore survivor relatives, probably out of suppressed guilt. The young woman, from a German Jewish refugee family, spoke a comprehensible if grammatically inaccurate German. Before the visit she purchased food and flowers to bring as a gift. During the visit she showed a genuine interest in, and kindness toward, the old rejected man, probing gently his situation before the war and his views on family, politics, and life. At the end of the visit they agreed to meet again, which they did. On the way out the young man decided to propose.

These acts of kindness by a young woman, who could have avoided the visit altogether and who, having gone, had no reason to be other than polite, were acts motivated by an inner kindness, by the blessing of Abraham. She could not have known how they would affect the young man. Nor, if she had known, could she have put on such an act. Blessing flows naturally and it is the presence of blessedness, expressed in small acts of unassuming kindness, that should be the critierion of a good marriage partner.

Mystical Parenthood

The reading for this week begins, "These are the progeny of Isaac the son of Abraham; Abraham enabled the birth of Isaac" (Genesis 25:19). This verse raises many questions: What are the "progeny"? The word can also mean "stories"; if so, what are they? Why, if this is to be a story of Isaac's progeny, does it begin with Abraham who is his father? What does it mean to say Abraham "enabled the birth" of Isaac? And so on. The rabbis proposed many answers, and Levi Yitzḥak followed suit with responses of his own.

In Jewish mystical tradition Abraham represents God's grace, God's love for us insofar as that love is totally unmerited on our part. God gives it to us freely; we do not deserve it. This grace is a powerful enlightenment. While the tradition recognizes the importance, indeed the indispensability of this grace, it remained somewhat skeptical about it. Grace is of the other-world; it is too powerful for this world. And so Levi Yitzḥak taught that, in his early years, Abraham was fully exposed to it. During that period he was called "Abram." But, in order to enter this world of progeny and history, Abraham had to compress the grace that was in his life; he had to draw strict limits for it. In the process, the enlightenment was attenuated. This compression and attenuation, however, enabled Abraham to enter the world of our reality and, eventually, to have children. The sign of his movement from pure enlightenment to practical enlightenment is signaled by his change in name from "Abram" to "Abraham." The extra Hebrew letter *hey* enabled him to be a "father of nations," to enter this world. Even after Abraham entered the world, though, he remained the person motivated by grace, reaching out to everyone, traveling in search of souls.

Isaac, in the Jewish mystical tradition, represents the fear of God, the avoidance of contact with the profane so that one can dwell in the awe of God. He does not undergo a name change; he is stable. He does not leave the holy land; he does not wander in search of souls.

Jacob, the third patriarch, is the mixture of the two. He combines the pure and practical grace of Abraham with the fear and awe of Isaac. He encompasses both sets of qualities. He is expansion in grace and compression in awe. Grace is embodied in his name "Jacob"; awe is embodied in his name "Israel." And, since he is the fusion of both, he alone of the patriarchs has two names, both of which continue to be used to refer to him. This combined new quality is, as Levi Yitzhak has mentioned in connection with his teaching on Rosh ha-Shana, "compassionate love" or "loving compassion."

The "children of Israel," then, are those who compel God to compress Himself from grace and awe into the third quality, love. They are the ones who, by their very generation out of the patriarchs, evoke in God Himself the move from grace and from fear to loving compassion. This is the meaning of "Abraham enabled the birth of Isaac"—that the action of Abraham was such that it enabled Isaac to have a child called Jacob, that the influence of Abraham was such that the pure and practical grace he embodied enabled the fear and awe of his son to combine with his own grace and to create a third person imbued with loving compassion.

What a strange way for moderns to view the responsibilities of parenthood. It is not simply providing a home, clothing, inheritance, and so forth. Nor is it creating the educational opportunities and outlets for the personality. It is not even giving psychological support. Parenthood is enabling a child to give birth to another child. It is creating a spiritual momentum that can sustain itself into the following generation. It is embodying a spiritual quality with sufficient strength to generate a counter-quality with the vision of a fusion in the third generation. A parent, Levi Yitzhak teaches, must enable his child to give birth.

Each individual personality, too, goes through a certain spiritual development from pure grace, to practical grace, to fear-awe, and finally to compassionate love. We live as infants in a world of pure grace. Slowly we compress this grace and grow into awe and reverence. Finally, if we have the strength, we develop the ability to move dialectically between expansive grace and compressed awe into true loving compassion. Even God, the tradition teaches, goes through these phases. Even God passes through Abraham, Isaac, and Jacob. And it is the "children of Israel," Levi Yitzḥak teaches, whose very presence compels Him to expand, to compress, and to respond in compassionate love.

A Kabbalistic Meditation

Hasidic tradition, and Levi Yitzḥak as a part thereof, was reticent about its strictly kabbalistic teaching. Such instruction was reserved for the elite and, when it appeared in public, it was presented briefly and qualified by such phrases as "and he who understands will understand," or "examine it and you will find it easy." The reading of this week affords us a clear glimpse into Levi Yitzḥak's kabbalistic teaching, for he takes the dream of Jacob and systematically interprets it in that mode.

The passage reads:

Jacob left Be'er Sheva and went to Ḥaran. He came upon the place and spent the night there because the sun had set. He took one of the stones of the place, put it at his head, and lay down in that place. He dreamed that there was a ladder resting on the ground whose head reached to the heavens with angels of God going up and down it. And the Lord stood over him and said, "I am the Lord, the God of Abraham your father . . ." Jacob arose early in the morning and took the stone which had been at this head and set it up as a monument, pouring oil on its top. (Genesis 28:10–18)

Levi Yitzḥak prefaces his exegesis by saying that this reading always falls in the month in which Ḥanuka is celebrated. The word "Ḥanuka" comes from the Hebrew *ḥinukh,* meaning "education." Education, in turn, means preparing something to be a vessel capable of sustaining the presence of holiness. Jacob's actions, then, are "ḥinukh." They are intended to prepare a vessel for the holiness which is about to flow into it. In his words: "Jacob, our father, set his intelligence, thought, and mind on this matter because he yearned to bring it from potency into actuality, from its root into its branching out, so that the Community of Israel be planted as a complete structure."

What is it that Jacob is preparing for holiness? According to kabbalistic doctrine, God is composed of ten sefirot, ten aspects of being. They are not all alike, nor are they static. They are, rather, different aspects of His personality, so to speak, and they are interactive. The upper three are the holiest, the lowest is the interface between God and the universe. (See figure on page xix) Kabbalistic language provides a series of symbol-words for these sefirot. "Community of Israel" is the symbol-word for the lowest of them. Levi Yitzhak, then, understands Jacob to be preparing, through meditation, the lowest aspect of God to receive holiness from the upper aspects of God. In language closer to modern understanding: Levi Yitzhak understands Jacob to be meditatively preparing the outer level of God's personality for an influx of holiness from the inner levels.

Jacob's actions, then, are to be interpreted as a kabbalistic meditation. Levi Yitzhak recognized, however, that these actions also had two historical levels of meaning: they took place in biblical time *and* they had a general historical meaning, symbolizing the relationship between God and the Jewish people. He maintains, therefore, that the narrative must be understood on its kabbalistic level as well as on its two historical levels. The material, though very complex, is worth pondering.

The meditation began while Jacob was still in Be'er Sheva. He meditated first on the unity of the Community of Israel, historically and kabbalistically. But, while doing so, he caught a vision of the suffering of the Community of Israel: the destruction of the temple and the exile, in its kabbalistic as well as its historical sense. At this point the exegesis begins:

- "Jacob left Be'er Sheva"—Jacob ceased meditating on the seven divine sefirot;
- "and he went to Haran"—Jacob meditated on that suffering and anger [using a play on the words Haran, a place name, and *haron*, anger];
- "he came upon the place"—Jacob encountered the suffering of God Who is with His people in their suffering [drawing on the rabbinic use of *maqom*, "place" meaning "God" and upon Isaiah 63:9, "in all their trouble, He is troubled"];

- "he spent the night there because the sun had set"—the light of his meditation had been dimmed because of the pain of Israel and of God; his ecstasy was interrupted;
- "he took one of the stones of the place and put it at his head"—Jacob meditated on this [understanding "stones" in the sense of letters as in *Sefer Yetsira*] and put it in his thought [head];
- "he dreamed"—Jacob, in his meditation, overpowered the sense of oppression at the pain and destruction he saw;
- "there was a ladder resting on the ground whose head reached the heavens"—this teaches that the roots of the exile reach even into heaven, drawing away divine energy;
- "angels of God were going up and down it"—this teaches that there are some souls who experience return to God because of the exile itself and that there are also souls which experience descent because of it;
- "the Lord stood over him"—although Israel is in exile, God is with them [drawing on Psalm 98:15];
- "I am the Lord, the God of Abraham . . ."—when God saw that Jacob had set his thought on these matters to set them right by meditation, He renewed His promise to Jacob;
- "he set it up as a monument"—Jacob worked meditatively to erect a completed structure;
- "pouring oil on its top"—Jacob drew down the divine energy, which is called "oil," from the sefira of Wisdom, and drew down its vitality and holiness upon everything else to unify all the sefirot, bringing the flow from potency to actuality.

The delicate play of interpretation is hard to catch. On the historical level, Jacob meditates on Jewish history trying to overcome the pain of Israel and God Who accompanies Israel in its woes. On the strictly kabbalistic level, Jacob meditates on the outermost aspect of God, trying to help God meditatively overcome the pain He experiences, thereby drawing on the inner strength of the less-exposed aspects of His being.

For moderns this is very difficult to grasp: that Jacob, and by implication the Jewish mystic, can meditatively set his thoughts on events and change them by drawing on the divine energy; and, on the strictly kabbalistic level, that the mystic can meditatively set his thoughts on aspects of God and help God Himself attain an inner stability by drawing God's inner energies to the surface, so to speak. Yet, this *is* classical Jewish kabbalistic doctrine and Levi Yitzhak, as an heir to that tradition, preached it. In my own prayer life, I have had occasion to meditatively recite certain verses which, according to kabbalistic teaching, kindle the lights in each of the aspects of God's being and I have felt the intensity and truth of this way of worship. Levi Yitzhak, however, also teaches that only at the beginning of a person's way of worship is it helpful for one to be enflamed by the thought that the world depends on the worshiper. Later, however, one reaches the stage where one no longer thinks of that but concentrates on God alone.

Dealing with the Evil Impulse: A Juxtaposition of Levi Yitzḥak and Freud

This reading deals with the confrontation between Esau and Jacob. The younger brother has bought the birthright for a pot of porridge, has manipulated his way to receiving the blessing, has had to flee, and is now ready to return. While away, however, he has become very rich as befits one with a blessing. The older brother has sworn to kill him. What should Jacob now do as he approaches the borders of the holy land, knowing that Esau is coming armed toward him?

Rather than answer this question directly, Levi Yitzḥak turns to an old tradition that interprets Esau as the "evil impulse." According to this tradition, the meeting that is about to take place is really between Jacob's good impulse and his evil impulse. It is an encounter in spirituality, not in political history.

Jewish tradition teaches that the evil impulse is, in the first instance, the sexual impulse. "Were it not for the evil impulse, men would not marry and build houses" (Bereshit Rabba, 9:6). "When the evil impulse attacks a man, he should pull it to the house of study" (Talmud, Kiddushin 30b). The sexual dimension of the evil impulse, then, is part of creation; it is natural. It needs to be channeled, as do all natural impulses. When properly contained it is positive; but it can also be distracting and even destructive.

In a deeper sense, however, the evil impulse is the compulsion that makes one deny and defy God's authority. It is a very subtle force, appearing in many guises. It may appear as anger against God and Torah, or just generalized anger which includes God and Judaism. Or it may appear as depression which dulls the will, blackens the spirit, and causes whatever joy one has to seem pale and listless. Or it may appear in a spurt of wild happiness that denies the bounds of reality. Or it may appear as intellectual doubt, which surrounds one with unanswered questions. It may even appear as super-piety, which self-justifyingly arrogates authority to itself. Jewish tradition knows that the evil impulse has many, many faces, though the common denominator is rebellion from God—intellectual, moral, social, and ritual.

How does one deal with this subtle impulse to rebellion? How does one cope with the complex compulsion to sin? "The heart of humankind is convoluted and compelled; who can know it?" (Jeremiah 17:9). This must have been in the mind of Levi Yitzhak and others as they pondered the proper ways to deal with the evil impulse.

Levi Yitzhak suggests several types of response. On one level he teaches:

The rule is that, when a person begins to draw close to God, one's evil impulse begins to dominate him or her. In this situation, one should think that, through his or her worship of God, one will [certainly] attain to the blessings of this world. In this way, the evil impulse is subdued and cannot undermine one's clinging to God. Afterwards, when one is already attached to God, then one's worship can be only for the purpose of bringing pleasure to God and not for the blessings of this world.

Levi Yitzhak's proposed therapy is simple: make peace with the evil impulse, recognize it for what it is—a rootedness in the pleasures of this world—and make use of it for spiritual purposes. The evil impulse, even in its subtle sense, is part of creation, hence it can be used for good. It is natural, if base, and can be turned to spiritual purposes.

Interpreting the confrontation between Jacob and Esau as an inner spiritual engagement, Levi Yitzhak interprets the relevant verses. Jacob sends messengers ahead with an offering to Esau with instructions that, when Esau questions the messengers, they are to say that this is an offering from Jacob (Genesis 32:17–18):

- "When my brother Esau"—When the evil impulse, who is called Esau;
- "meets you"—meets the holy thoughts [and good deeds] who are the true messengers;

- "and asks you, 'To whom do you belong? Where are you going? And what is all this that comes before you?' "—it will ask, "What are all these holy thoughts [good deeds, and piety]? For what purpose are they? [Is it not only to receive the benefits of this world?]"

- "You shall say to him, 'It belongs to Jacob, your servant;'—one should respond, "We are the messengers of Jacob; through good deeds we are created. Do not speak against Jacob because of his good deeds (and holy thoughts)."

- " 'It is a gift sent to my master, Esau' "—"This goodness also touches you [the evil impulse] for, through good deeds [and holy thoughts], one acquires the blessings of this world and these are a gift to the evil impulse."

Levi Yitzhak's advice for dealing with the impulse to rebel against God and to seek the pleasures of ths world, then, is to propitiate it: to be egotistical but within a calling to God; to seek wealth, honor, and public recognition but only in the service of God; to pursue pleasure but in a religiously constructive sense. Levi Yitzhak advises us to be religiously realistic; to pay the devil his due, so to speak.

Levi Yitzhak proposes another, more sophisticated conception of the evil impulse and a way to deal with it. He does not mention it here, but it occurs elsewhere in his writings and is drawn from his view of creation. Evil, in kabbalistic thought, is not simply the product of the sinful action of people. Nor is it the absence of good. It cannot be, on the other hand, a positive independent force in creation. Rather, evil is the result of the shattering of the vessels. That is, when God first attempted to radiate His power into the universe, it could not absorb that power. The boundedness that tried to contain Him shattered. The shattered boundedness and the now-fragmented divine energy became part of the background of the second (successful) attempt at creation. This background evil is called "the shells" and the background divine fragments are called "the sparks."

The background evil in the cosmos is the root of the evil of this world. It is the source of the vitality and energy of evil deeds. The impulse to deny and defy God, then, does not derive simply from the human psyche. It is, rather, a part of the background structure of the universe; the human psyche only draws upon it. The evil impulse, in kabbalistic thinking, is a manifestation in the human sphere of a flaw in creation. It is, however, a part of creation and hence, like everything else, derives its being and existence from God.

Levi Yitzhak's advice for dealing with the evil impulse in this sense is to examine the evil deed, to explore its roots in the human psyche, but then to meditate on its roots in creation. This meditation will lead to the realization that all evil is essentially a derivative of the divine energy. Evil, in its most profound sense, is contingent upon God for its very existence. There would be no shells if there were no sparks. Having reached that point, and it is not an easy one to attain, one must turn to the divine which is in or behind the evil, to the spark in the shell, and meditate on that. This will lead to the realization of the omnipresence of God—God is everywhere, even in the impulse to rebel against Him. Reality is one. At this point, evil ceases to be grasped as an independent seductive force; it collapses ontologically and falls by the wayside psychologically. One's consciousness is, rather, filled with God. Pondering over the fact that even our evil impulse receives its vitality from God and that we can penetrate beneath its evilness and touch the underlying divine energy is another way of dealing with the evil impulse. This redeeming of the sparks, however, is only for the initiated.

For moderns, the idea of an evil impulse sounds very strange, almost medieval and superstitious; perhaps this is based on the traditions that personify the evil impulse in a satan-type figure. But the real concept, as we have seen, goes much deeper. The evil impulse, as Levi Yitzhak taught it, is not far from such Freudian concepts as compulsion, id, and death-instinct—concepts which are common parlance in modern culture. It is best, therefore, to take Levi Yitzhak's words on that level, as symbols of a deeper layer of human awareness.

How effective are these two ways of dealing with compulsion (although there are others)? I think that those of us who have been through psychoanalysis are left with the feeling that the traditional ways for dealing with compulsion are inadequate. The psychoanalytic way is to understand the origin of compulsions and, when that fails, to go back and understand the origin of the failure. The human heart really is convoluted and compelled (Jeremiah 17:9), and there are levels upon levels of origin and motivation.

One of the basic assumptions of Freudian analysis is that resistance (here in the form of compulsion) is due to personal trauma or to transference distortion. I think Levi Yitzhak would not disagree that personal trauma and transference distortion (though he did not know this term) could be possible sources of resistance. But he adds another source: resistance is really a distraction from the good, it too being rooted in the good. Put differently: resistance (sin) is really a fear of the knowledge of the good, a diversion thrown up by the psyche to cover our instinctive positive knowledge of the transcendent, the divine. Levi Yitzhak would not argue against the functional definition of psychoanalysis. He would argue that everything, even psychological distortion, exists within the broader setting of the meaningful, the good, the transcendent. God, he would teach, is the ultimate ever-present basis of all reality, even psychological reality. The spiritual impinges upon us, even if we do not consciously seek it. Jonah, not Oedipus, must be the model.

This difference of opinion between Levi Yitzhak and Freud leads to other differences. In psychoanalysis, the ultimate value is the right of the individual to unhindered enlightened self-development. Levi Yitzhak would disagree: It is humankind's obligation to hold itself open to the transcendent that is primary. It is humanity's fulfillment within the scope of creation that is ultimate.

Freud did not deal well with the realm of the numinous. For him the transcendent was a projection and the holy an illusion. Levi Yitzhak would not disagree that people project characteristics into God. He would assent to the proposition that our understanding of God is molded by our perception of our parents (though he would not have thought about it that way). For Levi Yitzhak such projection is idolatry; it is a distortion of God as He truly is and even as He has revealed Himself. But Levi Yitzhak would not admit that the penetrating awareness we have of God is itself always a projection or an illusion. He would argue (perhaps with Rudolph Otto) that holiness is a category of awareness on its own—subject to human distortion, but real nonetheless. (Freud seems to have adumbrated this type of analysis in his consideration of the feeling of beauty as nonprojective).

Finally, as noted, in psychoanalytic theory therapy is knowing the roots of resistance. Levi Yitzhak would argue that knowing the roots—even the divine roots—is not enough. There must also be a constructive stage of therapy in which one commits oneself to a view of the world that ranks certain things as evil and hence condemns those impulses that lead in that direction, and which positively ranks both certain goals and the compelling motives that lead us toward them. Freudian theory is weak on this point and psychoanalysts are divided on how this reconstructive phase is to be accomplished.

How does one, in full neo-Freudian consciousness, appropriate constructive values and encourage strong adhesion and aversion thereto? Levi Yitzhak suggests prayer at this level of therapy; that is, an attempt to put one's residual resistance into a larger framework of meaning and power, into the larger context of humankind's place within creation, revelation, and redemption. Prayer puts us within the perspective of God and this enables us to see ourselves, even our sinful resistance, differently. Prayer is one of the stages of therapy, Levi Yitzhak teaches; it is part of the process of repentance. Accordingly, he interprets Jacob's prayer as he goes forth to meet Esau as follows: " 'God of my father Abraham and God of my father Isaac . . . Save me, please, from my brother, from Esau' [Genesis 32:11] . . . Save me, please, from having Esau become my brother. Let it not come about that the evil impulse be my brother." Prayer is an integral part of the way we deal with the evil impulse.

I have spoken for Levi Yitzhak and, while he could not have known Freud, I think he would argue as I have outlined. For myself, I agree that the awareness of God is primary and not only projective; that we do however project and, in the process, distort the transcendent; and that one important element in dealing with the evil impulse (compulsive behavior) is placing it within the larger framework of meaning. This we accomplish through thought, meditation, and prayer.

Dealing with Fear

This reading begins with the words, "And Jacob dwelled in the land of the sojourns of his father." The Hebrew word for "sojourn" *(megure)* can, however, be read from another root to mean "fear" (as in Jeremiah 20:10). This leads Levi Yitzḥak, following Naḥmanides and others, to understand this verse to say, "And Jacob dwelled in the fears of his father, Isaac."

This is a very profound insight. To modern ears, it sounds as if it were taken directly from Freud. In large measure, we do live "in the fears of our parents." In the simplest sense, we absorb such fears as acrophobia or fear of the dark. But, in a more complex sense, we also take on such apprehensions as the fear of competition, the fear of failure and success, and the fear of ridicule. In a still deeper sense, we draw into our being the unexpressed fears of our parents about their sexuality, about their parenting, about their loyalty to their own parents, and about the deeper meaninglessness of their lives. Parents who were insecure—and all parents are insecure, because they are human—communicate these insecurities; we, the children, take these into ourselves by a living osmosis. And we will surely pass on our own fears and anxieties to our children. We do, indeed, dwell in the land of the fears of our parents.

What was Jacob's fear? Isaac, his father, had been bound on the altar and nearly sacrificed to God. Isaac had known the truly awesome power of God. Even if he had never spoken of it to Jacob, the son would have known. It is Jacob who refers to the God of his father as "the Fear of Isaac" (Genesis 31:42,53). The tradition also teaches that Isaac never questioned this truly awesome demand, that he submitted to the will of God with a full heart. Again, even if the father had never spoken of it to the son, the latter would have known of the total devotion of that moment, of its utter givingness. And so Levi Yitzḥak teaches that, in spite of God's promise of protection, Jacob feared that he would not

be able to worship God properly, and hence that he would bring
disaster upon himself and his family.

"Every person must worship God at all times and at every moment,"
says Levi Yitzhak. "One should be joyous always if he or she sees that
Israel enjoys the blessings of this world. And if, God forbid, it is the
opposite, one must share the pain. One should also worry always
whether sin will cause one to stumble and not worship the Creator as
one should." Levi Yitzhak's prescription for this basic element in the
human condition, then, is twofold. First, he teaches that fear is not bad;
that guilt is not to be avoided—even the primitive deep fears and guilts
that we absorb into our being from our parents. Fear is not the best
way of life but it is a natural part of it.

Second, Levi Yitzhak teaches that such anxieties must have a framework, a dimension of transpersonal meaning. Our personal fright and
anxiety must exist within the history of God's relationship to the Jewish
people. When it is well with them, we are joyful; and when it goes
ill with them, we suffer with them. When the Jewish people sings, we
sing; when they cower, we cower. Our personal anxieties are real, but
meaning-less. Our personal fears are poignant, but without a greater
setting. Only God's relationship to Israel gives significance to our lives,
and only when fear is rooted in significance is it worthy of our human
energy. Meaning is a function of chosenness, not an assumption of
personal judgment.

This thought, too, is very profound. Moderns tend toward an understanding of therapy and meaning that is oriented toward the individual.
It is necessary to spend a great deal of time excavating personal fears,
those drawn from one's own experience and those drawn from the
experience of one's parents insofar as they have been absorbed into one's
own psyche. But what is one to do with these fears? There is no life
without fear. There is no life without the transmigration of the subconscious of the parent to the child. But, there is also religious context,
which takes up these fears and puts them into transpersonal history.
There is also social and spiritual reality, which sanctions and guides
anxieties, giving them form beyond the self. And there is holiness,
which gives meaning to a life which is otherwise only personal. This
is the way toward which Levi Yitzhak is pointing.

A Lesson in Being Kind

In this reading, the story of Joseph and his brothers gathers momentum. The narrative, after all, is not about the Egyptian economy but about the history of God's people. Joseph provides against the famine which finally touches the holy land. Jacob must send the family to Egypt to buy grain. The brothers appear and are brought before Joseph, who has been watching for them, knowing that providence has ordered matters so. They come into the presence of the Egyptian lord, not recognizing Joseph. They bow down, in partial fulfillment of the God-sent dreams. What does Joseph feel? What does he do and say? Levi Yitzḥak considers only one of the relevant verses: "And Joseph saw his brothers and he recognized them, but he made himself a stranger to them . . . " (Genesis 42:7). The words "recognize" and "made himself a stranger" are of the same root, though they have opposite meanings. This is common in the Semitic languages and rare, though not unknown, in the Indo-European languages. (The best example in English is "cleave," which can mean "to cling to" and "to split.") Why did Joseph "make himself a stranger" to his brothers, Levi Yitzḥak asks?

The Scripture comes to teach us the righteousness of Joseph, for Joseph had dreamt that his brothers would bow down to him as it says . . . though the brothers did want Joseph to rule over them. It is human nature that, when a person beats another and the latter knows that it is he who has beaten him—that is, that the vanquished knows that by the hand of his adversary he has been defeated, then he [the vanquished] is bitter and he is greatly pained. But, when one is vanquished by another and one does not know by whom one is vanquished, then one is not so bitter. Now, here, Joseph had vanquished his brothers in the fulfilling of the dreams which he had dreamt and, in truth, they did not want Joseph to beat them so that they would have to bow down to him. Here, we can see Joseph's righteousness for, when they bowed down to him and it turned out that he had beaten them . . . and he knew that they would be bitter, Joseph, the righteous one, "made himself a stranger to them" so that they would not be bitter at the victory he had achieved over them and it would appear to them that they were bowing to a stranger. In truth, Joseph was a king and they were not pained because they thought that they were bowing to a king. This is the meaning of the verses: "They bowed down to him . . . he recognized them but he made himself a stranger to them" . . .

It is further possible that this is the reason why Joseph, the righteous one, did not let his father know that he was alive and had become a king. For Joseph knew that the dreams would be fulfilled and that his brothers would come and bow down to him. And, if he had made it known to his father then, when the brothers had come and bowed down to him, they would have experienced pain in that he had vanquished them, for the knowledge of the father would also have been the knowledge of the sons. Therefore, he did not let his father know . . .

There is so much truth in the side of human nature that Levi Yitzḥak has shown to us. Even nice people, when they get a chance to crow over someone, they usually do so—especially if there has been a history of animosity between them. It is very rare that we really can lord it over someone else, especially an enemy; and when we can we usually do so. It is, as Levi Yitzḥak says, human nature (Hebrew *derekh ha-teva'*). But that doesn't make it right. Joseph, who in rabbinic tradition and especially in kabbalistic tradition is known as "the righteous one" because of his resistance to the wife of Potiphar, would certainly not have behaved that way. He would have set a good example for all of us. And indeed he does so by hiding his identity so that his brothers not be embarrassed. (There are other reasons for this too; see the next reading.) Interestingly, at the end of the Joseph story, after the death of Jacob, the brothers sense that their position is weak, they come to Joseph, bow down again—this time in full awareness of who he is—proclaim themselves his slaves and ask his forgiveness. Joseph does not seem surprised but responds, "Do not be afraid, for do I stand in the place of God? You planned evil against me but God designed it for the good so that it would happen this day that a great people be kept alive" (Genesis 50:15–20). Again, Joseph eschews the ego victory and protectingly comforts his brothers.

The problem of why Joseph did not ever contact his father is a vexing one. The novelist Thomas Mann wrestles with it too, pointing out that Joseph did not try to escape from the Ishmaelite caravan, nor did he contact his father discretely even when he later had the power to do so. Levi Yitzḥak sees the answer to this problem in Joseph's kindness. Thomas Mann sees it in the mystery of providence at work in Joseph's life; he must wait for the dénouement before revealing himself. The next reading returns to this theme.

Joseph and His Brothers: Three Levels

With the opening lines of this reading, we reach the climax of the story of Joseph and his brothers. Benjamin has been brought to Egypt, has been caught with Joseph's cup, and is to be kept from returning to his father, Jacob. All effort by the brothers to understand what is happening to them has failed. Now Judah steps forward and in sixteen verses makes the speech that brings this story to its climax. What did he say? How does he resolve the decades of human tension that make up this story?

Judah recounts the simple facts, including Jacob's warning that, should Benjamin not return, the brothers will have sent their father to the grave in great sorrow. Judah admits that to return without Benjamin is to sin personally against his father, since he has assumed responsibility for him. And he pleads to be imprisoned in Benjamin's stead so that he not have to return and see the anguish of his father. Why does this simple récit work?

Commentators from the earliest rabbis to the latest scholars have struggled with this. So have such great novelists as Thomas Mann, one of the best commentators on this story. My own instinct is to say that Joseph accepted what had been done to him as somehow within the design of Providence. He says as much to the brothers further on. He holds no grudges. People do not control their own fates except in a very modest way, and Joseph realizes that. Perhaps, in some remote corner of his mind, he realizes that he may even have deserved some of what happened to him.

For Joseph, the whole entrapment scheme revolves around Jacob: How could the brothers have done to Jacob what they did? How could they have taken his favorite child and told him that the child had been killed? How could they have caused their father so much anguish, especially since Jacob probably suspected that the hand of the brothers was behind Joseph's disappearance? This, it seems to me, is Joseph's question. If so, it explains the success of Judah's speech for, in it, he talks only of the suffering that the imprisonment of Benjamin will cause to Jacob. In his speech, Judah acknowledges that they caused their father pain once and that to do so again is simply unthinkable. With that, the story reaches its dénouement.

But is that the end of the meaning of the story? Or is the story of Judah's appeal to Joseph significant on a deeper level? Here Levi Yitzhak comes to our aid. The story, he teaches, is not just a narrative of family tensions. It is rather a paradigm of Israel's relationship with God. The Jews are always trying to be good children to their heavenly Father. They sin from time to time but they love Him nonetheless. Yet fate seems to play all sorts of games on them. Destiny mocks their good intentions. And so they are always in danger. Joseph, says Levi Yitzhak, is the Holy One, blessed be He, and Judah is the Community of Israel. Judah, the leader of the Jews, the saint of the people, steps forward in this perplexing moment when the winds of fate are blowing ever so irregularly and addresses God disguised as capricious destiny. His address has three elements: the simple fact of the goodwill of the children and their love for God their Father, the admission that they have caused Him grief, and the simple prayer that he, the saint, may be acceptable as a sacrifice and substitute so that the Father not be pained even more. Love, confession, and prayer, Levi Yitzhak teaches, are the only power the Community of Israel possesses. They are also the basis of the power of the zaddik, the saint.

There is something very poignant in this vision. History works against the Jews. And, when they confront it, they can only claim their goodwill, confess their sins, and pray that through them God be spared further anguish. The vagaries of life also work against the saint. He or she can only confront its irrationalities and lay claim to goodwill, confession, and prayer. I think, in this connection, of the rebbes of the holocaust. Can they have done anything more than Judah did? They had only the affirmation of God's fatherhood, the confession of their sins, and the prayer that their lives be acceptable atonement. They can have wanted only that God not have to see what was happening to His children.

This story is also, Levi Yitzḥak says, a kabbalistic text. In that mode of thinking Joseph, the Holy One blessed be He, represents God's inner self while Judah, the Community of Israel, represents God's outer self. The one is Tiferet; the other Malkhut. We are all familiar with the phenomenon of inner and outer selves from our own psychology. We talk to ourselves. We think to ourselves. We wrestle with our inner thoughts and feelings, struggling to bring them to expression. God too, kabbalistic mysticism teaches, has these moments when He must talk to Himself and try to decide what to do. This story, then, is really the story of God arguing with Himself about the fate of the Jews. One part of Him is severe and wants to see the people punished while the other part wants an ongoing relationship tempered with realism. As Judah steps forward, Malkhut finds voice. As Judah admits God's fatherhood and the people's sinfulness and then pleads for atonement, Malkhut too admits that, in His innermost self, God can demand the ultimate, but pleads that He ought not to do so. As Judah speaks of love betrayed yet present and yearning, so does Malkhut. And then Joseph, the Holy One blessed be He, is moved. Then God, in His innermost being, is touched, is filled with love, and is reconciled with His children.

This vision too is beautiful. What happens on earth, even in the most perplexing cross currents of fate, is a reflection of what goes on on-high. An act of saintliness here is reflected in a similar act in God Himself. Our story is personal, familial; it is also national, historical; but it is also mystical, divine.

The Vicissitudes of the Life of Prayer

Levi Yitzhak devotes several interpretations in this week's reading to the topic of prayer. Was it, perhaps, because there is now again a long period of time between holidays and, hence, a relatively dry period spiritually? Levi Yitzhak does not say but his observations on the prayer life are very astute.

"Judah, your brothers will acknowledge you . . . the sons of your father will bow down to you" (Genesis 49:8). "Judah," Levi Yitzhak teaches, is the quality of Malkhut, God's face to creation, which is perceived by the souls of Jews. And "your brothers" is the Jewish people who are called that by God as it says, "for the sake of My brothers and friends" (Psalm 122:8). The verse from this reading, then, is speaking about our prayer to God. It is not simply Jacob's blessing to his son. Levi Yitzhak continues:

It is known that every person must strengthen his or her heart with the faith that the Holy One, blessed be He, certainly does not reject, God forbid, the prayer of any member of His people even though He is "great, powerful, and awesome" and even though "silence [alone] is worthy of Him." Rather, the words of His people, even of one who is, God forbid, on the lowest of the rungs, is precious to Him and the Creator, may He be blessed, takes pleasure in this.

Yet, let not anyone think, "If the goodness of the Holy One, blessed be He, is so great, why then should I pray with a broken and contrite heart? Without that, God will also accept my prayer!" It is forbidden to think this way. Rather, one should think, before praying, how many angels He has, each of whom is equal to one third of reality. And yet each of them is as a mustard seed in comparison to the angel that is above . . . And all of them are as nothing in comparison to His throne of Glory. All ask, "Where is His Glory?" You, human being, let your ears hear what your mouth is saying, "They [the angels] all are beloved, they all are specially created, they all are powerful, they all do God's will in fear and in awe" [the daily liturgy]. On realizing this, one should tremble and faint when standing to pray before the great King. And it is proper that one's limbs shake. Similarly, after praying, one should think, "How can I dare to bring out of my mouth useless words and enjoy them? Have I not just spoken before the great and awesome King? And will I not have to speak again before Him Whose Glory fills the universe?" [If one does all this], then it may come to pass that one's prayer be acceptable before Him, may He be blessed, and that one's requests be filled for good.

From this kind of praying, the Creator, may He be blessed, receives pleasure which, in turn, causes a flow from Him to all the worlds, for everything depends on the deeds of the lower beings and upon our prayers . . . our words are very precious to Him . . .

Levi Yitzhak goes on to teach that there are two types of prayer: one which we do because *we* experience the pleasure of the joy of our enthusiasm and we want to devote ourselves always to this enthusiastic worship of God so that we continue to experience joy and derive pleasure therefrom; and the other which we do only because it causes joy to God, because *He* experiences pleasure at our worship of Him. This latter is a higher form of worship. The two types are embodied in the rabbinic rule that, when one comes to "Blessed are You" (at certain points in the liturgy), one bows on the word "Blessed" signifying the bringing down of God's blessing for our own joy, and one straightens up on the word "You" signifying the raising of our prayers to heaven for God's benefit, so to speak. This is also the true meaning of the "you" in the verse from this reading: "Judah [God], your brothers [Your people] will praise you [You]." They will lift their prayers to You, for You.

"There is a general rule though," Levi Yitzhak teaches, that everything that is with us constantly, even if it is infinite goodness itself, will not always generate great pleasure because it becomes a habit. So it is with those who worship God always: Sometimes the Creator, may He be blessed, contracts the brightness of His Presence so that it not be continuous for them. Later, though, they rise to greater heights . . . It is as if the Creator were at moments hidden so that the righteous will have the joy of not having Him with them always, as it says, "From Asher [from what is now], his bread will be fatter [his joy will be greater] [Genesis 48:20]."

Anyone who prays regularly is familiar with the vicissitudes of the prayer life described by Levi Yitzḥak. Anyone for whom prayer is not simply a personal or communal ritual knows the moments of trembling and fear, of pleasure and joy, and of hiddennes and barrenness too. God's presence is not constantly sensed by us. He is always there but we do not always know it. As a result, there is a certain doggedness, a certain sense of persevering and persisting, to our prayer life. We try, we fail, and we try again. We stick to God. As Abraham Joshua Heschel indicated, "Faith is loyalty to God."

Memory helps us in the desert, for we remember Him when He was close. Sometimes we live on such memories a long time. That is why adolescents should be encouraged toward religious experience. We live in a very secular world; they will have their fill of it in due time. The teenage years are the time for intense religious experience, for building a spiritual memory to sustain us when life's needs catch up to us and press in on us. Modern parents don't always appreciate this. That is also the function of holidays: to enable us to devote ourselves more fully to God, to build a store of memories of Him which will sustain us in the moments when we don't sense Him directly. Moderns forget that too. Life, Levi Yitzḥak reminds us, is a returning toward God in prayer and meditation.

EXODUS

Distance From Life

In this week's reading, Levi Yitzḥak uses the classical rabbinic preaching method of weaving two verses together to generate one meaning. The first verse is taken from the reading. It describes the action of Moses' sister after her brother has been put into the floating cradle: "His sister placed herself a distance away to know what would happen to him" (Exodus 2:4). The second verse is taken from Jeremiah (31:2): "From a distance away the Lord appeared to me." How do these two verses relate to one another? Of what are they speaking?

"The rule is," Levi Yitzḥak teaches,

that, when [the beings of] the worlds are attached to their material nature, then they are not able to grasp the true worship of the Creator, blessed be He. But, when they distance themselves and strip away their material nature, then they are able to grasp the true worship of the Creator, blessed be He. This is hinted at in the verse from Jeremiah: "from a distance away"—when one is distanced from one's material nature; "the Lord appeared to me"—the Lord appears to him or her. This is also hinted at in the verse from Exodus: "his sister" [coming from the root "to mend"] signifies the capacity for attachment; "she placed herself a distance away" signifies that one must distance oneself from one's material nature; "to know" [as in the verse "And Adam knew Eve his wife"] signifies total unification; and "what would happen to him" [understanding the word "what" to be a reference to the Ein Sof, the Infinite], signifies the continuous emanation of vitality to him from the Creator, blessed be He.

The exegesis presented here may seem far-fetched to the modern reader who prefers to take the text at its simpler narrative level. Or it may seem to be asethetically pleasing to one who appreciates this homiletic art form. In either case, Levi Yitzḥak's meaning is clear. He has taught us a basic lesson in spiritual living: that we cannot truly worship God when we are steeped in, and significantly oriented toward, the nonspiritual side of our being.

The nonspiritual dimension of our existence is very broad. We have the need to make a living and we spend a great deal of energy thinking about our careers, balancing our income against our expenses, and just plain doing the work of our jobs. We also have significant psychological needs: for love, for food, for sex, for bodily vigor. These too occupy our actions, our planning, and indeed our most intimate fantasies about who and what we are. We also have social and intellectual needs which move us to meet people, to keep up with the news, to read books, to be active in organizations, and to perfect ourselves as conversationalists. All these needs generate a great deal of motion and even anxiety in our lives. This is not bad; it is part of living. Judaism does not espouse a monastic existence geared to retreat from life, to achieving inner calm and balance, at the expense of living in the real world. But the material dimension of our being does becloud the spiritual if we let it become central; and it is all too easy to do just that.

There is a time to "place oneself at a distance" from all this, Levi Yitzhak teaches, not to "relax" but "to know the action of the Infinite happening in our lives." There is a time to bracket the material dimension of our lives in favor of an opening of our awareness to the presence of God in our lives. This is Levi Yitzhak's lesson.

Knowledge of God

One of the most perplexing sentences in the Bible occurs in this reading as God initiates Moses into his prophetic career: "God spoke to Moses and said to him, 'I am YHVH. I appeared to Abraham, to Isaac, and to Jacob as El Shaddai but [by] my Name, YHVH, I was not known to them'" (Exodus 6:2–3). Noting that part of the text of Genesis does indeed speak of YHVH interacting with the patriarchs, modern biblical critics proposed that the verse here teaches that in some traditions YHVH did speak to the patriarchs and in some He did not. This led them to conclude that there were two main traditions of the patriarchal stories: those with "YHVH" and those with other names for God such as "Elohim," "El Shaddai," and so forth. This became known as "the documentary hypothesis" of the origin of the biblical text.

The contradiction between the plain sense of this verse and the facts of the Genesis narrative did not escape the rabbis. But, since it was an article of faith that the Torah was a unitary whole, they had different answers. The interested reader can find this whole controversy in various books, beginning with the encyclopedias. Levi Yitzhak's exegesis does not deal with this problem, but tries to interpret the spiritual dimension of the two verbs used in the sentence: "appeared" and "was known."

On the one hand, Levi Yitzhak teaches that God is completely unknowable. "No thought can grasp him at all," as the Zohar says. On the other hand, he teaches that "anyone who wishes to be worthy and to come to some comprehension of Him has no choice but to come to Him by means of three types of service: study of Torah, prayer, and acts of charity. These are, so to speak, the letters of God's Name." How do these relate? "By doing these acts, one can come to the point of recognizing that He is above all letters."

There are, however, two paths to the knowledge of God: The first is through the aforementioned acts of service. In this mode, we know

God through His letters, through His Names, through His revelation. We study Torah and we come to know Him. We pray the words of the tradition and we come to know Him. And we do acts of charity and kindness and we come to know Him. The second path is the recognition that follows acts of service. It is the moment "which comes automatically, after great labor and enormous effort in the service of God through Torah study, prayer, and acts of charity." It is the moment "in which there is no understanding or knowledge but only attachment and annihilation of reality."

This distinction between the two paths to the knowledge of God is the true meaning of the verse in Exodus: "I appeared to . . . as El Shaddai" refers to the Names of God which are known and knowable. The verb "appeared," a passive form of "to see," is used. This aspect of God can be "seen," can be comprehended, can be known through acts of service. "To know God," in this sense, is to know Him through sacred action. "But [by] My Name, YHVH, I was not known to them" refers to the ineffable, unknown, and unknowable dimension of God. This aspect can not be "seen" or comprehended. It is beyond the letters and the acts of service. It can only be experienced in the annihilation of reality. "To know God," in this sense, is "to be be bound up with" as in the verse, "And Adam knew his wife, Eve." It is an experiential bond that, in its totality, effaces identity. God, Moses is told, was "seen" in His knowableness by the patriarchs; but He was not "known," experienced in His unknowableness by them.

With this exegesis, Levi Yitzhak has not only provided a spiritual insight into the passage, he has also given us direction in the spiritual life. Life should be a devotion to the way of service—Torah study, prayer, and acts of charity and kindness—so that one may reach beyond that to occasional moments of knowing God experientially.

How much time do you spend daydreaming, fantasizing? Most of us spend a lot more time at it than we are willing to admit even to intimates. Add to that the time we spend watching television or reading adventure literature, for that too is a form of allowing ourselves to take on a heroic dimension we really do not have. Classical rabbinic Judaism did not approve of this. Such time was a "waste of Torah." Whatever time one would devote to fantasy should be directed to study. There

Preparation, Chosenness, and Hierarchy

In describing the plague of darkness, the reading of this week tells us: *ve-yamesh hoshekh* (Exodus 10:22). The translators and the commentators have had trouble with this phrase. The traditional rabbinic understanding is that the darkness was so deep that it was actually tangible. Whatever it was, the next verse goes on to tell us that, in the dwellings of the Israelites, there was light and not that special darkness.

Levi Yitzhak reaches deep into the rabbinic and mystical tradition and explains that:

The radiance of the Creator, blessed be He, is infinite. And, when it came into His will to create His universe so that He be called "loving," He contracted His radiance according to the quality of the receiving beings: for the world of the serafim, according to their capacity; for the world of the *hayyot*, according to their capacity; for the world of the [other] angels, according to theirs; and so on for all the heavenly worlds. They, however, are always on one level of being, according to the capacity to receive the radiance with which they were endowed on the day of their creation. They cannot look upwards from their rank. This is so that they not be annihilated by the radiance of the infinite. Nor can they look downwards—as it says, "With two wings they covered their face and with two wings they covered their feet" [Isaiah 6:2].

Israel, His holy people, however, by the study of Torah and the doing of His commandments, can make "garments" with which to [absorb His radiance and] rise from one level of being to another. But the wicked and the non-Jews do not have the Torah and the commandments and so they, too, are always on one level of being. Therefore, when God wishes to break the wicked, He shows them His radiance. Since they have no "garments" with which to [absorb His radiance and] rise from one level of being to another, they are defeated.

This is the secret of the verse [in this reading]. God's "darkness" is His is some truth to this. Imagine how much we would know if we spent all our fantasy time in study! Torah was, and is, the center of classical rabbinic Judaism. Fantasy was, and is, the center of modern culture. (Just think of the advertising, leisure, and sports industries, or of the romantic movement in literature, music, and drama). These cultures conflict; the battle is over human energy and time.

Jewish spirituality revitalizes Jewish fantasy. It makes us dream again of a real and imminent messiah. It makes us dream again of a world whose riches exceed the poverty-in-wealth and oppression we know in this world. And it makes us have visions of a moment of being bound up with God, of being annihilated into Him. Jewish spirituality revives our hope of a relationship with the ultimate Being, a relationship that goes beyond the bounds of all human intimacy. Human beings can "see" God, Levi Yitzhak taught, and through that seeing can "know" God. Whether we are moderns steeped in the sin of fantasy dictated by our culture, or whether we are rabbinic Jews, steeped in an almost idolatrous relationship with the tradition, the call of Jewish spirituality is to revive the truly spiritual power of the human imagination.

contracted radiance and "ve-yamesh" means "He put aside." Thus, He put aside His contracted radiance and revealed His full radiance. The Egyptians had no Torah and commandments and, so, they were struck down but the Jews, who had "garments" made of Torah and commandments, had "light" in their dwellings. This is also the secret of the saying [Talmud, Nedarim 8b], "In the end of time, the Holy One, blessed be He, will bring out the sun from its hiddenness. The righteous will be healed by it and the wicked will be judged by it."

There are many things that we can learn here. First, note Levi Yitzhak's reversal of the plague of darkness to one of divine light. It is very well done. Also, note that pure spirituality is not a simple influx of God's love, or a superabundance of good feeling. Receiving the divine light requires "garments." It requires preparation, protection. Experiencing the intense presence of God demands a life devoted to Him. It is not for amateurs. This is classical teaching in all mystical traditions. Moderns, who believe that everything must be easily available, would do well to remember it.

Second, Levi Yitzhak took seriously the doctrine of the chosen people. The Jews are special, not by birth or race, but by having been chosen by God. Their chosenness is inextricably bound up with the covenant. And it is, therefore, the covenant that gives them special access to God—an access that is superior to that of the wicked, of the non-Jews, and even of the angels. Moderns are embarrassed by this doctrine. We have been brought up in an egalitarian ideology that teaches that all people are equal, especially religiously. No, says Levi Yitzhak. The Jews are different and special.

I do not wish to mitigate Levi Yitzhak's teaching of chosenness. It *is* the teaching of the tradition. But I wonder whether, internal to the tradition, there is not room for the non-Jew who is spiritual to have access to God's primal spirituality. Judaism, unlike most other religious traditions, does provide for the non-Jew's access to true morality. Such persons are called "righteous gentiles" and they are considered to have a share in the world-to-come. But it seems to me that the tradition ought also to provide for the genuine spirituality of the non-Jew. It is a different spirituality: for Christians, it is mediated by Jesus; for others, it is mediated by other forms. Holiness is universal; the numinous is part of the image (Genesis 1:26). Would Levi Yitzḥak really be willing to say that all non-Jewish spirituality is delusion? Does the tradition not admit that, while non-Jewish spirituality is not open to the fullness of the divine, it nonetheless may partake of it in some way? Does not the covenant with Noaḥ, and with Adam, bind all humanity not only to the way of morality but also to the way of spirituality?

Third, I have always been unhappy with the notion that the world of the angels and dead souls is a static world, that these beings cannot rise from one level to another. If God is pure spirituality and true morality, all levels of being must be that in diminished measure. Beings in the worlds between us and God must be spiritual and moral. They must have the power to act, even the power to err; perhaps they must have even the power to sin. Otherwise they are not part of the great chain of being that begins in God and penetrates downward to our world. I prefer a structure that provides for beings with increasing levels of spirituality and morality, and power. I prefer angels who are more than we and less than God in every sense of the word.

Some moderns reject the idea of a hierarchy of being altogether. Some prefer the view of a static heavenly world of only bliss (or punishment) because that is the traditional teaching. Both of these lines of reasoning have the effect of making our efforts here absolute. This, however, seems to me to be a form of anthropocentrism that, I think, the tradition would reject as hidden idolatry. A universe of varying levels of spirituality and morality, of diverse power, and of increasing responsibility seems to me to be more within the plan of the creation.

On Miracles: An Extended Comment

After being saved at the Red (or Reed) Sea, the Jews sang a song of praise to God which is contained in this reading. It is introduced by the words: "On that day, the Lord saved Israel from the hand of Egypt" (Exodus 14:30). What is the import of the phrase "on that day," asks Levi Yitzhak? Is it merely a phrase identifying the time of redemption, or does it have some special spiritual significance?

There are miracles which derive from the part of God that is immanent in the universe, from the part that is inherent in the laws of nature. The miracle of Purim is of this type. But there are also miracles that derive from something above nature, which derive from the radiance that transcends all worlds. The former are revealed. The latter are hidden because the radiance is hidden from created beings.

There are, then, two types of miracles: those in which God works through nature and history and those in which God violates nature's laws and creates something new.

The miracles wrought through nature and history can be both personal and communal. Purim is the story of a communal natural miracle: Haman is a Jew-hater. He hates Mordecai's resistant presence. He rises to power in the court. And he bribes his sovereign into approving his persecution of the Jews. All this could, and does, happen anywhere; it is natural, historical. There are no mighty plagues, no prophetic warnings; just hatred and intrigue. As the setting is natural and historical, so is the dénouement. Esther, the Jewess, is in a position of power. Her uncle alerts her to the danger to herself and her people. She artfully unmasks the perfidy of Haman and the sovereign orders his destruction and the protection of the Jews. Here too, there are no supernatural miracles, no theophanies, no God wreaking vengeance on the enemies of His people. There is the counter-intrigue of Esther and Mordecai. All this could, and does, happen anywhere; it is natural, historical. The tradition notes that the Book of Esther is the only book in the Bible in which the Name of God does not appear. He has worked through the natural course of events, through the historical characters. His action has been providential, not supernatural.

Still, the story of Purim is not quite natural; it does not quite follow the rules of history. We do not view the place of Esther in the plot as the Queen, chosen by contest, as a "historical accident." Neither do we view the rapid rise to power of Mordecai as an accident. Rather we view these events as the hand of God, as providence at work in the affairs of humanity. Hence, the story of Purim is also a miracle and one thanks God for it.

Much the same is true of the establishment and continued existence of the State of Israel in our time. These did not, and do not, come about by an act of God, directly from heaven. Rather they were, and are, accomplished through the goodwill of the nations of the world and the blood of Jewish soldiers willing to defend their people and their land. These are natural, historical causes. Yet it was, and is, not statesmanship and bravery alone that defends the Jewish state. Rather, we see in this action the providential hand of God; and in this sense the State of Israel is a miracle.

There are also personal natural miracles. We observe the delicate sprinkling of color in early spring, or we breathe the first oxygen-refreshed air after the leaves have grown, or we watch the stately change of costume creation assumes in the fall. These are natural, yet personal, miracles. So is the recognition of the complete otherness of a child, the seeing of its independent self-responsive being. So is the in-breaking of laughter into our lives, and the recognition of our blessedness, and the sense of power at having accomplished something, particularly if that deed has spiritual as well as social meaning. These too are miracles inherent in our existence, in our createdness. There is also wonder, amazement, and being astounded at the very fact and mystery of perception and consciousness. These too are natural, personal; yet not quite natural, as the daily liturgy phrases it, " . . . and for Your miracles that are with us everyday, and for Your wonders and goodnesses that are with us at all times, evening, morning, and afternoon."

Another form of miracle wrought through nature and history is very personal. It is one familiar to many of us. My own life has been filled with moments where I have been at the right place at the right time in order to represent God, the tradition, or the Jewish people. I have never had a prophetic word telling me, "Go and say, 'Thus said the Lord.' " But life has conspired to have me placed in certain places at certain moments. Does the phrase "life has conspired" make any sense? Does the explanation "it was coincidence" make any sense? No; rather, a religious person says, "I sense the presence of God in my life, moving mysteriously." Or to put it the other way around: the sense of God's presence is not only in moments of prayer and mystical consciousness but also in the everyday warp and woof of life, in the flow and direction that our lives take. We do not know in advance what God has in mind. Nor do we always understand His purpose in moving us through life. We certainly are not the beneficiaries of any supernatural violation of the laws of nature. But His presence implies involvement, relatedness, and concern, and we are aware of it. That, too, is a miracle, a natural historical miracle, for it works in us, through us, even if pain and suffering should obscure our vision.

But there is also the supernatural miracle: the rupturing of the laws of nature and history, the in-breaking of the divine power into creation. These are the miracles that are hidden because the radiance of His power by which they function is hidden. The miracle of the splitting of the sea is one such miracle. "On that day" it happened. " 'That' implies hiddenness and 'day' implies radiance," says Levi Yitzḥak. The meaning of the verse, then, is this: With the radiance of the hidden world, God created a miracle that was beyond nature and, by it, saved the Jewish people. Levi Yitzḥak means to teach that the miracle of the splitting of the sea was not an "ordinary" natural miracle but an intervention into nature and history by God. As textual support, he cites the Passover Haggadah: "Not by an angel and not by a messenger, but the Holy One, blessed be He, in His own presence and His own self, redeemed the Jews."

Modern people have two distortions of the concept and role of the supernatural miracle in religion. Those who are rationalist—and we have all been trained in a rationalist world—tend to be skeptical of supernatural miracles. There is no such thing as the "super" natural. There is only nature, or creation, part of which we know and part of which we do not know. Yet we have confidence in our ability to know even the currently unknown, given enough time. Those who follow this line of thought are particularly sensitive about using the supernatural miracle as a foundation-stone for religious identity. A phenomenon of which we are, in the very least, skeptical cannot serve as the cornerstone of our spiritual personhood.

Other moderns, however (and many of us fall in this category to a greater or lesser degree), have an intuition or experience of God at the core of their spiritual lives. For those for whom this is true, supernatural miracles verify experience, miracles "prove" faith or, at least, support it. We welcome the supernatural as some form of evidence that the uncanny experience of God that forms the core of our religious identity is true. We welcome historical miracles such as the splitting of the sea and we approve of personal miracles because both reinforce faith.

Both approaches, however, contain deep dangers. The rationalist runs the risk of excluding the uncanny, the great mystery of creation; the experientialist courts the danger of superstition, of seeing the hand of God where it is not.

Levi Yitzhak dissents from both views. He reminds us that there is a world of hiddenness, of unrevealed energy, and this world does not manifest itself often. Once in a very great while, the power from outside intervenes in creation. Such an event is palpable when it happens; indeed, it is frightening. It is not ordinary, natural, providential. And it is not intended to convince us of anything, nor to strengthen our faith. Such acts are acts of hiddenness, of veiled radiance. They come into our universe at His behest; they serve no person; they have no human purpose. It is to these miracles that we must address ourselves. It is to the Passover-type miracle, with all its supernatural plagues, its prophetic warnings, and its unnatural splitting of the sea, that we must turn our being.

We cannot experience the power and presence of God when He split the sea; that is past. We can only hold ourselves open to the hidden power of God, to the veiled radiance that lies just beneath the surface of creation waiting to break in and create something new. Sometimes, however, we can have a glimpse of what such moments may have been like. It has happened to me that, as I read the great song ritually, suddenly I felt the Presence and the Power—as a meager flame to the great fire. My voice trembled, and others knew too. The miracle-then was real-now, as the reflection-now was direct light-then. For a moment, it was "on that day," "by the radiance of that hiddenness."

On Spiritual Counseling

At the beginning of this reading, Moses' father-in-law comes to visit him. Yitro notices that Moses must sit all day and deal with the people.

And he said, "What is this that you are doing with the people? Why do you sit alone while all the people stand and wait for you from morning to night?" Moses replied to Yitro, "The people come to me to seek direction from God" ... And his father-in-law replied, "That which you do is not good. You shall surely wither, you and the people, for it is a difficult a thing which you do." (Exodus 18:14–18)

Levi Yitzḥak ignores the verse in which Moses explains that he is rendering judgment in legal cases and develops a spiritual interpretation of Moses' actions, one which flowed out of his own life and, in a lesser sense, flows out of the life of all who do religious counseling.

When a zaddik speaks with those who are beneath him in spiritual level, their presence confuses him. However, if one is a great zaddik, he can elevate their souls by his speech with them. This is difficult work. Now, Yitro saw that the people were "standing and waiting," that is, that they were remaining on one spiritual level and not advancing from degree to degree in the service of God. Therefore, he asked, "What is this that all the people stand and wait on you? They are all in the position of standing and waiting, that is, on one level." To this Moses replied, "They come to me so that I can rehabilitate them and I raise up their souls with speech." To this Yitro replied, "It is a difficult thing which you do, to raise the souls of people who are spiritually lower than you."

Levi Yitzḥak has in mind a highly technical usage when he speaks of Moses "rehabilitating" the souls of those lower than he. To "rehabilitate" means to reach into the soul of another, by meditation, and to raise that soul from its current level of spirituality to a higher one. This is the kabbalistic concept of tikkun. It can be done for the soul of another person and it can also be accomplished for the spark of the divine in any existing thing. Thus to make a blessing over bread, with the proper meditation, is to "rehabilitate" the bread—that is, to reach into its divine core and to consecrate that core to God. The ultimate tikkun is the rehabilitation of the Jewish people and, indeed, of the whole cosmos. This will occur in the days of the messiah. Rehabilitation, in its technical sense, can be accomplished only by a real zaddik, as Levi Yitzhak indicates.

Those of us who do spiritual counseling understand, many times removed, what Levi Yitzhak means. Spirituality is very personal. It suffers when it must grapple with the vulgarities of the world. The spiritual person develops the sense that "I sleep but my heart waketh" (Song of Songs 5:2).[1] She or he learns that one cannot, indeed one must not, avoid the world of trouble and oppression. But it does pull one down.

Spirituality is also very sought after. Most people live quite comfortably in the world of diminished spirituality. But they know there is something there, they need it, and they search for it. They seek it, quite naturally, in those who have a sharper sense for it. Such seeking persons come, not with intellectual problems of faith or law, not with social or economic problems, not even with sexual or psychological problems—though these too may surface in discussion. Such seeking persons come searching for the spiritual. To counsel them is to fight mightily to remain open to them. It is to struggle to remain present to their presence. Just being there spiritually is the most basic step. It is also the most difficult. The techniques of spirituality are easy to teach; being present is harder.

The modern day spiritual person is a faint shadow of Moses, as understood by Levi Yitzhak. She or he is also a dim reflection of the zaddik, of Levi Yitzhak himself. The compassionate understanding of sensitive friends like Yitro helps.

A Flaming Heart

Toward the end of this reading, Moses goes up on Mt. Sinai. The Glory (Presence) of God rests upon the mountain and the text describes it as follows: "The appearance of the Glory of God was as a consuming fire" (Exodus 24:17). Levi Yitzḥak, setting aside the descriptive meaning of the verse, interprets it spiritually.

A person, in his or her worship of God, may He be blessed, through Torah and mitsvot, brings great joy above. And so, when a person wants to know if God, may He be blessed, has joy from this worship, the criterion is this: If one sees that one's heart burns like a fire and that one feels religious enthusiasm always to worship Him and that one has a passion and a will to worship the Creator, then it is certain that God, may He be blessed, has joy from that person's worship. Such an individual is helped by heaven and holy thoughts are sent to that person's heart. This is why it is written "and the Glory of God was as a consuming fire"—for the sign, if one wants to know if one has seen the Glory of God and if the Holy One, blessed be He, is happy with one, is "a consuming fire," that one's heart burns like fire.

This is a very audacious statement. First, it unequivocally casts the criterion for proper spiritual behavior on the individual. Each person—not the community—is the judge of whether his or her worship is acceptable to God. Second, the criterion set up is a subjective one—a feeling of religious enthusiasm, not an accumulation of objective proper deeds. Both of these motifs run strongly against the rationalistic, objectivistic understanding of Judaism prevalent in usual orthodox circles as well as in modernist circles.

There are further implications: that the reason for studying the Torah and doing the commandments is to create a parallel subjective feeling in God and that, in some way, the lesser (yet real) motivation for doing these things is to bring oneself to the feeling of "burning heart." These implications, too, are far from the usual understanding of why one observes the tradition.

Yet it is exactly this emphasis on real, personal religious experience that is the crucial element in Jewish spirituality. One does what one is supposed to do in order to give God pleasure. One does experience a sense of "burning heart" when one does these things. And one does use this experience as the criterion for the truth of what one has done.

The subjectivism and individualism may not be far from some forms of modern consciousness, but the spirituality of this experience is very strange to modernity. How much of that which we do can be characterized as "a religious enthusiasm always to worship Him . . . a passion and a desire to worship the Creator?" How much of our ritual or ethical behavior can be said to fall into that category? How much even of our prayer life is suffused with that ardor? Modern religiosity has a routine quality about it. This protects religious experience from too much subjectivity, but it also deprives spiritual life of a vital factor that reinforces, motivates, and helps to form an ideal. We need to ask, how do I know that my acts are acceptable to God?

The Wrongness of Withdrawal

Rabbinic tradition did not accept the chronological order of the Bible narrative here. It understood the incident of the golden calf (Exodus 32–34) to have followed immediately upon the end of the previous reading (Exodus 24), and it understood the sections dealing with the sanctuary and the priestly garments (Exodus 25–31) to follow the story of the golden calf. The sanctuary was thus understood as a concession by God to the people's need to have a focus for their worship and, perhaps, as an act of reconciliation between God and the people following the incident of the sin of the golden calf.

Levi Yitzḥak accepts this rabbinic understanding of the chronology of the Torah and he points out that the reading opens with God commanding Moses to speak to the people of Israel (Exodus 25:1–2). Why did God have to command Moses to speak to the people, Levi Yitzḥak asks? This is the first time that he addresses them as a people, with something positive, since the great revelation on Mt. Sinai. Why did Moses need to be commanded?

The righteous leader guards carefully his speaking to the masses of the people. For, when one speaks with the masses, they can disturb him from his continuous meditation on God, may He be exalted. If, however, it is the case that an individual can be uplifted by his speaking with the righteous leader, then the latter is permitted to speak to him. In fact, through speaking to someone about one's continuous meditation on God, one can make an impression on the other and bring him, too, into the realm of holiness.

This is what happened to Moses: When the people sinned with the golden calf, they ceased being in the holy state they had attained at Sinai and returned to their impurity. And so Moses was afraid to speak with them. Therefore, God commanded him "Speak to the people of Israel" meaning, "They are the seed of Israel, children of Abraham, Isaac, and Jacob. By your speaking with them, you will uplift them to holiness and they will again cling to My Name. Speak to them."

This problem of the zaddik being disrupted from his continuous meditation on God *(devekut)* seems to have bothered Levi Yitzhak. He speaks of it often. It is very understandable. Most people are mundane. Many are anti-intellectual and anti-spiritual. Some are even vulgar. The average person is just that: average. Spirituality, on the other hand, for all its power, is very tenuous. It is an awareness but it is fleeting. Being spiritual is a commitment to that awareness, but the commitment has its ups and downs. It is hard to persevere with spirituality in the face of daily tasks, distractions, and outright sin and temptation. Spirituality requires a certain reservedness, a certain distance from the world and from people. To love one's neighbor as oneself—to share his or her sorrow, pain, and joy—is to get so involved as to run the risk of losing one's spiritual center.

No one, however, not even Moses, can escape this burden. He, too, must return to the people. He, too, must speak to them and help uplift them. So must any serious righteous leader. "You shall be holy" and "love your neighbor as yourself" are in tension. They follow one another; they imply one another. Neither, alone, is sufficient; neither, alone, transcends the other. It is an old idea but, because the temptation to isolation in spiritual and intellectual ivory towers is so great, it bears repeating.

Levels of Spirituality

The previous weekly reading dealt with the instructions for setting up the tabernacle in the desert. Moses is told to speak to the Jewish people and to ask for contributions. Then he is shown a model of the tabernacle: the ark and its covering, the table and its utensils, the great menorah, the cloth curtains that formed the walls with their rings, the supports for the curtains with their bases, the great inner curtain for the holy of holies with its support and bases, the main altar, and the roof of the whole tabernacle. In this week's reading, Moses is given instructions about: the oil to be used in the great menorah, the priestly vestments including those of the high priest, and the incense altar. He is also instructed how to consecrate the priests so that they may serve in the new sanctuary.

The rabbis noticed two strange things: that Moses is mentioned only once at the beginning of last week's reading and not at all in this week's reading. Furthermore, last week's reading begins with, "And God spoke to Moses . . ." while this week's reading begins with, "And you shall command . . ."—the pronoun in place of the name and the command in place of the address. Why is this so? What is there about the items enumerated in this week's reading that evokes such a different manner of communication? Most of the commentators indicate that the purpose of this is to ensure that Moses himself will be responsible to supervise the four activities mentioned here (preparation of the oil, making the priestly garments, consecrating the priests, and constructing the incense altar). Levi Yitzhak, however, had his own interpretation.

Two phrases give us a clue to the meaning of this passage, Levi Yitzhak teaches: (1) "May He Who makes peace in His high places make peace for us and for all Israel" (daily liturgy). This teaches that He can only make peace for us when we turn to the high places, that is, when we turn to the heavenly roots of our existence. In this context, Levi Yitzhak says that one must look to the biblical narrative as a metaphor for the heavenly realm. (2) "When Moses consecrated the priests, he served in a garment of the purest white color" (Bamidbar Rabba 12:10). Whiteness, Levi Yitzhak teaches, is not a color. It is the hue that receives all others. It is the "nothing" of the colors. The text, then, means that Moses, while consecrating the priests, was in a mystical state of cleaving to the Ayin, to the Nothing, to the God beyond all expression and conceptualization.

Bringing all these thoughts together, Levi Yitzhak teaches:

The tabernacle stood over against Israel. Hence, Moses was able to cling to the speech of God and to understand its construction by the use of his own intelligence. The priestly garments [and the oil and the incense which are the center of the priestly worship service], however, were beyond Moses since he himself was not a priest. He, thus, had to meditate upon them, annihilate himself in the transcendent Nothingness of God, and be guided by His commandment.

The explanation is already clear, but Levi Yitzhak intends us to look a bit deeper. In the world of Jewish kabbalistic mysticism, Israel (the tabernacle) represents the lower seven sefirot (aspects of God), while the priestly garments together with the holy oil and incense represent the upper three sefirot. The ultimate meaning here, then, seems to be that Moses was accustomed to mystical meditation on the lower realms. He is, therefore, addressed in speech and by name. He was not, however, accustomed to mystical meditation on the highest realms. He had to annihilate himself into the inexpressible and inconceivable aspect of God to grasp them. God wants Moses to know both dimensions. Hence Moses is not addressed by name, nor is he spoken to. He is guided, commanded.

The modern mind has largely lost not only the hierarchy of sefirot of the kabbalistic tradition, but also the sense that the divine comes in shades of intensity. We think of God as a single experience, not as a range of experiences some more intense than others, and some so intense as to be painful or frightening, even annihilating. In this respect, moderns are naive. If human relations vary from the banal to the ecstatic and participate in levels of barely conceivable complexity, so should our relations with the divine. Levi Yitzhak teaches us here that there is a difference between tabernacle with its appointments and priestly service with its accoutrements; that there is a difference between levels of spiritual awareness, even between levels of mystical awareness. To know the tabernacle, the lower levels of spirituality, is not the same as knowing the priestly service, the upper levels of spirituality. That is a very important lesson, even if we only grasp it on its periphery.

On Charitable Giving

In this reading, the Jewish people commits the sin of sins, the worshiping of the golden calf. Why and how this happened is a very profound subject. More meaningful, though, is God's reaction. He is angry but He comes down and teaches Moses a prayer that Moses is to recite at this moment of greatest trouble and danger for the people. It reads: "Lord, Lord—God Who loves compassionately and cherishes, Who is patient and overflows with grace and truth. He stores up grace for thousands of generations. He forgives rebellious sin, purposeful sin, and inadvertent sin. He cleanses" (Exodus 34:5–7). This prayer of God's became central to the Jewish penitential liturgy. Levi Yitzḥak devoted a great deal of time to interpreting it (see 177–79).

Jewish tradition divides the qualities of God invoked in this prayer and understands the number of them to be thirteen. There are also thirteen well-known rabbinic hermeneutic principles for interpreting the written Torah. Only one of them is relevant to Levi Yitzḥak's interpretation here, the "analogy." This hermeneutic principle allows the rabbis to draw analogies between biblical contexts such that some practical principle in law may be derived.

"Now," Levi Yitzḥak says,

my master, my teacher, my rabbi, our rabbi and teacher, Dov Baer [of Mezeritch], taught that these thirteen qualities of God are one with the thirteen hermeneutic principles by which the Torah is interpreted. Thus, the quality "Who loves compassionately and cherishes" is parallel to the hermeneutic principle of the analogy. For the rule is that the rich man must have compassionate love for the poor man. To do this, the rich man must compare himself to the poor man. He must cling to his pain and his oppression. For by comparing himself to him, he puts himself on an equal plane with him and his compassion is aroused. So it is with the Creator, may He be blessed, as it says, "I am with them in time of trouble" [Psalm 91:15]. This is the unity of "Who loves compassionately and cherishes" with "analogy."

This is a very profound comment for several reasons. First, there is the beautiful insight into the nature of charity. Second, the interpretation shows the learnedness of this hasidic tradition. It is not only the beautiful story but also the context of the interweaving of the thirteen qualities with the thirteen hermeneutic principles. And third, it is not only the deep insight into human nature but the extension of it to God's relationship to us.

Let us return to the insight into the nature of charity. How profound! Why do we give money to charity? For some, it is a matter of social obligation: that is what being part of a community means. For others, it is noblesse oblige, a duty of the privileged. For some, charity is a way to personal recognition. For others, it is guilt. All these are false motivations, Levi Yitzhak instructs us in the name of his teacher. Deep down, we give because of some analogy we make between ourselves and the human recipients of our charity. Deep down, beneath our conscious thoughts, we have put ourselves, very briefly, on the same plane as the oppressed. And so we give.

A lot of our charitable giving is to causes. Almost all of it is mediated through institutions. I thought for a long time that this was in order to attain a degree of efficiency. But if Levi Yitzhak is right, this giving at sumptuous community dinners or elegant cocktail parties to causes and through institutionalized bureaucracies is nothing but a protective device. It is meant to protect us from the pain of the analogy with those we help. We escape their suffering by giving in comfort. We even give with a certain generosity in order not to have to sustain the analogy between us and them (note the language of "us" and "them"). How much more difficult would it be for us to drive up in our fine cars and warm coats and actually distribute food to the needy and the homeless. How impossible would it be for us to have to look them in the eye, and hold that moment of dialogue in our memories and souls. And the oppressed? And the imprisoned? And those we maim in war?

Charitable giving, Levi Yitzhak teaches, is not real giving until we recognize the compassion that underlies it. Charitable giving has no deep meaning until we make the analogy between ourselves and the oppressed. For only that analogy awakens our compassion, and only our compassion enables us to give as we ought to give.

The analogy and the compassion are also the key to God's love for us and to our appeal to Him.

On Building a Sanctuary

The reading of this week recounts the actual construction of the sanctuary in the desert. The call for free-will gifts is sent out. The workers are appointed. And the people start bringing the materials for construction. The enthusiasm is, however, so great that the people bring more than is necessary and so Moses has to order an end to the presentation of gifts. "And the work was enough for all the work to be done, and an excess" (Exodus 36:7).

"How can something be 'enough' and 'an excess,'" asks Levi Yitzhak? "If it is 'enough,' it is not 'an excess' and if it is 'an excess,' it is more than 'enough.'" The verse, and indeed this whole section dealing with the construction of the sanctuary, must have deeper meaning. Levi Yitzhak develops this by teaching, "The construction of the sanctuary was akin to the creation of the heavens and the earth." Using this principle, he develops two important lessons.

At creation, everything derived from the power of the Infinite and so it was capable of expanding indefinitely, without border or limit. Therefore God, may He be exalted, was forced to say "Enough!" and to give order and boundary to all the worlds. For this reason, He is called "Shaddai" [usually translated, "Almighty"], that is, "He Who said to His universe: 'Dai,' 'Enough.'" [Talmud, Hagiga 12a]

The first lesson, then, is that at the creation of the world and at the construction of the sanctuary, there was a holy impulse at work that was truly infinite and that God, and then Moses, had to set a boundary to it and had to give it form before it could be useful. This is taught by the word "enough."

According to the Talmud (Berakhot 55a), Bezalel, the chief architect of the sanctuary, was not only a consummate artist (from which the famous art museum and art school of current-day Jerusalem derives its name) but also a deeply spiritual person who had been instructed in the art of meditating upon the letters of creation and combining them to form objects. The construction of the sanctuary, then, was accomplished by his meditating on the letters and using them together with the presented materials in order to construct the various objects of the sanctuary, just as God had used the letters and primal elements to meditate and combine the objects of this world.[1] Here too, Levi Yitzḥak teaches, Bezalel imitated God in saying "Enough" to the divine energies at his command, thereby giving them form and shape.

In a still deeper mystical sense, the construction of the sanctuary was an attempt to rehabilitate the world. It was an attempt to set right the sin of the golden calf. It was an undertaking which would allow the Jewish people, and through them all humankind, to correct its waywardness. Bezalel not only had to imitate creation, but he had to effect a rehabilitation and reconciliation between God and humankind. Yet he could not do it alone, Levi Yitzḥak taught, and so he left "an excess." Moses and Bezalel left room for the reconciliatory action of all the righteous through the ages. The second lesson, then, is that the acts of rehabilitation of the later sages and saints, too, are acts of construction of the sanctuary. The acts of reconciliation by subsequent righteous people are also a direct mystical imitation of God. Therefore the verse speaks of "an excess."

Sanctuary building for most moderns is usually limited to endless meetings of building committees and fund-raising efforts. Drawing up plans for efficient use of space and providing for requisite financing are uppermost. How many square feet for this? How much for that? Contracts and bids. Sometimes aesthetic questions arise, but they are left to the architect and his committees. Where is the sense of the energy of the Infinite to which we must say "Enough?" Where is the sense of the power of reconciliation which has been left us as "an excess" to embody in our buildings? We may joke, or look enviously, at Moses' "fund-raising campaign." But have we looked at the meditation that he and Bezalel used in constructing their sanctuary? Have we considered that building such a structure is not an exercise in engineering and finance but an imitation of God, a creation of the world?

It is not only the building of sanctuaries from which the dimension of the spiritual is missing. It is lacking in most "religious" art. When a Torah is written, the scribe must have holy thoughts. He must wash his hands when he comes to the Name of God. His *kavvana* is part of what makes a Torah scroll not just an aesthetic object but a holy object. (Catholic tradition incorporates this idea in its differentiation between religious art and icons. The latter derive their meaning from the meditation of the artist, not from the aesthetic value.) Similarly, religious music: Is there a difference between singing Verdi's religious music and his secular operas? Does it make a difference if it is done in a church or concert hall? I think that Levi Yitzhak would answer "Yes." God has left us "an excess," a power to build sanctuaries, to rehabilitate and reconcile humankind and God in works of architecture, art, and music.

The Evil Eye and the Good Eye

There is an old superstition, "No blessing rests upon that which is numbered or counted" (Talmud, Ta'anit 8b). The depth of this superstition is not to be underestimated. I remember that my grandmother, who did not come from a particularly observant home, would always add a warning phrase whenever she mentioned the names of her children or grandchildren. And I know Jews who will not answer the question, "How many children do you have?" Counting and numbering are deeply symbolic patterns of human behavior, pregnant with fear and joy.

Levi Yitzhak would never have contradicted the Talmud, but he does reply to the quotation with one from the Song of Songs, "Your eyes are [as the] pools of Heshbon" (7:5). Using puns and reading "pools" as "blessings" and "Heshbon" as "counting," Levi Yitzhak interprets, "Your eyes bring blessings even upon that which is counted." From this, he launches into an analysis of how the wicked and the righteous bring blessing and curse with their glance.

The root of the evil eye is to be found in the case of Balaam—on every place upon which he cast his eye, a curse fell [Zohar I:68b]. For, when a wicked person casts his eyes upon something, he separates it from its root above, from its source of vitality. Because of the desire of the wicked person for it, the object of his or her regard becomes "counted." (To this, the talmudic saying is addressed.) . . . But the [good] Jew of each generation sees and looks with the power of the Creator which is within him or her and, in so doing, attaches the object to its origin in the divine world. With this type of looking, he or she brings blessing and divine flow from above on that object even if that object is counted and numbered. To this, the verse refers, "Your eyes bring blessings even upon that which is counted." In this manner, one must understand the beginning verse of this reading, "These are the accounts of the sanctuary which were rendered at the bidding of Moses" [Exodus 38:21]. For everything was counted several times and an accounting was made, yet there was blessing on it and the Shekhina dwelled in it.

This is a very sharp analysis of both the reading from the Torah and the superstition about counting. Levi Yitzḥak is well aware of the superstition. He is also alert to the facts of the sacred text. And he knows that superstition has no root in genuine faith. So, first, he rules out refraining from counting under all circumstances. Second, he differentiates counting that brings blessing from that which entrains evil. And, third, he makes us understand that the former is desirable and the latter to be avoided.

What makes counting evil? It is the passion and intent, *kavvana*, of the wicked person. Such a person casts an eye which is intended to encompass the object for his or her own purposes. It is a selfish, ugly act. The eye of the evil person sees only his or her own benefit. Such a glance brings only evil. And what makes counting good? It is the intent, *kavvana*, of the good person. Such a person casts an eye which is intended to penetrate to the divine core of the object, to see it for what it is in relation to God and His creation. This is a holy act. The eye of the good person sees beyond the surface to the unspoken divine depths. Such a glance brings blessing.

There is so much truth in this insight. The essence of pornography and family abuse is in the passion for exploitation in the eye of the beholder. To see another as an object of one's base passions, one must block out the divine presence in the other. One must concentrate on the other as an object of the seer's passion. There is a story told of a woman who was asked by an S.S. officer to state which of his eyes was real and which glass, on pain of death. She looked at him and properly identified the glass eye. On being asked how she knew that, she replied, "It looked more compassionate." We can always tell the evil eye when we see it. And we always know the evil eye in ourselves when it prompts us to act.

Conversely, there are some people whose very glance has healing power. There are those who, simply by casting their eyes upon us, make us feel that we are in the presence of something special; indeed, that we are ourselves something special, better. Such people see through to some deeper layer of our selves. They sense a dimension of our existence that we normally hide even from ourselves. To tell the truth, if we take the time and effort, we too can look at people that way. We too can look deep into the soul of the other and see the presence that is there. We cannot read the inner thoughts, but we can sense the divine root that is present in the other. We can always tell the good eye when it is set upon us. And we can always tell when we are using that capacity ourselves.

In America it is considered proper to "look the other person right in the eye." I've always wondered why this is such a great virtue, to be "eyeball to eyeball" with someone. What does it prove? What is being communicated? So often such a glance is devoid of any spiritual substance. So often it is a glance that is emptied of the content of the other's personhood in favor of an assertion of social presence. It is neither a good eye nor an evil one; it is impersonal. Is that better? Levi Yitzhak would say, "No." Better to try to use one's good eye and, if not, be modest and look away.

LEVITICUS

The Real Meaning
of the Sacrifices

This reading begins a long section dealing with the sacrifices. To moderns, the whole passage is a mystery. We think of animal sacrifices as "primitive," as a level of human culture which we have surpassed. Yet, in a basic way, the sacrificial system allowed those who participated in it to deal with death, and blood, and God, and food in an intimate and very concrete way. Worship involved a real death and, without that death, there was no ritually acceptable meat as food. Sometimes I think that people in those days were closer to the ground, closer to the basic realities of life, and God.

Levi Yitzḥak begins his homily with the generalization, "The sacrifices were in the pattern of the divine flow of blessing." He goes on to explain:

By the acts which people had to do—to plant and to sow, to raise cattle and to sacrifice—the Creator, blessed be He, caused the flow of blessing to descend upon them. For Israel is worthy, because of their good deeds, that the Creator, blessed be He, send down upon them His blessing. When Israel was in the desert, however, they were in the state that the Holy One, blessed be He, showered His blessing upon them because of His great grace as in the case of the manna and the well of water for, in these, there was no action of humans at all. In the land of Israel, by contrast, the flow of blessing that they received was a function of their deeds . . . This flow, which comes to a person as a function of his or her acts, is the source of true happiness and joy for that person.

This is an interesting insight, that the blessing we receive in the desert of life is a function of God's grace. We do not work for it; it is His gift. But the blessing we receive in the land, in real life, is a function of our own work. We deserve it, and it is a source of joy. It is as the Psalmist says, "When you eat of the sweat of your brow, you shall be happy and it will be well with you" (Psalm 128:2). So often we think that life owes us something, that blessing is somehow natural, that it is coming to us. Or we think that it is enough to cast ourselves upon God and His great mercy. That is not so, Levi Yitzḥak teaches. Blessing, if it is to be a source of joy, must be a function of our labor. We must work for it. Note that, in contrast with much of Christian thinking, the blessing received in response to work is better than grace, that is, the blessing received freely of God's bounty. This is a basic concept in Jewish theology.

The true meaning of the sacrifices, then, is not "sacrifice" but work and labor, act and deed. It is the work of preparing that which we will offer God. And it is the deed of offering it, of giving to Him the very life of that which we have raised, which is the sacrifice. This labor and deed, properly done, are true spiritual worship. This work and act, understood in their concreteness and in the context of God's word, are true religious service.

Grace, Blood, and the Sacrifices

In this reading, Moses dedicates the sanctuary. The ceremony is quite precise (Leviticus 8 and 9): Moses takes the priests, their vestments, the oil of anointing, and three sacrificial animals. These he brings to the sanctuary. He then takes the high priest, washes him with water, and puts all the vestments on him. Next he takes the oil and anoints the parts of the sanctuary and then the high priest. Then he does the same for the other priests. All is now ready for the sacrificial service. The first animal to be slaughtered is the bull of the sin-offering. This is a large animal, appropriate to the occasion. The high priest and the other priests lay their hands on its head. Moses then slaughters it, sprinkles its blood on the altar, and offers up the necessary parts in the proper places. The second animal to be slaughtered is the ram of the whole-offering, again an impressive animal. The priests lay their hands on its head, Moses slaughters it, sprinkles its blood on the altar, and burns the entire offering there.

The third animal to be sacrificed is also a ram, the ram of consecration. Again, the priests lay their hands on its head. Moses slaughters it and smears its blood on the right earlobe, the right thumb, and the right big toe of each of the priests. He then takes the appropriate parts of the animal and puts them in the hands of the priests who raise them up as an offering to God. Certain parts are then burned on the altar, while others are set aside to be eaten by the priests and Moses. Finally, Moses mixes the blood on the altar with the oil of anointing and sprinkles the priests and their clothing to consecrate them. This ceremony is repeated for each of seven days, during which the priests may not leave the sanctuary. On the eighth day, Aaron officiates. He takes a sin-offering and a whole-offering, which he sacrifices on behalf of himself and his household. He then takes a sin-offering, a whole-offering, and peace-offerings, which he sacrifices on behalf of all Israel. A very impressive investiture ceremony.

There is so much that we do not understand about this consecration. What are these sacrifices? Is there meaning to their sequence? Why the right earlobe, the right thumb, and the right big toe? The biblical text is accompanied by signs which indicate how it is to be chanted. When Moses slaughters the ram of consecration, the note indicated on the word "and he slaughtered" is very ornate and very rare. It occurs only four times in the Torah: once when Lot "hesitates" on leaving Sodom (Genesis 19:16), once when the servant "prays" for a sign in choosing a wife for Isaac (Genesis 24:12), once when Joseph "refuses" the advances of the wife of Potiphar (Genesis 39:8), and once here (Leviticus 8:23). Why is this place so special? Is there any connection between these four situations? The text of Levi Yitzhak, here, is cut off and the editor indicates that material is missing. The fragment available deals only with the nature and sequence of the sacrifices.

Before approaching Levi Yitzhak, we must note the following concerning the dedicatory sacrifices offered by Moses: The first sacrifice is a sin-offering. It is intended to purify and make atonement for the altar. The altar has never been used; it is not holy. In fact, it is profane and has been touched only by workmen who were not consecrated. So it must first be purified, its sinfulness atoned for. The blood of the bull does that. The second sacrifice is a whole-offering, a holocaust—that is, an offering that is wholly burned, totally given to God. It is intended to be a sign of complete submission to God. The first offering after purification, then, is wholly to Him from Whom all things come; it is pre-lapsarian, so to speak. The ram serves that purpose. The third sacrifice is the consecratory offering, part of it is offered to God and part of it is shared by the celebrants. This sacrifice is the first of the communal rites; it inaugurates the sanctuary and formal worship. Again, a ram is used. In a certain sense, then, each of the three dedicatory sacrifices is a "first"—the one which atones and purifies; the one which is offered in wholeness and total purity, before the sanctuary becomes a representative of the community; and the one which consecrates and inaugurates communal, covenantal, regular contact with God.

The sequence, then, is sin-offering, whole-offering, and consecratory-offering. Note that, on the eighth day, Aaron follows the same sequence: a sin- and then a whole-offering for the priests, and a sin- , a whole- , and peace-offerings for all Israel.

Levi Yitzhak noted carefully the sequence of these offerings and, as was his custom, concerned himself with the spiritual interpretation thereof. In the fragment available, he dealt only with the first two:

The sin-offering precedes the whole-offering. This is because the sin-offering is a direct light from the upper world to the lower world while the whole-offering is a light which returns from the lower world back to the upper world. Therefore, the whole-offering is wholly burned, as it says, "He sacrificed the whole-offering and did it properly." [Leviticus 9:16]

The "direct light" is the flow of God's energy toward us. It is one-sided; it is His grace. God's grace, Levi Yitzhak teaches is, however, intertwined with the sin-offering. It purifies and atones. By contrast, the "light which returns" is energy from God which we return to Him through meditation, through contemplative doing of deeds (mitsva with kavvana). Humankind's response to God, Levi Yitzhak teaches is thus intertwined with the whole-offering. It must be whole-hearted, of one piece, given in purity and concentration. Seen globally, God's grace and our concerted response are the two poles of the spiritual worship of God, just as the sin-offering and the whole-offering are two poles of the sacrificial worship of God. This is a very powerful thought because it clearly implies that neither God's grace nor our concerted response alone is sufficient. Rather, God and humankind need each other for true worship and true blessing to take place.

Finally, Levi Yitzhak teaches that in the divine economy, grace precedes full response. God acts, then we respond; His free-will love comes before and evokes our purity of heart. This too is a spiritually powerful thought—that God's grace is prior to our response, that atonement precedes the fullness of spiritual life. At times I think that, without that moment of precedent grace, we would never attain the purity of even one moment with God.

How strangely beautiful to hear the bloody ritualistic killing of animals transformed into a strong theology of atonement, grace, and response.

Keeping Kosher and Prophecy

Kashrut is the noun and *kosher* or *kashér* is the adjective used to describe the dietary laws which Jews observe. No pattern, except perhaps the prohibition on intermarriage or the Sabbath, runs as deep in Jewish consciousness and in the gentile perception of the Jew. The separation at table, the prohibition on sharing certain foods, is certainly one of the major barriers between Jew and gentile, in the minds of both. How does this work, and why?

The rules are quite simple: (1) One may not eat certain animals at all. They are listed in this reading, Leviticus 11, and again in Deuteronomy 14. (2) The permissible animals must be properly slaughtered and treated. The trachea and gullet must be slit by a knife so sharp that it won't nick a fingernail (this is a completely painless death) and the blood must be removed by draining and salting. Finally, (3) one may not mix meat and meat products with milk and milk products. Even dishes and silverware for the one may not be mixed with those used for the other. This is derived from Exodus 23:19; Exodus 34:26; and Deuteronomy 14:21.

Applying the rules is very complex: What is the rule for animals not listed? What is the status of an animal that dies an accidental death? Is fish considered meat or milk? What is chicken? What of artificial products such as dairy creamers, which are not milk? What will be the rule about artificial meat, when such a thing is possible? What is the status of vegetables? How does one correct a mixture of meat and milk (and there are hundreds of cases imaginable), if at all? There are many more. One needs a special education in this area to answer these questions. At Passover time, when one is forbidden to eat any leavening substance, the rules are even more complex.

Jews have long felt a need to defend or deny these rules. In modern times, some Jews look upon these laws as remnants of an earlier stage of Jewish civilization which can, and should, now be discarded. Others just follow the rules like a tribal taboo. Still others seek reasons for the laws of kashrut. The reasons given over the centuries are legion: They were, and continue to be, health regulations which protect those who observe them from certain illnesses. They were, and are, a folk pattern that distinguishes Jews and hence provides a means for, and a sense of, personal and group identity. They were, and are, God's command, and one simply does not disobey God's word. Many peoples have dietary restrictions, including Muslims whose restrictions are close to ours, so Jews can, and should, have such restrictions too. They are part of a mystery and create a sacramental aura to all eating. And so on. Levi Yitzhak offers a reason I've never heard before:

"God spoke to Moses and to Aaron, saying to them, speak . . ." [Leviticus 11:1]. What is the meaning of "saying to them"? [In connection with the verse describing the drawing forth of Moses from the water], Rashi [the great medieval commentator to the Bible] says: " 'Shall I go and call a nursing woman for you from among the Hebrews' [Exodus 2:27]—the Egyptians took Moses to many Egyptian women to nurse but he would not drink because he knew he was destined to speak with God and be a prophet to Israel." And the holy Nahmanides [another great medieval commentator] said [in connection with this section on forbidden animals], "The reason the Torah forbade us these animals is that . . . in the future, the Holy One, blessed be He, will speak with each person of Israel as it says, 'Your sons and your daughters shall prophesy' [Joel 3:1]." From these we learn that, since God is destined to speak with the Jews, it is not fitting that the mouth which will speak with Him should now eat forbidden foods. This is the meaning of "saying to them"— that I shall one day "say" to each of them . . . therefore, they shall not now eat any forbidden food.

Keeping kosher is not, Levi Yitzhak teaches, a matter of health regulations, either ancient or modern. Nor is kashrut a matter of self-identification. It is not even simply a matter of observing God's word. Keeping kosher is a way of preparing oneself to receive the word of God. It is a way of cultivating the bodily habits that will make one a fit receptacle for the divine Presence. What one eats, counts. What one says, counts. The mouth, as the popular stories would have it, is the gateway into and out of the body. To eat properly, and to speak properly, is to guard the gateway of the body. Someday, God will address us. He will speak to us and we will speak with Him. And our bodies, as well as our minds and hearts, must be ready. We must be whole when He comes.

Putting Forth Seed, Being Pregnant, and Birthing

This reading begins with the period of impurity and the sacrifice to which a woman who has just given birth is subject. The text clearly says that, for a boy, a woman must undergo a two-stage impurity of seven days and then thirty-three while, for a girl, the time of impurity is fourteen and then sixty-six days (Leviticus 12:11–15). Moderns try to reinterpret or discard this misogynist piece of legislation; premoderns accepted it and even developed its internal logic. Thus the Zohar *(ad loc)* teaches: "From the time that a woman becomes pregnant until the day that she gives birth, she speaks only of her desire to give birth to a boy." Levi Yitzhak, speaking from deep within the tradition, accepted the implications of the biblical text. He does not deal, here, with the differential time of impurity, but devotes one of his homilies to an explication of the zoharic expansion of this text.

I heard from my teacher and rabbi, Dov Baer [of Mezeritch], may his soul be in Eden, the following interpretation: The sages, may their memory be a blessing, said, "The Jews nourish their Father in heaven as it is written [Proverbs 10:1; 15:20], 'A wise son causes his father to rejoice.'" This means that, in our doing the commandments and good deeds, we cause pleasure to the Creator, may He be blessed. This is the "nourishment" that the Jews give to their Father in heaven, for pleasure is, so to speak, nourishment. [Levi Yitzhak continues], it is, therefore, fitting for each and every Jew to do the commandments and good deeds so that the Creator, blessed be He, have pleasure from these deeds.

The Holy One, blessed be He, has myriads of angels who say "Holy, holy, holy . . ." in fear and in awe yet He desires the deeds of humankind. The matter can be explained by analogy: Certain princes have a special bird which speaks the language of men and all who hear are astounded and say to others, "Come, hear, and see something truly unusual." The meaning is easy . . .

Now, each person contains within himself or herself three moments: putting forth seed, being pregnant, and giving birth. "Putting forth seed" occurs when one is aroused in one's heart to worship the Creator. "Being pregnant" occurs when one has decided to do such a deed. And "giving birth" occurs when one actually does the commandment or good deed. This is as the sages, may their memory be a blessing, have said [Talmud, Rosh ha-Shana 4b]: "The verse [Psalm 45:10], 'A princess [Hebrew, *shegal*] stands at your right with a crown of pure gold,' must be interpreted as follows: Because the Jews love the Torah more than the gentiles love sex [Hebrew, shegal], they merit a crown of pure gold" . . .

[Combining all these insights, one learns that], from the moment a person is aroused and decides to do a commandment or a good deed [puts forth seed and becomes pregnant] until the moment that one actually does that deed [gives birth], one speaks only of one's desire to do a deed that will bring pleasure to the Creator [give birth to a boy] which will, in turn, bring energy and blessing upon all the worlds.

I am always astounded at the intricacy with which Levi Yitzhak weaves texts from the Bible, the Talmud, the Zohar, and here even his teacher into one whole. This is an art form. It is complex—but, then, Jewish commentary and Jewish spirituality are a discipline of the learned. I am also continuously amazed at the ease with which Levi Yitzhak transforms even the most arcane subjects and quotations into a single clear spiritual insight.

Here, Levi Yitzhak's point is simple: Putting forth seed, pregnancy, and giving birth are spiritual moments in the life of every serious person. The processes of sex, conception, and birthing are not the monopoly of biologists or of only one gender. Everything is a way to the service of God. What, then, are these three moments: the impulse to do something, the decision to do it, and the actual performance of the deed. How simple. All of human existence is composed of these three moments. Impulse is not enough though it is indispensable. Decision is not enough though it too is indispensable. The act is the measure of the impulse and the decision. Deed fulfills will and desire. Furthermore, impulse-decision-deed must be placed within the framework of the spiritual, the bringing of joy to God, in a word—within the service of God. And finally, the reason for this is because He wants it that way.

Moderns may reject the misogyny of the sources, but we must take seriously the spiritual insights that this system generates.

On Sexuality: An Essay

One of the fundamental principles of Judaism is separation. We separate day from night, Shabbat from the rest of the week, meat from dairy, wool from cotton, the holy from the profane, and man from woman. The effect of separation, whether it be Shabbat from the work week or woman from man, is to enhance our awareness of the differences between the two. Thus the distinctions made throughout Judaism between man and woman serve to reinforce sexual identity and to increase our awareness of the other.

Certain rules in the tradition govern the cycle of permitted sexual expression between husband and wife; they are rather straightforward. Intercourse is prohibited from the onset of the menstrual period, an average of five days, to seven days following its cessation. Following this period of abstinence, the couple may engage in intercourse essentially without restriction until the onset of the next menstrual period. The average couple, then, experiences twelve days of separation followed by a period of reunion.

The biological and psychological effects of this cycle, however, are complex. Women have a hormonally induced ebb and flow of sexual desire. But, while the period of abstinence serves to heighten a woman's desire, it occurs during the low point of her desire cycle. By contrast, men do not have a cycle of sexual desire and thus they are not biologically buffered from the sexual tension generated by twelve or more days of abstinence. Instead, a man experiences ever-increasing sexual tension. Further, a man is forbidden to engage in autoerotic behavior. Although, technically, a woman may do so, a woman who is spiritually motivated in her observance of these laws would not make this choice. For her, that would constitute an abuse of sexuality. Finally, as sexual tension varies, one's perception of one's spouse varies from the intensely physical to the deeply spiritual to the peacefully comfortable. The marital sexual cycle is thus characterized by an ebb and flow of relationship, by alternating periods of tension and release, of closeness and separation.

If sexual tension within the marriage is not handled with sensitivity and delicacy on the part of both members, the strain on the marriage can be extreme and can lead to a difficult situation. The sexual energy that builds throughout the period of abstinence is at risk of being discharged as anger, hostility, and even as overt physical violence. For both, this could lead to what can legitimately be termed demonic behavior. Sex could become a mode of domination or a vehicle to express anger and frustration. Sadomasochism could creep into subsequent sex acts. Sex and abstinence could become a compelling mode of reenacting past trauma. Sex and relatedness could become a way of expressing so much that was never intended.

Much of rabbinic writing on the topic of sex is devoted to finding ways of controlling and channeling this energy into socially acceptable outlets and of preventing further increase of sexual frustration within the relationship. Realizing that sex and abstinence can become a symbol for many emotions, the rabbis attempted to constrain the destructive elements in many ways: The husband is required to satisfy the wife sexually; should he fail, a woman has grounds for divorce. The tradition clearly acknowledges male dominance as right and proper; a man is commanded to impregnate his wife. Sex must be had in modesty, not in orgy. Certain ritual acts which have subconscious sexual symbolism are practiced—swaying during prayer, treating the Sabbath as a queen, and so forth. Prayer, study, and other positive social acts are encouraged. Women are expected to dampen their visible sexuality in clothing and behavior. Discussion of sexual topics is allowed, but only within the frame of the tradition. It is especially meritorious for a couple to have intercourse every Sabbath during the permitted times (Talmud, Bava Qama 82a; Ketubot 62b), thereby ensuring that at least twice a month there will be less confusion about sexual expectations, and hence less possibility of manipulation. The strongest check against the misuse of sex, however, is the requirement that, during intercourse, one ought to think certain thoughts. This brings us to Levi Yitzḥak's homily.

The reading of this week announces the following provision:

"When sperm issues from a man, he shall wash his entire body in water and remain [ritually] impure until the evening . . . If a woman has intercourse with a man such that sperm has issued from him, both shall wash in water and remain [ritually] impure until the evening" (Leviticus 15:16–18). "At first reading, this would seem very strange indeed," says Levi Yitzḥak:

How can the Torah have commanded that one be ritually impure after normal intercourse when that act is a specific positive commandment of God, may He be blessed ["Be fruitful and multiply," Genesis 1:28]? Rather, the essence of the matter is that the emission of sperm in normal intercourse does not make one ritually impure since it is a command of God. However, since it is all but impossible for a person to subdue his or her impulse and to master it so that one not think of one's own pleasure at all but think only of the command of God, there is a certain impurity attached to the act of intercourse. For one almost always thinks also of one's own pleasure. This is the impurity in the sexual act and, for this reason, the emission of sperm in normal intercourse conveys ritual impurity.

The matter may be compared to a great and mighty king who had two artisan-servants. He commanded them to make a certain thing for him. They both did as the king commanded but they acted out of different motives. The first did the bidding of the king in order to give the king pleasure in having his command fulfilled. The second fulfilled the command because he wanted on his own to make that object. He did it for his own pleasure, not to give the king the pleasure of the obedience of his servants. The first, in his action, accepted the kingship of the king; the second did not. So it is in the matter of intercourse: one person thinks only to fulfill the command of the King while another thinks of his or her own pleasure [although it coincides with the command of the King]. Therefore, the emission of sperm in normal intercourse conveys ritual impurity.

When one contrasts this attitude of Levi Yitzḥak with such modern books as Alex Comfort's *The Joy of Sex,* one cannot help but be aghast. As moderns, we look upon Levi Yitzḥak's attitude as the height of neurosis: There *should* be *no* joy of sex; that is, no enjoyment of sexual pleasure in, of, and for itself. When actually engaged in intercourse, one should repress all thoughts of personal satisfaction, and think of God. Our questions tumble out: What could possibly be wrong with pleasure in wholly licit sex? How could a person even do such a thing—not think of pleasure and only think of God? Is that not also an insult to one's partner? Is there no area of activity where we have our privacy from God? Levi Yitzḥak and Alex Comfort couldn't be further apart. And we, participants in both worlds, couldn't be more hard-pressed to judge between them.

On second thought, the idea is not as neurotic as it seems. A great deal of sex is lived out in the thoughts that accompany the act. We never do anything without having something in our mind, and that includes eating, playing, walking, and even sex. This multiple layering of consciousness, and our ability to control it, is called *kavvana*.

Sometimes, during sex, we have thoughts of loving and sharing, of giving and taking. Sometimes, we have thoughts of being loved and dependence, or of strength and protectiveness. Without such thoughts, sex is biological; it is not love.

But that is not all that may be in our minds during sexual intercourse, as Freud has taught us. Sometimes we have thoughts that can only be called sexual fantasies. Sometimes the fantasy is acted out, sometimes it remains intramental; but it is present in a large percentage of moments of sexual satisfaction. The reason for this, as psychoanalysis and honest common sense confirm, is that sexual activity itself is not always sufficient to generate culmination of the sexual impulse. When it is not, we help that fulfillment along by fantasy. Why do we do that? Why do we mix reality and fantasy in the effort to achieve fulfillment? There are as many reasons as there are human psyches. But all of them, upon reflection, are what we would call neurotic: a fear of impotence, a mild sadomasochistic impulse, a need to purge excess vital energies, a compelling urge to reenact some moment of childhood, and so forth.

Actually, in most adult situations, sex is only secondarily biological. It is primarily an expression of something else: love (and that means many things), a need to be loved (that too has different meaning for different people), or a series of more or less neurotic impulses. There is always a mix of the biological and the mental, of the physical and the psychological. Sexual activity, for all of modern society's vaunting of it, is derivative in its inner motivations.

What would constitute appropriate spiritual accompanying thoughts? What would be appropriate religious *kavvana* during sexual intercourse? Before answering the question, imagine what such an approach could do for us: no more trying to make sex say "I love you," no more wondering if we are also being loved, no more preoccupation with enjoying oneself or with achieving orgasm, no more sadomasochistic motifs, no more compulsion to unending pleasure (how many orgasms are enough?), no more guilt feelings or frustrations about fantasied infidelity, no more reduction to childhood-generated situations, and so on. And positively: the sense of living a total religious life, a lack of embarrassment in having God with us even at the most intimate of moments, a way of living that places heightened sexual tension within a larger whole, and a sense of being part of a greater command, plan, and meaning in the universe. The idea that consciousness of God and sex should be associated, and not dissociated, is an important suggestion.

How does one achieve such a state? What *should* be in one's mind if one wants to unite spirituality and sex? One approach is to recognize that God is implicit in any natural act, that He is present whenever we satisfy a need of the body that He has created. Another is to recognize that God is present in the body, need, and person of the other. More explicitly, however, we can turn our consciousness to the presence of God during sex as we do it during prayer, or study, or any other human act.

The analogy is to our consciousness when we bless someone. We do not simply pray for the other person or recite a liturgical formula. To truly bless someone, we must first empty our minds of all the distracting thoughts that assail us. Then we must invoke God's presence. We must concentrate on God, opening ourselves up to His love and power. When we feel it, and it does not always happen, we must then make ourselves into vessels, into conduits, for that power. It flows through us; we do not command it. Then we must make ourselves aware of the person we are blessing, his or her presence, her or his being. Finally, we must allow the presence of God to connect with the presence of the other through us. We must allow the power and being of God to flow through us to the innermost recesses of the other. And we must sustain that moment of conveying blessedness. This is what it means to bless someone.

The same holds true for the sex act. One must empty oneself of the physical concerns of the moment; one must make oneself aware of God's presence; one must open oneself to the presence of the other; one must enable oneself to be a vessel for the divine energy; and one must sustain that moment of presence-blessing. This is the *kavvana* of the sex act that Levi Yitzḥak is proposing. It is the way of bringing God and spirituality into our most intimate moments. It is not easy, surely not; but it is the ideal.

It is a strange temptation that Levi Yitzḥak sets before us, a choice, a gentle urging in the direction of the divine, a calling to our better selves. Levi Yitzḥak is right: sexuality itself does not convey impurity. It is the thought and the motivation behind it that are the source of our own inner purity and impurity. It is the consciousness that accompanies sex that is at once the check on our abuse of sexuality and the measure of the wholeness of our spirituality.

Reason and Unreason in the Commandments

Toward the end of this reading, the following verse occurs: "You shall observe My statutes and My laws which, if a person do them, he or she shall live by them; I am the Lord" (Leviticus 18:5). That there are two types of legislation can be readily seen. What are they? Why are they in this particular sequence? And why are they followed by the promise that whoever observes them shall have (true) life?

Levi Yitzḥak's comment is very clear and direct:

The "statutes" are the commandments that have no [apparent] reason while the "laws" are the commandments that do have [apparent] reason. Now it is true that, when a person observes a commandment that does not have an [apparent] reason, she or he is purified by this to understand those commandments that do have [apparent] reasons. But, when a person, God forbid, does not observe the commandments that have no [apparent] reason, then he or she has no power at all to understand the commandments which do have [apparent] reason and, so, to observe them. This is the meaning of "you shall observe My statutes . . ."—when you do the commandments that are "statutes," i.e., those which have no [apparent] reason, your mind will be purified to understand and to do the "laws," i.e., those commandments which do have [apparent] reason. This is further hinted at in the closing stich, "which, if a person do them, she or he shall live by them"—that is, that he or she will understand that [all] the commandments are the source of his or her vitality.

The point, in two parts, is deceptively simple: First, there are "rational" commandments, that is, those that seem to have reason. There are also "irrational" commandments, that is, those that seem to be without any rhyme or reason. Observing the former takes no great commitment. It takes no great courage not to steal or kill and it takes no special faith to render thanks to God. Observing the latter, however, requires real commitment because they seem to make no sense. Second, observing the "irrational" commandments "purifies us" or "purifies our minds," that is, observing the "irrational" commandments actually helps us understand that all commandments fit into one whole. To put it differently, observing the "irrational" commandments makes them "rational" experientially; they come to fit within a larger pattern of religious commitment and meaning. Similarly, observing the "rational" commandments on nonrational grounds makes them "irrational" experientially; they lose their commonsense meaning and they too fit into the larger whole. The real import of both the "irrational" and the "rational" commandments thus becomes clearer. And we come to this by observing the "irrational" mitsvot, not the "rational" ones; they "purify" us.

Is this true? Does bending our will to the "irrational" element in religion make the whole more intelligible, including the "rational" parts? In the enlightenment strain of modern culture, thinkers would answer "no." The irrational has no special call on us; in fact, it is a destructive force in human knowledge and living. All of science, even psychoanalysis, is devoted to rationalizing the irrational. In the romantic strain of modern culture, thinkers and poets would answer "yes." The irrational is the truly human. After all, machines can think and so can animals. Learning to live with the irrational is the art of life. Consider Dali's painting, or Stravinsky's music, or the sheer incomprehensibility of the holocaust, or the irrationalities of child-raising, or caring for aging parents. I think Levi Yitzhak is right: Learning to accept the seeming irrationalities of life, of God's scheme of things, purifies us in a strange way. It frees us to live a little more fully. After all, if we are created in God's image and He is one of us (so to speak), we must learn to live with His irrationalities too.

But there is more. One of the central concepts in Jewish thinking, especially in Levi Yitzhak, is the idea of "servanthood." We are God's servants; the same Hebrew word means "slave." Accepting God's irrationalities, therefore, becomes a living action-symbol of our servitude to God. This is where moderns rebel against the kind of religion that Levi Yitzhak teaches. We are not slaves and do not see ourselves bound as servants to a Master. We can accept irrationality, even capriciousness, in human relations because we know that behind the irrationality is the common bond of humanity. But pure imposition of will upon us is unacceptable.

The easiest way to understand this is to contemplate the overwhelming anger we feel when thinking of the absolute power wielded by the concentration camp guards or other such figures. The analogy does not hold completely, of course, because we do not understand God to be cruel. But the absoluteness of the demand for obedience is the same. Perhaps our resistance even to beneficent absolute authority stems from the childhood experience of the absolute authority of the parent. I understood this clearly when I saw a production of *Alice in Wonderland* some years ago in which the Queen of Hearts was portrayed as a mother figure. The capriciousness of life for a child must be overwhelming.

Our objections notwithstanding, Levi Yitzhak, following classical rabbinic thought, teaches that there are "statutes," commandments without any (apparent) reason, and that we are bound to observe those too. Furthermore, the observance of this irrational dimension of God's will "purifies" us because it makes clear to us our status as His servants, our utter dependence upon Him for all vitality and existence. Servitude, not rationality, is the issue. "Experiential rationality," not intellectual consistency, is the crux.

Fear, Awe, Reverence, and Knowledge

The reading for this week begins with the verse: "Each person should fear [have reverence for] his or her mother and father; and you shall observe My Sabbaths; I am the Lord, your God" (Leviticus 19:3). There are two problems here that deserve attention: (1) There is one word in Hebrew for fear, awe, and reverence. What does this mean? What is the relationship among these three phenomena? (2) To the rabbis, the juxtaposition of fear of (reverence for) parents and the observance of the Sabbath was noteworthy. To moderns, steeped in the ethical as opposed to the ritual, this is more than strange. The answer to both questions lies in the fact that premodern Jewish culture did not distinguish between fear, awe, and reverence—at least, not in the same way that we do. The rabbis distinguished between "upper fear" or "transcendent fear" (which we would call awe or reverence) and "lower fear" or "fear of punishment." I have commented on this elsewhere in this book. Also, premodern Jewish culture did not distinguish between "ethical" commandments and "ritual" commandments. All are contained in the Torah; all are given by God; and hence all are equally spiritual, equally binding. In both cases, then, the problem is in the way moderns approach the text, not in the text itself.

Levi Yitzḥak accepted the integration of ethical and ritual commandments, yet he too was puzzled by the juxtaposition of fear/reverence of parents and observance of the Sabbath. He addressed the problem by first making an astute observation about fear/reverence and then commenting on the verse:

The rule is that he who has fear of something must have some little knowledge of it; i.e., that he who has fear of something is not able to grasp all of it because the thought is greater than one's ability to grasp [but he must have some inkling of knowledge about it]. So it is with the worlds: they have fear/

reverence of God which means that they do not grasp all of His essence but they do understand a fractional part of it; [that is,] from the pouring forth and shining [of existence] upon the universe, [they understand] that there is a Being above all Who is ultimately beyond comprehension. The first aspect— that the worlds comprehend but a little of His essence so that they may be in fear and reverence of Him—is called "father and mother." The second aspect—that His pouring forth and shining upon the worlds is an indication of His ultimate unknowability—is called "Sabbath," for "Sabbath" means the ceasing from all work when, nonetheless, the activity of thought continues.

This, then, is the meaning of the verse: "Each person should fear his or her mother and father"—that the little knowledge that the worlds have of Him is the source of their fear and reverence; "and you shall observe My Sabbaths"—that this [little bit of knowledge is the knowledge of His unknowability which] is derivable from His emanation of existence to the universe.

Levi Yitzhak's insight begins with the recognition that we do not fear the unknown; rather, we fear the partially known. We do not reverence that which is completely beyond our ken; we feel reverence for that of which we have some knowledge but which yet points beyond itself to something much greater which is unknown and unknowable. We do not experience awe in the presence of the unperceived, but in the face of that which alludes to a reality greater than ours. Fear, awe, and reverence are our response to intimations of transcendence. They are our acknowledgment of our fragmented perception of that which is beyond our very being.

We cannot be ignorant of God, Levi Yitzhak reasons, for we sense the presence of His vitalizing energy in all the worlds of creation. At the periphery of our awareness is that little bit of knowledge, that "mother and father," which evokes fear and reverence. Yet behind the "mother and father" is the "Sabbath"—the continuous flow of His Presence in creation which is testimony to His ultimate unknowableness. The paradox is complete: We cannot be ignorant of God but He cannot be known. God can be sensed, and we do know Him, in the reverence we feel as we contemplate the multitude and continuity of His blessing upon all creation.

What Is True Prayer?

This week's reading contains the commandment to count seven full weeks from Passover to Shavu'ot. This period, called the "counting of the *omer*" or the *sefira*, links the celebration of God's redemption of the Jewish people to the commemoration of His revelation to us. From what point, however, does one start counting the omer? The Bible clearly says: "You shall count for yourselves, from the day after the Sabbath, from the day on which you bring the omer offering, seven sabbaths; they shall be complete" (Leviticus 23:15). The reader, by now accustomed to Levi Yitzḥak's acute examination of the biblical text, will note many problems: Why count "for yourselves"? What is "the day after the Sabbath"? Was it the same as "the day on which you bring the omer offering"? What was the "omer offering"? Why "seven sabbaths" and not "seven weeks"? Why must they be "complete"; what if they are not? If the reader has seen several of these problems, he or she is entering into the spirit of traditional Jewish examination of the biblical text. For our purposes, we will only ask the second question: What is "the day after the Sabbath"?

Jewish tradition was divided on the meaning of this phrase. One view, which later was declared sectarian, claimed that the first Sabbath after the Passover holiday was what was meant. Rabbinic tradition, however, understood "Sabbath" in a general sense and interpreted the point for the beginning of the sefira to be the day after the first holy day of Passover. Since Passover lasts seven days, the counting began on the second day of the holiday. The reasons for this need not detain us, but the decision left the rabbis with the biblical word "Sabbath" understood in the sense of "holy day." This, in turn, led to many interpretations of "the day after the Sabbath." And it is to Levi Yitzḥak's interpretation of that phrase that we turn.

Levi Yitzḥak has two interpretations of why the second day of

Passover should be called "the day after the Sabbath." First, he teaches that this is not a reference to an ordinary Sabbath but to the Sabbath of creation, for the inner logic of creation was only made clear after Passover. God had intended, right from the beginning, to have a chosen people and to save them in the eyes of all the world. This occurred on Passover, and so the first Sabbath of creation did not achieve its full reality until after the redemption from Egypt on the first night of Passover.

Second, Levi Yitzhak teaches that:

The chief desire of the Jewish people is to be able to worship God, may He be blessed, with a whole heart. And, when they approach Him in prayer, their deepest request is to be able to worship Him fully. At such moments, they forget to pray to God, may He be blessed, for their physical needs [of food, clothing, and shelter]. There is, however, another aspect [of their spiritual life] when they do ask God for sustenance and their needs. But the aspect [of their spiritual life] in which they ask to serve only God is called "Sabbath," for the Sabbath is like the world-to-come, having no root in this-worldliness. This, then, is the meaning of the verse: "After the Sabbath"—when you are in a stage of "after-Sabbath," you may ask for your needs.

During the counting of the omer [which is the "after-Sabbath" activity], we ask for blessing and goodness for ourselves. And on the holiday of Shavu'ot, we raise all these requests for our needs to the [level of] the total worship of God, may He be blessed. For on the holy day of Shavu'ot, we [again] pray to be able to worship God fully. For this reason, the Torah says [of the holiday of Shavu'ot]: "when you offer up a new offering" [Leviticus 23:16]—that you should offer up all the prayers for your needs that you have made during the counting of seven weeks [Hebrew, shavu'ot] on the holy day.

This is a profound typology of prayer on two grounds. First, some moderns have the feeling that it is somehow "selfish" to ask God for our own needs. Not so, says Levi Yitzhak. It is a natural aspect of one's spiritual life that one pray for food, clothing, children, health, success, money, and personal happiness. It is not the highest form of prayer but it is natural and important. Second, to most moderns, the highest form of prayer is praise—praise of God in nature, in history; as creator and judge. Not so, says Levi Yitzhak. The highest form of prayer is the deep wish to serve God with a whole heart, the yearning just to be His servant. But it must be a passion so deep that one forgets all one's personal needs, even the needs of one's community.

How shallow most of our prayer seems in comparison—the hymns, the responsive readings, the listless silent meditations, the social-ritual liturgy. Do we think we have no need deep enough to pray for? Or are we so content in our service of God that we think we already serve Him "with a whole heart"? Levi Yitzḥak urges us to reach out from the middle ground we occupy and to pray both for our specific needs and for that totality of devotion that characterizes true spiritual service to God.

"A Sabbath unto the Lord"

The reading for this week contains the laws which project the idea of Sabbath onto the use of the land and onto the institution of slavery. Everyone and everything is entitled to a Sabbath because all are created. The Bible thus provides that a slave can serve only six years. If he insists, he can stay seven times seven years, but then he must go (Leviticus 25:35–55). The reasoning is straightforward: "They are My slaves whom I brought out of Egypt" (Leviticus 25:42). Similarly, the land must have a Sabbath (Leviticus 25:1–34). It must lie fallow once in seven years and it cannot be sold in perpetuity. Here too the reasoning is direct, "For the land belongs to Me; you are sojourners and wayfarers with Me" (Leviticus 25:23). Note that, in setting the character of this fiftieth year, the jubilee year, the Bible uses the phrase that was later inscribed with a slight variation on the Liberty Bell, "You shall proclaim liberty throughout the land to all of its inhabitants" (Leviticus 25:10).

Levi Yitzhak was very sensitive to the fact that, in this reading, God asserts His kingship and dominion over all. He notes that the pericope begins with the phrase, "the land shall have its Sabbath, a Sabbath unto the Lord" (Leviticus 25:2) and it closes with the phrase, "you shall observe My Sabbaths" (Leviticus 26:2). What is "a Sabbath unto the Lord" and what does God mean when He calls these days "My Sabbaths"? Levi Yitzhak answers the second question first:

During the enslavement in Egypt, Moses, seeing the terrible labor of the Jews, asked Pharaoh to let the Jews rest one day a week. He chose the Sabbath as that day of rest. Then, when we were commanded to observe the Sabbath at Mt. Sinai, he rejoiced in his portion for he had thought of this before it had been commanded . . . Therefore, God now said, "you shall observe My Sabbaths" [to teach that] Israel should rest on the Sabbath, not as a respite from their work but only because God, may He be blessed, has commanded them to rest on the Sabbath.

This is also the meaning of "the land shall have its Sabbath, a Sabbath unto the Lord." It is the way of the world that one plows a field one year and leaves it fallow the next so that it be fruitful for planting. Therefore God, may He be exalted, said "a Sabbath unto the Lord" [to teach that] in the sabbatical year the land should rest, not for the good of the land but as "a Sabbath unto the Lord"—because He, may He be blessed, commanded it.

Levi Yitzḥak has here returned to one of the central motifs in his theology: that utilitarianism is not spiritual. When one acts for one's own ultimate good, that is rational, even praiseworthy if the good of all is also taken into account; but it is not religious. To qualify as spiritual, an act must be done *only* because God commanded it. To qualify as religious, a deed must be an act of obedience, of servanthood. His examples are clear in their very simplicity. The Sabbath for people is not to afford respite from work (if so, one could choose any day, or rest every day, and define the Sabbath accordingly). It is to afford an opportunity for servanthood. Similarly, the Sabbath for the land is not to replenish natural resources but to enable even the land to be a servant of God.

As often as we have seen this idea, it is still strange, especially to modern ears for whom the power of decision lies with the individual person and his or her perception of what is good and fitting. As long as we observe any commandment because it is beautiful, or because it is good for us in any way, we are observing it at our own pleasure. And it makes no difference whether one is orthodox, conservative, or reform (or Jew, Christian, or Muslim). The only justification for doing any religious deed is that God wants us to do it. It is not reason and consensus or authority and trust that count, though each has its place and role, but commandedness. What a difficult standard Levi Yitzḥak has set!

"Walking" with God

The reading for this week, the last in Leviticus, begins with the phrase, "If you walk in My statutes and observe My mitsvot and do them, I shall give you your rains in due season" (Leviticus 26:3–4). Why, asks Levi Yitzḥak, does the Torah add the phrase "and do them?" Of course, if one walks in God's ways and observes His commandments, one is "doing them." "Doing," reasons Levi Yitzḥak, must be something other than "walking" and "observing."

When a person truly performs a mitsva, without any inner reservation, then it may happen that he or she may attain to the higher state of doing another mitsva in the same manner. And, then, he or she may attain to yet a higher state. Therefore, the righteous are said to "walk," that is, they proceed from level to level of holiness. This is also the meaning of [the phrase in the Sayings of the Fathers, 4:2], "one mitsva elicits another."

In this initial interpretation, Levi Yitzḥak has taught that the word "walk" used in the verse does not mean simple observance of the mitsvot. It means the full observance thereof, the doing of mitsvot with an inner purity, the living of Jewish ritual with a sense of God's holy presence. Levi Yitzḥak, however, has also taught that this "walking," this way of being Jewish, this method of observing mitsvot must be habit-forming, that one must accustom oneself to it and grow in it. If a person observes one mitsva in this way then, in the words of Ben Azzai, that act elicits another mitsva to be done in the same way. Growth in inner spirituality is true "walking."

The older I get, the more I hear the resonance of Levi Yitzḥak's insight. We live lives that are so secular, so devoid of spirituality. We are so pressed for time to do this and to do that that we barely know what the word "spirituality" means. How many synonyms can we think of for the word "spiritual?" When was the last time we used the word? How many people do we know whom we would call "holy?"

When we say our prayers, do we feel "holy?" Would we use the word "spiritual" to characterize even our prayer, much less the rest of our life? We do not "walk" in God's ways in the sense that Levi Yitzḥak teaches. We do not have the habit of holiness, the custom of spirituality. But that is what Judaism is really all about: the presence of God in our lives and our response to that presence. To reach that level of awareness, we must learn to "walk" spiritually, to make a habit of this "walking," and to grow in it. This is Levi Yitzḥak's first lesson from the reading.

How does Levi Yitzḥak interpret the terms "observe" and "do" that also occur in the verse from this week's reading? He begins by quoting from the Talmud (Kiddushin 40a): "The Holy One, blessed be He, takes a good thought and combines it with the deed." This means, Levi Yitzḥak teaches that, "when a person thinks and, in thought only, takes it upon himself or herself to do a mitsva, then God considers it as though the person had done the deed right away." Then, taking the Hebrew *shamar* in the sense in which it is used when Jacob "takes note" of Joseph's dream, Levi Yitzḥak teaches that "to observe" (also shamar) is not really to act but "to think, to take note." Finally, combining these two thoughts, he interprets the verse as follows: " 'If you observe My commandments,' that is, if you think that you will do them, even though you have not done them yet, then 'and do them,' that is, I will consider it now as if you had already done them, for the good thought is always combined with the deed."

Levi Yitzḥak's second lesson from the reading, then, is that intending to do a mitsva is itself a mitsva, that intending to do a mitsva right is itself an especially good deed. Here, too, our lives are like a great desert. We say our blessings and observe our traditions without much spiritual thought and holy intent. We "fulfill our duties," as the common phrase would have it. We "do what is expected." But is that what the Holy One, blessed be He, wants of us? Does He want us only to do His will mindlessly? Certainly not. He expects us to pray when we recite a prayer. He expects us to rejoice when we do a mitsva. He expects us to praise Him when we observe His commandments. I always point out to my students that Jewish New Year cards are the lowest form of Jewish religious culture. They create the pretense of accomplishing something related to the Day of Judgment. But what can a Rosh ha-Shana card do, other than fulfill some social function which has nothing to do with the Day of Judgment? Observance of mitsvot, Levi Yitzhak teaches, must be accompanied by thought, by intent. So much so, that God will even give us "advance credit" for the intent alone, if it is pure. He will combine it with the deed for us.

One may not, to be sure, neglect doing mitsvot. But if we really intend to do a mitsva correctly—with proper intentionality—and then we get sidetracked, if something intervenes between plan and execution, God will still count the thinking as if we had also done the commandment. Jewish living requires *kavvana,* and *kavvana* creates spiritual growth.

NUMBERS

Microcosm-Macrocosm and Holiness

The reading of this week contains the details of the census of the Jewish people in the desert. The astute reader will notice that the numbers do not add up properly and should consult the commentators for an explanation. For Levi Yitzhak, the noteworthy point is that the tribe of Levi was not counted together with the rest of the Jews (Numbers 1:47–49). Why was this tribe singled out for a separate census?

Levi Yitzhak begins his answer by remarking that the Torah contains 248 positive commandments and 365 negative commandments, yielding a total of 613 mitsvot. This division corresponds to the traditional biological division of the body into 248 limbs and 365 connectors. (I am not sure how these last figures are arrived at, but they were regarded as authoritative.) "The rule is," writes Levi Yitzhak, "that, just as there are 248 physical limbs and 365 physical connectors, so there are 613 rational [that is, having articulated form] lights for the service of the Creator. They are called 'spiritual limbs [and connectors]' and the Creator, blessed be He, pours forth [blessing] continuously on these rational lights." With this remark, Levi Yitzhak has touched upon one of the oldest themes in religion, one deeply rooted in Judaism especially in kabbalistic mysticism: that the human body is a microcosm, an image of the greater divine world, and that the divine (the Torah, in this case) is a macrocosm, an image of the human body. Man is the image of God and God is the image of man.

Levi Yitzhak does not dwell on the microcosm-macrocosm image here, though he surely accepts it. But I cannot leave it without registering my dissatisfaction with it. My objection is more psychological than dogmatic. One of the advantages of being human is that we are not God, that we do not have His responsibilities. We may, and should, aspire to imitate some of His qualities but there is a certain qualitative leap between us and Him, a gap that defines both us and Him. I am human and I have all I can do to be human. I do not want to be God, or to have Him reside in me. Mystics have always found great beauty and reward in this microcosm–macrocosm idea, but it leaves me ill at ease.

Levi Yitzhak continues, "Some persons grasp only the rational lights while others grasp and see the pouring forth that comes from the Cause of causes even to those rational lights . . . Israel stands for the rational lights while the tribe of Levi stands for the pouring forth which comes from the Cause of causes even to the rational lights." Here, Levi Yitzhak has developed another of his fine typologies of holiness and solved the problem in the weekly reading at the same time. He teaches that there are two types of people: There are those who perceive the Torah and the commandments, all of which are "lights" and are "rational," that is, have some articulated form. And there are those who are able to pierce through to the stream of being that flows beneath even revealed reality and which is, on that account, prerational, unarticulated and unarticulable. These two types are not miscible; they must be counted separately. Hence the separation of the census of "Israel" from that of the tribe of "Levi."

Here I find myself in agreement with Levi Yitzhak. There are those for whom God is His Torah, for whom the divine is incarnated in the commandments. That is what the word revelation means; that is what the revealed will means. Such persons maintain that all we can ever know is the revealed will. And there are those who recognize that God cannot be contained even in His own revelation; that His being transcends His will. Such persons maintain that we can know, or have an intimation of, this ineffable aspect of God too. The Jew, Levi Yitzhak teaches, must assert both: God is Torah and beyond. And the Jew must be both: Israel and Levi.

"May the Lord Bless You and Keep You"

This week's reading contains the blessing with which the priests were told to bless the children of Israel. The text reads:

And God spoke to Moses saying, "Speak unto Aaron and his sons saying, 'So shall you bless the children of Israel. Say unto them: "May the Lord bless you and keep you. May the Lord cause His face to shine upon you and may He be gracious unto you. May the Lord lift up His face unto you and grant you peace." ' And they shall set my Name upon the children of Israel and I will bless them." (Numbers 6:22–27)

Levi Yitzḥak's problem with this text is in the introductory phrase, "So shall you bless . . ." Why "so"? Why not, "These are the words with which you shall bless"? Or why not, "With these words shall you bless . . ."?

In searching for an answer, Levi Yitzḥak calls upon a short homily by the founder of the hasidic movement, Rabbi Israel Baal Shem Tov. The latter's homily, based upon Psalm 121:5, "The Lord is your shadow," is as follows: "Just as a shadow does everything that a person does, so the Creator, blessed be He, does, so to speak, everything that a person does." To this Levi Yitzḥak adds that a person should always act in such a way that God has pleasure in his or her actions, that God would be proud of that person. "For it is well known that, when one prays only for oneself, one is as a receptacle; that is, one's hands are spread out with the palms up and the back of the hand down. But, when one prays only to give God pleasure, then one is as one who pours blessing; that is, one's hands are spread out with the palms down and the back of the hand up." (Levi Yitzḥak is interpreting the way the priests hold their hands when blessing the people—index and middle finger together and smallest and ring finger together, each grouping separated from the other; palms down and backs up.)

Levi Yitzhak means to make three points here: that true blessing is a pouring-forth of an energy we receive, a channeling of divine power; that this type of blessing gives God pleasure, it makes Him proud; and that such an act evokes a shadow movement by God, a parallel response of poured-forth blessing from Him.

How often have I as a father blessed my children? How often have I as a rabbi blessed a congregation or a bride and groom? In doing so, I have often evoked the deepest hopes that I have for the person I have blessed. I have often invoked God's blessing for a specific situation. I have always tried to purify my inner self and to invoke God's presence. I have even tried to be a conduit for God's power to another. But I have never thought of giving God pleasure in my blessing someone else or of making Him proud when invoking His Name. I have sometimes prayed to give God pleasure. I have sometimes observed the commandments to make Him proud. But I have never blessed anyone with that in mind. Levi Yitzhak teaches us that a prayer or a blessing must be more than sincere; that it must have more than serious content, more than appropriate *kavvana*. A true prayer, or a true blessing, must be for the glory of God. It must transcend the one who prays and the one who is prayed for. Only then will it evoke the shadow movement of divine response.

For those of us who practice religion, this is an important insight. For it is all too easy to think that, when we have attained an inner purity, we have attained spirituality. Or, when we have achieved a certain candor in prayer, we have achieved something religiously important. Not to speak of the danger of ritualistically reciting the proper formulas believing that, in so doing, we have accomplished an act of piety. To bless and to be blessed is not a social matter. Nor is it a receiving. It is a pouring, of God, for God. To pray and to be prayed for is not a matter of substance and content. It is an address of God, for God.

The Manna and the Messiah

The history of Moses' leadership of the Jews in the desert is one of complaint by the people. Life in the desert is difficult and, although they have seen great wonders and miracles, they cry out again and again for the comforts of Egypt. In this week's reading, the text notes: "and the Jews also cried out, 'Who will give us meat to eat? We remember the fish which we ate freely in Egypt . . .'" (Numbers 11:4–5).

Levi Yitzhak opens his comment with a question: "Why is the taste of fish juxtaposed to the cry for meat?" The answer he gives is as follows: "They tasted in the manna any savor that they wished" (Talmud, Yoma 75a). But they could taste only those savors that were already known to them. They held them in their thought and were able to taste them in the manna. Any food that they had not tasted, they did not know the savor thereof and, hence, could not taste it in the manna.

Now the taste of kosher meat, that is, of meat properly slaughtered and salted, is different from unkosher meat. But in Egypt they had eaten unkosher meat, and hence they did not know the taste of properly prepared meat which had been commanded them upon Mt. Sinai. They did, however, remember the taste of fish, because fish was prepared no differently after Sinai than before. Therefore, they said, "Who will give us meat to eat? We remember the fish which we ate freely in Egypt . . ."

This [corresponds with the saying of the rabbis that] the Holy One, blessed be He, will make a feast for the righteous in the end of time composed of the great leviathan and the wild boar and the son of the geese and ancient wine. In reality, the Jews will eat manna at the end of time just as they ate it in the desert. Therefore, the Holy One, blessed be He, will prepare a feast for them from these things so that, afterwards when they eat the manna, they will be able to remember the savor of these foods and taste them always in the manna.

I find it difficult to believe that there is a deep and mystical truth hidden in Levi Yitzhak's teaching here. Rather, we are witness to a deep love for the text and the tradition being woven into one fabric. The biblical text is a bit peculiar, but it could stand ignored. The rabbinic traditions about the taste of the manna and the eschatological supper could also be left quietly alone. But, in the world of Levi Yitzḥak, these traditions are very much alive and no biblical text is simply ignored. So he evolves a wonderful homily which does give the verse meaning, and then he weaves into that homily the living eschatological dimension of human existence. The manna was more than food; it was the miracle food that could taste like everything. It will be the food of the eschaton too. The homily requires imagination, love of the text and tradition, and a willingness to live the text, the tradition, and reality from an eschatological perspective. Modern spirituality lacks all three of these qualities; without them there can be no true religious life.

The story is told that, when one of Levi Yitzḥak's children was engaged, the prenuptial agreements specified that the wedding be in Berditchev. Levi Yitzḥak tore up the document and ordered it rewritten with the wedding set in the holy city of Jerusalem and, if the messiah should not come in the meantime, then the wedding would take place in Berditchev. That is living in the eschatological dimension of human existence.

The Divine Invokes the Divine

This reading tells about the spies Moses sent into the holy land. It begins, "Send for yourself men who will spy out the land" (Numbers 13:2). From the point of view of the tradition, Moses had no need of spies because God would assure the victory of His people; why then does he send them? I think moderns would reply, "God helps those who help themselves and Moses' responsibility was to properly prepare the military aspect of the campaign to occupy the chosen land." This response, however, is a little too quick because that was an abnormal period of history. In those days, God Himself did intervene—witness the exodus, the delivery at the sea, and so on, up to and including the miraculous defeat of Jericho. The question of the tradition, then, is theologically not so farfetched: What does the Torah mean when it says that Moses sent spies?

Levi Yitzḥak chose to answer this question from within the Jewish mystical tradition:

The rule is that, when a Jew comes to a place and worships God there, all the divine sparks which are residual in that place are ashamed in his presence because he, in his worship, reveals the root and principle of the power of the Creator . . . He, then, easily conquers the sparks . . . However, in order to do this, a person must rid himself of all baseness so that the sparks will indeed be embarrassed in his presence; then he can conquer them. This is the meaning of the sending of the spies—that they had to "send forth," that is to rid themselves of their baseness in order to redeem the sparks.

Before we can understand the full power of this interpretation, we must know that, according to the Lurianic strain of Jewish mysticism, when God created the world, He at first did not succeed. The result of that first attempt was a fragmenting of the then-existing universe into "sparks of the divine energy" and into "shells of boundedness." Even after the second, successful attempt at creation, the sparks and shells of the first remained. Humankind's purpose, according to this stream of Jewish mysticism, is to go through life finding and meditatively redeeming these remnants of the first creation, the divine sparks. This became a central doctrine in Jewish religious thought and there even existed, for a brief period, a man who believed he was the messiah and who set about redeeming the sparks hidden in the world. Many people followed this false messiah because they were attracted to the idea that the fragmented existence in which we live could be redeemed by mystical means. Later, secularism continued the belief in a fragmented "alienated" existence but proposed political or psychoanalytic modes of redemption.

Levi Yitzhak lived at the edge of that mystical tradition. He believed that there were sparks, that they could be redeemed by mystical action, but that such action was the task only of the zaddikim, the great leaders of hasidism. He was one of those leaders and he gives us here a glimpse into his "calling," into the messianic dimension of his existence.

What has Levi Yitzhak said? He has said that the divine is indeed in all of creation, even in strange places. And that the divine spark can be redeemed by a Jew coming and invoking God's direct presence through prayer. This happens when the remnants of the divine recognize the divine invoked by the praying Jew, are embarrassed and then rejoin the divine. The key to successful action in this arena is, Levi Yitzhak says, that the person praying rid himself of all baseness, of all shell-ness, of all materiality. That act of "stripping oneself of baseness" is the prerequisite for the act of redemption. Without purifying oneself, one cannot redeem anything.

Moderns are skeptical about Levi Yitzhak's doctrine of sparks and purificatory and then redemptive action, though I suppose a truly inspired preacher could go into the Sodom of the pornography and prostitute districts of a city and preach the word of God even there. We should, however, not be so skeptical, because there is a way for moderns too to understand Levi Yitzhak. There are people whom each of us know who have a certain aura of the sacred about them. In their presence, we would not curse or indulge in profanity. It is also true that each of us has a varying amount of this aura and that we too can evoke and create this presence of God in our own lives and in the lives of others. When we do this, those with whom we have contact are themselves "raised." They are drawn toward the God-presence which we invoke. It is strange but true—the divine invokes the divine. This is, I think, what Levi Yitzḥak can mean for moderns when he talks about invoking the divine in others. It is not what he originally meant, but it is the underlying motif of his teaching. It is not easy, but it is a vision of what human existence can aspire to.

In order to invoke the divine in ourselves and then in others, Levi Yitzḥak teaches that we must rid ourselves of the baseness in our existence. That is very true. We are all tempted by the luxuries and even by the vulgarities of modern society. The advertising industry makes its livelihood by trying to tempt us to that life; so does the pornography industry. Yet we must shed all this if we are to live holier lives. Sometimes I envy those who live in cloisters and ghettoes; they are insulated, at least in part, from the temptations of the world. Yet all of us must learn to strip away the materiality of our existence. Levi Yitzḥak is right: to be able to invoke the holy, we must "send forth" our baseness.

The Paradigmatic Rebellion

This week's reading deals with the paradigmatic example of rebellion. Korah, of a distinguished levite family, and Datan and Aviram of distinguished Reubenite families, join forces to challenge the leadership of Moses and Aaron. What was the nature of this rebellion? The text seems to indicate that they raised the following question: Why were Moses and Aaron chosen as leader and high priest respectively; why not Korah and his group? But the text is ambiguous and the commentators stepped in with suggestions. Some said that Korah challenged Moses' interpretation of the law. Some say he wanted to be a high priest. Some say he was jealous that he was not made a head of family. And so on. Levi Yitzhak places a spiritual interpretation on these events.

"There is a difference," Levi Yitzhak teaches,

between the generation of the desert and the generation which entered the promised land. The generation of the desert [Hebrew, *midbar*] drew its vitality from the word [Hebrew, *dibbur;* a play on words], for everything that was done for them was done by the word of God. But the generation which entered the land drew its vitality from the doing of the deed [of entering and conquering the land].

There was one exception: Joshua's conquest of Jericho, which is clearly a miracle. But that was due to the overflow of the spirit of Moses upon Joshua. Now, after the failure of the mission of the spies, God indicated that the entire generation which had left Egypt would not be able to enter the promised land (Numbers 14:35). "Korah," continues Levi Yitzhak,

when he saw that the generation of the desert was not to enter the holy land, ceased to believe that the Torah of Moses needs to be clothed [that is, take on form] in the world of actions . . . He believed only in the Torah of the world of speech but did not believe that, in the world of action, the Torah has need of clothing. Nonetheless it is so, as it says, "I am first and I am last." [Isaiah 44:6; 48:12]

Levi Yitzhak's interpretation of Korah's rebellion is, then, as follows: Korah had been a witness to the exodus, to Sinai, to the manna, to the supply of water in the desert, and to a host of other miracles. He had become accustomed to the miraculous presence of God, to the intensity of God's power in the life of the people. He had also seen the incident of the spies. There the people, in an act of repentance, had taken it upon themselves to wage war against God's enemies. God had punished them by condemning the whole generation to die in the desert. It seemed so illogical: the people had made an error in believing the report of the spies; they had tried to correct it by mounting an invasion of the holy land; and God had punished them. Korah, seeing this, despaired of living according to God in the real world. He knew that it is possible to live under God in the world of the word, but he questioned whether one can live under God in the world of individual action. He knew that one can live in the world of the intensely spiritual, the miraculous; he despaired of living in the world of action. Korah, Levi Yitzhak teaches, made a common double error: first, in identifying the peaks as more real than the valleys; and second, in assuming that, in the valleys, humankind is free to do as it sees fit, even in the Name of God.

This, Levi Yitzhak means to say, is paradigmatic rebellion: first, to accept the intense aspect of religious reality and to reject the mundane aspect thereof; to accept the miraculous word and reject the actional clothing thereof. And then to assume that actional living is "taking the law into one's own hands" and trying to outguess God's designs. Rather, Levi Yitzhak teaches, spirituality is living at the peaks *and* in the valleys; spirituality is hearing the word *and* clothing the Torah in obedient servanthood.

We too have a bit of Korah in us, as I think Levi Yitzhak intended us to see. We judge the peak spiritual experiences as more "valuable" than the mundane. Also, in the area of the everyday, we accept too glibly the right to act on God's behalf and, when we fail, we doubt God and His design. Servanthood is living in the world of action and following humbly His will; it is not living in the world of the word and arrogating that word to ourselves.

The Price of Anger

For the third reading in a row, we hear of the complaints and rebellion of the Jews in the desert. In the portion of Shelaḥ Lekha (Numbers 14), the people are frightened by the report of the spies; they want to return to Egypt. Moses pleads with God for them and He agrees not to destroy the people but insists that the generation of the desert shall not enter the holy land. The people again rebel and decide to mount an attack which fails. In the reading of Koraḥ (Numbers 16), a segment of the aristocracy challenges the leadership of Moses and Aaron. Again Moses pleads with God for the people and He agrees not to destroy all of them, only the ringleaders. Then (Numbers 17), the people rebel again, and again Moses takes steps to protect them and establish God's order.

In this reading, the people complain about lack of water but the action and outcome are different (Numbers 20:7–13). God tells Moses to take his staff and speak to the rock to give water. Moses takes the staff, gathers the people at the rock, and speaks to them, "Hear oh you rebels! Can we bring water out of this rock?!" Then Moses strikes the rock twice and water gushes forth. God then responds, "Because you did not believe in Me to sanctify Me in the eyes of the Israelites, therefore you shall not bring this congregation into the land which I have given them."

The text is very precise. In the earlier incidents Moses does not get angry with the people, but in this one he does. Also, he clearly defies God's command to speak to the rock, hitting it instead. Finally, this is deemed a sin and Moses is punished by not being allowed to take the people to the promised land.

What was Moses' precise sin? Levi Yitzḥak cites Naḥmanides who says that it was rebuking the Israelites so sharply. After all God, Who was angry at the first incidents, is not angry at this one; Moses should have been more patient. Levi Yitzḥak also quotes Rashi, who says that

Moses' sin was striking, and not speaking to, the rock. Levi Yitzhak, however, counters that these are really one and the same as follows:

There are two types of rebukers. The one rebukes with only good words; that is, one tells each Jew the greatness of his or her rank and the nobility of his or her origin, for the soul of the Jew is hewn out from above the throne of Glory. And one tells him or her of the greatness of the pleasure that the Creator, blessed be He, has from the deeds of each Jew. And one tells him or her of the greatness of the joy in all the worlds when a Jew does the command of the Creator. With this type of rebuke, the rebuker inclines the heart of the Jew to do the will of the Father and to accept the yoke of His kingdom.

The other type rebukes with harsh words meant to embarrass until he or she is forced to do the will of the Creator. The difference between these two is that one who rebukes with good words raises the soul of the Jew higher and higher, always telling of the righteousness and greatness of Israel—how great their power is on high. Such a person is worthy to be a leader in Israel. But one who rebukes with harsh words is not worthy of this state.

It is also true that, if one rebukes Israel with good words and recounts their greatness and righteousness, then all created things must of themselves do the will of Israel because they were created for that purpose. But, if one does not tell of the greatness and righteousness of Israel, then all created things must be forced to do that for which they were created.

Now Moses said here, "Hear oh you rebels"; that is, he rebuked them with harsh words and, therefore, he had to hit the rock to make it do that for which it was created . . . It is thus clear that Moses' first action caused the second, and it is all one . . . Therefore God said, "Because you did not believe in Me to sanctify Me . . ."

Levi Yitzhak's interpretation and meaning are quite clear: even when one is well provoked, one should not get angry; for anger leads to more anger and then, even if the goal is accomplished, a price has been paid in sanctity. To put it differently: true leadership requires great patience—not as an abstract virtue and not for the purpose of being concretely virtuous; not even because anger itself is wrong. Rather, anger distorts; it does not lead to the sanctification of God's Name. Therefore, one should be careful of it, especially leaders.

Jew-Hatred

The figure of Balak is well known to Jews throughout the ages: Balak is the Jew-hater, the person with a deep irrational fear and hatred of the Jews.

The verse is quite clear: "Moab was very afraid of the people because it was great, and Moab loathed the children of Israel" (Numbers 22:3). Why? As the commentators put it, "Why did Moab hate Israel, especially since Israel had been commanded not to attack them" (Deuteronomy 2:9)?

Levi Yitzhak offers three reasons for anti-Semitism. First, according to the tradition, wherever the Jews went, non-Jews chose to convert to Judaism. Balak's fear, then, is that as the Jews draw near, his people will desert him and join the Jewish faith. The basis of Balak's fear of large-scale conversion to Judaism is not any belief in the superiority of Judaism. Nor is it a worry over loss of numbers or the formation of a fifth column inside Moab. As Levi Yitzhak sees it, the Jew-hater fears the conversion of the non-Jew to Judaism because that very act changes the being of the non-Jew. The gentile, when he or she converts, becomes another person. She or he enters holy history, God's history. To accept the Jewish faith is to renounce the usual political-economic-social view of reality for the realm of the awesome. It is to become holy seed. In modern times, we have not had an active mission to the gentiles but, if we did, there would certainly be unreasoning resistance—because conversion is an ontological commitment, not simply a matter of mind or heart.

Second, because being Jewish is transhistorical (though it takes place within history), the mystical tradition teaches that the simple fact of Jewish existence is redemptive. Jewish being saves the world. Wherever Jews go, they bring God with them and their very presence redeems their environment. Balak, the Jew-hater, whose commitment is to power and domination, senses redemption coming. He is frightened and then filled with loathing at this people in whom is the spiritual presence which denies all earthly power.

Finally, Levi Yitzhak teaches, the logic of the Jewish redemptive presence means that the only good that can happen to the wicked is their downfall at the hands of the Jews. Jewish presence, to be fully redemptive, must mean Jewish conquest for, in that, God's Name is sanctified. And so Balak trembles and then hates.

In contemplating anti-Semitism in our own century, we can only acknowledge the wisdom of Levi Yitzhak. Nazi (and now Arab) Jew-hatred is not motivated by economic or cultural jealousy; if so, why exterminate? It is not political or national; if so, why portray the Jew as superhuman and subhuman at the same time? It is not even religious in the Christian sense of the word; if so, why humiliate before gassing? Jew-hatred, for Balak as for his modern embodiments, is hatred of God's redeeming presence. The Jew is God's chosen; she or he is His holy seed. Awe and redemption are His; we are His. Even the most wicked know this. They may claim, and indeed believe, God to be on "their" side. But in their spiritual subconscious, the wicked see the Jews and know that we are surrogates of His presence and rule—surrogates that must be wiped out before evil can prevail. Only the messiah can relieve the fear and loathing of the Jew-hater.[1]

On Being a Leader

As Moses draws toward the end of his career, he turns to God and says, "May the Lord, God of the spirits for all flesh, appoint a man to lead the community" (Numbers 27:16). The question arises immediately: why does Moses use this peculiar phrase, "God of the spirits for all flesh," when asking God to appoint his successor? Levi Yitzhak proposes two beautiful interpretations.

"The rule is," Levi Yitzhak teaches,

that one must always speak out in favor of the Jews in that they do not continually do the will of the Creator, as the angels do, because they are distracted by the need to sustain themselves. This is the lesson of Abraham, our father, who was a man of kindness and who spoke out in our favor when he gave the angels who came to visit him food to eat [Genesis 18]. He did so in order to show them the dependence of human beings on their material needs so that they not speak out against us. This, too, is what Moses meant when he prayed, "May the Lord, God of the spirits for all flesh." Humankind, because it is "flesh," is dependent upon its material needs and, because of that, it sometimes does not worship God continually. Therefore, Moses prayed, "appoint a man to lead the community," i.e., a judge and leader who always will speak out on behalf of the Jews . . . As You always speak out on behalf of humankind which does not worship You continually, so appoint a leader who will always speak out on behalf of Israel.

This is a typical Levi Yitzhak thought. People are distracted by their poverty, by their need to make a living, and therefore they cannot always serve God as they should. God knows this and forgives them. The people's leaders, however, are not always so forgiving. Moses therefore prays that God appoint someone who will be sensitive to their human condition and who will speak out in their favor in judgment. While Levi Yitzhak's community contained many poor people, basic human motivations have not changed; for, although most American Jews are not poor, they are nonetheless distracted by material, social, and political pressures. They need a leadership that will speak up on their behalf in judgment so that they not be "as sheep without a shepherd" (Numbers 27:17).

Another interpretation: "The rule is," Levi Yitzhak teaches,

> that the essence of the passion of the soul is to worship God. It is the body which has material passions. In truth, though, the body and the soul are both the handiwork of God. And, as there is power in the soul from God to do His work, may He be blessed, so there is power in the body from God to make the essential passion of the body to be also for the worship of God. We, therefore, have a claim against God—that He forgive us our sins since He has the ability to empower the body to submit itself to worship Him, may He be exalted. Now the soul, which yearns to worship God, is called the "spirit" . . . and the body is called "flesh" . . . Therefore, the text says, "May the Lord, God of the spirits"—You Who are He Whom all souls yearn to worship, may You be "for all flesh"—may You be He Who empowers all bodies to worship You.

Moderns tend to reject the dualism of body and soul. We think of the personality as one unit. Freud, however, showed us that matters are not that simple. Levi Yitzhak's psychology recognizes a movement toward God and one away from Him. All other movements are irrelevant. The soul is said to move toward Him; the body to move away. But even the body could move toward Him since it too is created. Moses' prayer, then, is the prayer that rises from the depths of any religious person. It is the plea for spiritual wholeness—that God be God not only of our souls but also of our bodies, not only of our avowedly religious strivings but also of our incontinent rebellious impulses. Every aspect of our being, even our resistance, derives from His vitalizing Presence. We need Him to help us be one in worship of Him.

On War and Wandering: An Initial Meditation

The Jewish calendar is a based on the movements of the sun and of the moon, in contrast with the Christian calendar which is based solely upon the sun and the Islamic calendar which only follows the movements of the moon. This results in a whole month being intercalated seven times in nineteen years. This, in turn, affects the lectionary cycle, making it necessary to have enough readings for each Shabbat of the intercalated year and to have to double-up on readings during nonintercalated years. This reading is one such doubled reading; it covers the pericopae of Matot and of Mas'ei.

War and wandering are the motifs of these two readings. Why does one go to war? How should one go to war? Indeed, are there wars which one must fight? Are there wars which are optional? And why does one wander for periods of one's life? Why are exile and wandering so central in Jewish theology and experience? These are the questions that Levi Yitzhak pursues here.

In pondering war, Levi Yitzhak—who was aware of the wars of the nineteenth century—noticed the verse, "And they went out against Midian as God had commanded Moses" (Numbers 31:7). He puzzled over the phrase "as God had commanded" and taught:

The rule is that there was a possibility that, in this war against Midian, alien thoughts might assail the Jews. They might want to make war so that they could take great spoils and capture great booty as indeed, in the end, they did take great spoils and booty. But the truth is that, when they went to war and fought, they did not have this intent at all. Their only intent was to fulfill the command of God as the verse says, "They marched on Midian as God had commanded Moses." [Numbers 31:7]

The war against Midian, Levi Yitzhak teaches, was a commanded war, a holy war. And it was carried out with the proper purity of motivation, with the pure intent to fulfill God's will which characterizes a Jew's observance of all God's commands.

Although Christianity has known the Crusades and various religious wars, and Islam has known the jihad for many centuries, the idea of holy war is repugnant to modern culture. Perhaps it is the pacifist element in Christianity; perhaps it is the violence of war in our century, particularly of the holocaust; perhaps it is the specter of nuclear war: but modern people rebel against the idea of a holy war, a commanded war. What is the traditional teaching of Judaism?

Maimonides, in his *Code of Law*, [1] sets forth the authoritative teaching of the tradition as follows:

(1) The king may not initiate a war unless it is a commanded war [Hebrew, *milhemet mitsva*). What is a commanded war? This is war against one of the seven nations [the Hittites, the Girgashites, the Emorites, the Canaanites, the Perizites, the Hivites, and the Jebusites; Deuteronomy 7:1], war against the Amalekites [see below], and saving Israel from the hand of an enemy who is oppressing them [Numbers 10:9]. In addition, the king can fight a permissible war [Hebrew, *milhemet ha-reshut*], which is a war fought with other nations in order to expand the boundaries of Israel and to magnify its greatness and reputation.

(2) The king does not need to ask permission of the court to conduct a commanded war; rather, he goes forth on his own at any time and he can compel the nation to go to war with him. But, in the case of a permissible war, the king can call up the nation only with the permission of the court of seventy-one [that is, the highest court].

(3) . . .

(4) It is a positive commandment to wipe out the seven nations [listed above] as it says, "You shall surely wipe them out" [Deuteronomy 20:17] and, whoever comes upon one of them and does not kill him or her, has violated a negative commandment as it says, "You shall not permit any person to survive" [Deuteronomy 20:16]. But all memory of these nations has been lost [that is, such commands no longer apply because these seven nations have been lost to history].

(5) Similarly, it is a positive commandment to wipe out the memory of Amalek as it says, "You shall wipe out the memory of Amalek" [Deuteronomy 25:19]. It is also a positive commandment to remember always their evil deeds and the ambush they set for Israel [Deuteronomy 25:18] in order to arouse enmity against them as it says, "Remem-

ber what Amalek did to you . . . do not forget" [Deuteronomy 28:17, 19]. From the tradition we have learned, "remember" is with the mouth; "do not forget" is in the heart [Talmud, Megilla 18a]—that it is forbidden to forget their hatred and their enmity [against us].

Un-modern and in a certain sense un-Christian as it may seem, the Bible clearly teaches, and rabbinic tradition concurs, that God commanded certain kinds of war and permitted others. He positively commanded: (a) the eradication of the seven nations, (b) the eradication of Amalek, and (c) the war of self-defense. He also permitted wars of expansion with the consent of the highest authorities. Furthermore, the Bible clearly teaches, and rabbinic tradition concurs, that the wars of eradication were total; there were to be no survivors (cf. also 1 Samuel 15).

What are we to make of this? Is God, and the tradition, really so bloodthirsty? Is the Jew really bound by the command of God to kill, to wipe out? On the other hand, these commandments are in the same Bible as the ten commandments and the holiness code; they are as divine, and one must take them seriously. The need, therefore, to accept and to make peace with these demands of God, irrational and even wrong though they may seem to us, is great. It is heightened by our sensitivity to the political situation in the Middle East, the ethical autonomy of modern humankind, and the dialogue with Christian pacifism.

It seems to me that we must start with the realization that God is no pacifist. He is a partisan—an active advocate for His people as well as for the values of justice and love that He embodies. He is "the God of war" (Exodus 15:3) and He expects, even commands war; that is, God expects and commands us to take even violent action to protect His people and to defeat evil. This notion is not completely foreign to moderns for we, too, sanction war in cases where it is waged to rectify gross injustice. We call this "just war." Moderns would agree, for example, that the war against Nazism was just, even to the unconditional surrender demanded and the extensive bombings. Such a war is "commanded," as the tradition would put it. Moderns would agree too, for example, that a war of genuine self-defense is a just, and hence a "holy" or "commanded" war. Modern people too, then, have a theology of war. We approve of Maimonides' categories (b) and (c), taking Amalek as a symbol of radical evil.

But what of the wars of conquest of the land (a), especially in view of the eradication clause; and what of the permissible wars of expansion? Biblical and rabbinic culture recognizes that God commands, even war. However, it also recognizes that God's command, even for war, can never be arbitrary or capricious; it must exist within His justice and His love. Acknowledging all wars, even those of conquest and expansion, to be God's will and recognizing His teaching of love and justice, the issue for thinkers in biblical and rabbinic culture, then, is not whether these wars offend human sensibilities, but whether they are consistent with God's will for justice and love.

The rabbis adopted two strategies to reconcile the command to make war with the command to do justice. First, they explained why one must wage such wars. Thus Maimonides explains God's position as follows: "Because they were the root and foundation of idolatry . . . so that we not learn from their heresy."[2] Maimonides' commentators explain that the purpose of the permissible wars of expansion must be to intimidate neighboring states from attacking Israel. Holy wars, then, have reasons and these can be debated. Second, the rabbis qualified the command to make war in order to insure that justice be done. Thus, for example, Maimonides limits the applicability of the law of the seven nations by ruling that they no longer exist. His commentators add further qualifications: that no people, even one of the seven nations, can be attacked without first offering peace[3]; that the commandment to eradicate Amalek does not apply until the days of the messiah; and so on. The basic attitude of the rabbis, then, is acceptance of God's will for war, together with explanation, interpretation, and qualification of that will to make it consistent with the rest of Torah teaching, to make it conform to God's justice and love. Rejecting God's demands as "ungodly" was not an option in biblical and rabbinic culture.

To follow the tradition, then, one must recognize that God is not a pacifist; but one must also know that God is no power-hungry spoil-starved warlord either. He acts for reasons—one must only find them. And He always acts within the teaching of His love and justice— one must only seek the necessary qualifications to make his special commands consistent with His general will for justice and love. To this

Levi Yitzhak adds a spiritual, intentional dimension. He teaches that, although God commands us to go to war and to give no quarter, He also commands that, in going to war, we do it only to let His will be done, not ours; that we accomplish His purposes, not ours. Levi Yitzhak instructs us that, although God insists that war, ugly as it is, be an option for the defense of His people and for the enforcing of social justice, He also demands that it be waged selflessly, with purity of motivation and intent. There can be no moral responsibility without power. God is the supreme judge. He must decide; He must enforce. And He demands the same of us, who are created in His image. In the modern world, where war is only a violent means of resolving human disputes—or worse, a naked grab for raw power—Levi Yitzhak reminds us that only God can command a war, that His command is always just, and that humankind's intention must be only to fulfill His will, His purpose.

The danger of this view, it seems to me, lies not in the law but in the authority that interprets and implements it. Who is to say what is God's will? Who is to say what war is commanded? Many have believed that they acted in His Name, and much blood has been shed in that cause. To this Jewish tradition replies, first, that there is no Torah without authoritative interpretation, that there is no revelation without approved commentary. Consensus protects; collective judgment insures against the distortion of His will. And second, even authoritative interpretation is subject to reason, argument, and further consensus. Thus, although the exercise of judgment is not easy, one is not free to desist from it. There is no escape, either for the individual or for the group, from having to judge whether a given teaching is within God's will or not. There is no flight from acting on that judgment, and from taking the consequences in the ultimate judgment, even in matters of life and death or war and peace. Consensus protects, but it does not guarantee. Authoritative interpretation helps, but judgment is inescapably ours.

Wandering and exile constitute the other theme of this double pericope. Wandering runs very deep in Jewish tradition. Abraham is a wanderer; so are his children and grandchildren. The Jews wander in the desert for forty years. Elijah is a wanderer. One of the earliest liturgical formulas begins, "My father was a wandering Aramean" (Deuteronomy 26:5). Exile, too, is a motif that surges in the depths of the Jewish soul. Moses threatens the people with exile if they do not obey God's command. Jeremiah goes into exile; Ezekiel into captivity. The rabbis interpreted the verse "I am with him in trouble" (Psalm 91:15) to teach that God Himself went into exile with His people, and He will stay in exile until the final redemption. The Zohar took this concept still further: God is in exile from Himself, alienated from His own being, as long as the exile of His people continues below.

To wander, to be in exile, to be a refugee, to be homeless—what purpose does this serve? Why must it be so? These questions lay heavily upon Levi Yitzhak, who knew that life is not secure and that no place could be a home to the Jews. He felt keenly the brokenness of life, the alienation of humankind from the divine, and he needed to see a reason, a purpose.

According to the mystical story of creation, God caused an empty space to be created within Himself. He then caused His light to penetrate into that space. But the forms the light took were not sufficient to contain His energy. They broke, and the forms and the light were shattered, falling into space. God's second attempt to cause light to penetrate space succeeded and our world was created. The original fragments and sparks, however, remain. Humankind's task is, according to this stream of Jewish mysticism, to find and meditatively redeem those sparks of the divine, to return them prayerfully to God.

Levi Yitzhak contemplated the verse, "And Moses wrote down their bringings-forth, their voyages according to the Lord" (Numbers 33:2), and noted that there are forty-two stops that the Jews made in the desert, corresponding to the forty-two letters in the Name of God. Integrating this with the mystical teaching of the sparks, he taught:

There are forty-two voyages that the children of Israel took as it says, "They camped in . . . , and they camped in . . ." This means that, when the Israelites camped in a place where there was evil fear, may God protect us from that, then they would worship God, may He be blessed, with exalted fear, fearing His power, glory, and might . . . and, when they camped in a place where there was evil love that had fallen there at the time of the shattering of the vessels, then they would worship God, may He be blessed, with true love

. . . and so on, with true greatness . . . In this way, they raised all the sparks that had fallen there and returned them to their root, to the holy place. This was the purpose of their wanderings in the desert. This, too, is the meaning of the verse: "And Moses wrote down their bringings-forth"—the bringing-forth of the sparks which they raised from the place of their encampment; "their voyages according to the Lord"—this was from God . . . that the purpose of their voyages was to bring up the sparks and to raise them to the source of holiness.

The purpose of wandering and of exile, then, according to Levi Yitzhak, is to enable the Jewish people to redeem the sparks of God that were left unintegrated in creation, to save the lost fragements of God which are scattered through reality. The purpose of exile and wandering is to enable the Jew to make God whole, to help Him end His own wandering and exile. At every stop in life, no matter how depressing, the Jew is not to look at his or her own discomfort, but is to seek the remnant of the divine inherent in that moment and to redeem it, gently, for God.

There is something both beautiful and tragic in this worldview. On the one hand, homelessness ceases to be a human discomfort; it becomes an imitation of the divine. To be a refugee is to be like God—a wanderer, in exile from one's home. It also places humankind in a very significant position, that of being able to help God, of being capable of participating actively in the redemption. On the other hand, there is something unreal, fantastic, about this way of coping with wandering and exile. We are accustomed to taking our fate in our hands, to entering history forcefully. The problem of the homeless and the refugee should be solved, by political action, in the arena of history. Jews have been saved in our day by Zionism not by mysticism, by political action not by meditation. We moderns need something more than Levi Yitzhak offers us in his interpretation of wandering and exile, although we must admit that even our best efforts have not solved the problem of Jewish homelessness (for example, behind the Iron Curtain) or the general refugee problem. We are still in exile; we are still wanderers.

DEUTERONOMY

Land, Language, and State:
An Excursus on Zionism

At the beginning of this reading, there occurs an interesting verse: "On the other side of the Jordan, in the land of Moab, Moses began to interpret the Torah" (Deuteronomy 1:5). Commentators, early and late, have wondered what the word "interpret" might mean. Levi Yitzhak notes that Rashi comments that Moses "began to interpret the Torah—into the seventy languages [of the nations of the world]." The natural question arises: Why, when the Jews were about to enter the holy land, did they need to know the Torah in the seventy tongues of the world? Why, as the people entered the promised land, did they have to begin learning the Torah in the languages of other peoples? Levi Yitzhak's answer is very subtle.

The language of each nation is the source of its vitality, the holy tongue belonging only to the Jewish people. In truth, the Jews heard the Torah on Sinai in Hebrew only but the Holy One, blessed be He, Who sees from the beginning to the end, foresaw that the Jews would someday go into exile. He, therefore, wrote into the Torah the languages of the other nations so that, through those words Israel, who would have a hold on their own vitality which is the language of the holy Torah, would be able to exist also in the exile . . . [For this reason] the rule is that the Torah sometimes contains words from the Targum [that is, in Aramaic] such as *yegar sahaduta* [Genesis 31:47] and words from the languages of the other nations such as *totafot* [with Talmud, Zevahim, 37b] . . . This is the meaning of "in the land of Moab" for, in the land of Israel, there existed only the holy tongue but, "in the land of Moab," that is, in the land of the nations outside of Israel, one must "interpret the Torah" into all languages in order to sustain the Jews in the exile.

Levi Yitzhak has made four points in this brief comment, each of which is profound. First, he notes that the source of the vitality of each nation is its language. Anyone who speaks more than one language or who translates can vouch for this. There are special turns of phrase that characterize a language and its people, and these expressions are almost untranslatable. Each language has an elegance of its own and a power of expression which is peculiar to it, and these constitute the identity and character of the people who speak it.

Second, Hebrew is the language of the Jewish people. Hebrew, the holy tongue, is the language of Torah, of the prophets, and of the Psalms. It is also the language of the Mishna and the Prayerbook, of medieval poetry, law, commentary, philosophy, and mysticism. The classics of Jewish civilization can only really be appreciated in their original tongue because Hebrew has a power and an eloquence of its own, as translators of the Bible and other Jewish classics know well. A Jew who reads, writes, and speaks in one of the tongues of the nations of the world is not fulfilled unless he or she also reads, writes, and speaks the language of his or her people, the holy tongue.

Third, the natural place for Hebrew is the land of Israel. The proper locus of the holy tongue is the holy land. There, the language and the environment resonate together. There, the echoes of the one rebound naturally from the landscape of the other.

And fourth, in the state of exile, the existence of the Jew is dependent upon the existence of the nations of the world; as long as the messiah has not come, the vitality of the Jews is deeply intertwined with the vitality of the peoples among whom they reside. However, while this is a characteristic of the state of exile, it is not wholly true, for the vitality of Jewish existence must still derive from the holy tongue, from the language of Torah. The Jew can touch the vitality of the nations of the world only through his or her own language. The Jew can participate in the existence of the peoples among whom she or he resides only through the medium of Jewish civilization.

I find myself in agreement with Levi Yitzhak on these matters: Language does define a person and a people; Jewish being is defined by the Hebrew language; Hebrew belongs most naturally in the land of Israel; and Jewish participation in the vitality of the exile must be rooted in Hebrew language and culture. It is to the third of these propositions that I wish to return—the land as the full and natural locus of the the Jewish people and its language.

Levi Yitzḥak was not one of the proto-Zionist rabbis. Settlement of the holy land is not a major motif of his preaching. He himself did not move there. He did not even visit the holy sites, as did some other hasidic rabbis. And, on at least one occasion, he interpreted a talmudic saying that favors settlement in the holy land in exactly the contrary sense (see 151–53). Nonetheless, he preached, without reserve, the chosenness of the Jewish people, the Hebrew language, and the land of Israel. Each is holy, in its chosenness, and the holiness of each is interrelated.

The holiday of Tish'a b'Av commemorates the destruction of the first and second temples. It has become a general day of mourning, for to it have been added the dirges written to commemorate other persecutions of Jews throughout history, including the holocaust in our time. The Book of Lamentations is read on Tish'a b'Av and, in commenting on the verse (5:19), "You, oh Lord, will dwell forever," Levi Yitzḥak writes of the interrelated chosenness-holiness of Israel the land and Israel the people:

How many times have kings tried to make of the land of Israel a well-settled place like other states but they have not succeeded! Why is this so? Because, in truth, the Holy One, blessed be He, created the whole earth and He decreed that some parts be settled and others be desert. Now, when a settled place is laid waste, it becomes a desert inhabited by wild animals and, when it becomes settled again, there are no wild animals in it as in the desert. The land of Israel, however, [is different]. When Israel dwells in it in security, it is settled but, when Israel is exiled from it, even though other nations dwell in it, it remains a desert . . . From this it is clear that the land of Israel belongs to us and it accepts settlement only from the Jews. This is the meaning of "You, oh Lord, shall dwell forever"—we trust that You will always dwell in the land of Israel . . . such that it will not accept the settlement of any other people but will remain a desert, for this land belongs only to Israel . . .

The primary axis of the land-people relationship, then, is not, according to Levi Yitzḥak, modern nationalism or international consensus. It is God's covenant with the people:

This Covenant is the central experience of Israel recorded in the Scriptures. But though it is located in certain specific historical contexts . . . it is felt to underlie the existence of Israel at all times . . . The Covenant has a bearing on the moral history of the world as a whole, proceeding as it does under divine providence from the beginning to the end of days. God is engaged: Man is tested. But within that universal drama Israel has its unique role . . . Israel becomes the covenant people *par excellence,* summoned to bear witness to the purposes of creation, to endure the messianic tensions of history, to undertake the task of building a sanctuary out of the materials of this world . . . Israel receives its vocation: that of becoming "a kingdom of priests and a holy nation"[1]

The force of this covenant, however, entails certain things: (1) The Jew can never be at home outside the covenanted land. Such territory, no matter how comfortably ensconced the Jew may be, is exile. It is beyond the pale of full covenantal history. (2) The land belongs to the Jews whether they are in it or not, whether their presence there is approved by international consensus or not. God wants us there; humankind's opinions are irrelevant. (3) The land is not ours to alienate. It is not ours to cede to anyone. Only God could grant it to someone else, though He has promised not to do so. And (4), the language of the people in its land is the language of revelation. It is the language of the foreparents and the prophets—Hebrew.

There is another dimension to the covenant of chosenness between God and His people and His land: the theological significance of a Jewish state. When the State of Israel was established, the chief rabbinate sought a formula for the liturgy which would leave open the possibility that this state might have messianic dimensions. In the prayer for the government, they ordained that the following phrase be used: "the beginning of the growth of our redemption." It is a strange phrase, cautious in its messianic claims yet allowing room for the action of people in bringing that moment closer to historical time. This phrase, however, captures well the sense of the modern Jew that the State of Israel is more than just another state. It is more than just a haven for persecuted brothers and sisters whom the world will not accept. The State of Israel does have messianic potential. We do not know, but it may well be the beginning of the redemption whose existence we must cultivate assiduously. In that sense, the State of Israel too is part of the covenant. It is certainly part of covenantal history.

Modern Jews, particularly those who live in the exile, are not comfortable with these implications. Such ideas force us to question the validity of our self-imposed alienation from the holy land. How can a Jew, living at the time of the third commonwealth, not own land and not pay taxes to a Jewish state when generations of Jews longed to do so and couldn't? Is the comfortableness of my life or the social and familial difficulty of settlement in the holy land sufficient reason not to go there? How can one ignore the importance of this moment in the grand scope of Jewish history? If Jewish living is important to me, and it is, how can I live a partial Jewish life in the exile when a full Jewish life is available to me in the holy land? How can I write in English when the language of my God, my people, and my history is Hebrew? Are not the prophetic issues of our time more pressing in their own historical setting than anywhere else?

Pondering the implications of the covenant also forces us to question the policies of the State of Israel in the areas of territorial concessions and Palestinian rights. Can the State of Israel concede territory to the Palestinians when our claim to that land rests on God's covenant and not on our ability to conquer and control it? Can a Jewish state, however, cede land if it is for the sake of peace? If it is for the sake of saving lives, is it not obligatory to cede territory, though on the clear theological assumption that such concession is temporal and not eternal? Where do the Palestinians fit in? Are they the biblical "resident-strangers"? Are they more than that? Do they have any claim on the land, especially one which might have a theological root? How do we apply the rules of justice and fairness, for our own sojourn in the land is conditional upon the covenant of land with justice?

Contemplating the implications of the covenant also compels us to reexamine the truth of such basic propositions of modernity as democracy and rule by consensus insofar as those usually serve as the ideological basis for the solution of current political problems. If Palestinians are resident-strangers, then they are second-class citizens, which runs against the democratic motif of modernity. Can we, in good conscience, act on this basis? Some Jews live in exile, but so does the State of Israel. How far, then, may one go in ignoring the consensus of world opinion in planning and evaluating our actions as a people and a state? Is the low profile the best profile? Does a high profile really hurt? Modernity moves us toward consensus, but is that good or covenantally right?

These questions are oppressive, but they must be faced by every modern Jew. For myself, I regret my life in the exile and I feel strongly that we Jews, inside and outside the land, must be guided by the implications of God's covenant with us. We must acknowledge the messianic dimension of the State of Israel. We must live there, or at least yearn to live there and feel guilty and unfulfilled if we do not. We must master and use the language of our people. We must not cede land and, if we do, we must be clear that such concession is temporary and for a limited political purpose. We must treat the resident-stranger with justice, granting him and her the rights the covenant accords. And, finally, we must follow our covenantal calling even if it contradicts some of the basic teachings of modernity. I do not know if Levi Yitzhak would agree with these propositions (I think he would); but his teaching of the sanctity-chosenness of the land, people, and language evokes in me a strong covenant-oriented Zionism.

On Being Chosen: A Post-Holocaust Reflection

In three well-known quotations in this reading, God is referred to by His two most important appelatives, "Lord" (the Tetragrammaton, the ineffable Name of God) and "God" (Elohim): once in Deuteronomy 4:4, "And you who cling to the Lord your God are all of you alive this day"; once in Deuteronomy 5:6, "I am the Lord your God Who brought you out of the house of bondage"; and once more in Deuteronomy 6:4, "Hear, oh Israel, the Lord your God the Lord is one." Commentators through the ages have speculated on the nuances behind these two ways of addressing God. Levi Yitzḥak, drawing on Maimonides, maintains that "Lord" (the ineffable Name) refers to the absolute simplicity and oneness of the divine, while "God" (Elohim) refers to God's guidance and providence over all that happens in the universe. To this Levi Yitzḥak, following hasidic teaching, adds:

The rule is that, although God created all the levels of existence, His guidance of them is according to the will of Israel: When Israel's will is to draw God's blessing upon someone, God lets His grace flow forth and, when Israel's will is that someone be judged, God fulfills that will and exercises judgment . . . Everything happens because of Israel and indeed, by Israel, is everything guided.

One of the meanings of Deuteronomy 4:4 according to Levi Yitzḥak, then, is: "You who cling [that is, have faith] that the Lord is your God Who directs the world according to the will of Israel have true spiritual vitality [life] in this world and reward in the next." And one of the meanings of Deuteronomy 6:4 according to Levi Yitzḥak would be: "Hear, oh Israel, the Lord is God Who directs the universe for the sake of Israel; that Lord is the absolutely simple one."

For those of us brought up in the spirit of modernity, this Israelocentrism is hard to accept. The Jews are, we are taught, another people—perhaps a special one, but not the center of the universe. The Jews, we are taught, have a history but they are not the center of world history, much less of all creation.

Another, and more serious, modern doubt: We can comprehend, if not fully understand, that the Lord is God—that God can, and did, choose the Jews and that, therefore, our destiny is not as the destiny of others. But how fully can we subscribe to this teaching of chosenness in the post-holocaust world? True, we have hobbled to survival, but it was after a terrifying blow. True, we have a strong state that will do its best to protect us in this indifferent and hostile world, but it is not omnipotent. True, the second world war was a war over chosenness, but the war was more terrible than anyone can even imagine. Can we really affirm our chosenness in the face of that terror?

The holocaust raises doubts in our mind not only about our chosenness, but also about God's justice and His mercy. Is there any way that His providential action in the holocaust can be seen as just, as merciful? We need to reflect on God's mercy, his *rahamim,* and our proper response to it.

The Hebrew language is rich in words describing mercy. A large number of roots—*rahem, hus, hamol, hitrazzeh, hitpayyes, hanon, hesed, erekh apayim*—occur in many forms—as beseeching verbs, as evocative adjectives, and as powerful nouns—in the Bible as well as in the liturgy. These roots imply others—*hoshi'a, hazzel, ga'ol, azor, zakhor*—which mean to save, to redeem, to help, and to remember. There are many more. God's mercy is described as the mercy of a parent toward a child (Psalm 103:13). He is called *ha-Rahaman, Rahamana,* the merciful One and *Av ha-rahamim,* the Father of mercy. His people, when they practice mercy, are called *rahamanim bene rahamanim,* merciful ones the children of merciful ones.

What are the types of mercy in the tradition? On what bases do we appeal to God for it? What are its limits? In the post-holocaust world, how adequate is this concept? Our appeal to God's mercy is twofold. There is the appeal from covenantal justice, which itself has two dimensions, and there is the appeal from helplessness.

In the very beginning there was God. He was all alone, but He was not unhappy. Yet, in the mystery of His being, there welled up in Him a desire to create, to have children. And so He chose to form the world and to create humankind. But bringing humanity into existence was not enough. God found that, because of His love for us, He had to give us guidance. And so He chose humankind again and gave us the covenant of Adam, and then the covenant of Noah, and then the covenant of Abraham. Finally, He gave us the Torah together with the obligation to interpret it. And He was pleased because some of us made the effort to mold ourselves to His revealed image, and displeased that many did not.

God's love, then, is of two kinds. From part of His heart there overflows a boundless unconditional love for His creatures. And from another part of His heart there flows forth a love engaged in human existence, a love devoted to parenting humanity. The former is called ḥesed, grace; the latter raḥamim, engaged love. The former was, and is, easy; it is of His unmoving essence. The latter was, and is, hard; it requires patience, understanding, and forgiveness.

Ḥesed, grace, motivated creation. It brought the world into being. Raḥamim, engaged love, motivated revelation. Moved by it, God gave us standards of action and measures of inner piety; He set forth His expectations of us, together with His obligations to us. It is a two-way street, a covenant between two parties. Later generations would quarrel about the details and emphases, but the basic terms would abide: We would not be alone; we would always know what He wants of us; and we could depend upon His engaged love to take into account our strivings and our failings. Justice and righteous judgment would be the bywords of our relationship.

Within this covenantal understanding, the key metaphor is "our Father, our King"—the fair Father, the just King. He can say, "It has been told you, oh humanity, what is good and what God requires of you" and we can say, "Shall not the Judge of the whole universe do justice?" He can command, "Choose life" and we can pray, "Grant us justice according to the law" (Micah 6:8; Genesis 18:25; Deuteronomy 30:19; daily liturgy[1]). The final judgment, as C. S. Lewis has remarked, is to be a moment of joy and triumph, for then, our devotion to Him and His love for us will be justified.[2]

Were it not for this covenant, we would not know what to do. We would be conscious of God's holiness, of His sublimity. We would know His beauty and His power. We would experience awe, reverence, and fear. But with what would we approach Him? What would be the protocol, the etiquette? What would be the expectations by which we could come into His presence and talk to Him? Even kings of flesh and blood have procedures; even earthly parents have standards on which relationship is based. Having His expectations in our hands, we have relatedness to Him with all the rights and responsibilities pertaining thereto.

This is the way of covenantal justice. We appeal to God's mercy, raḥamim, on the basis of the expectations of us that He has set forth and the rights that that expression gives us to justified recognition of our efforts. We appeal to God's raḥamim, mercy, on the basis of His raḥamim, His engaged love for us. "Our Father, our King, act for the sake of Your great 'raḥamim.' " "If we have no righteousness or good deeds, remember for our sake the covenant with our ancestors." "For You, God, are truth and Your Word is truth, valid forever."[3]

It should be noted that the appeal from covenantal justice is not limited to the just reward of our own fulfillment of God's expectations. The revelation was for all generations and the just reward is for all generations. The evil of one generation is not, however, transferable for any length of time. The collectivity of the reward is the "merit of the ancestors" and it, too, is part of the appeal to mercy from covenantal justice.

It is also the case that covenantal justice demands that we be merciful just as, and because, God is merciful (Talmud, Shabbat 133b; Luke 6:36).

This mutual responsibility between God and humankind for justice-with-love is difficult for some moderns to accept. There is a peculiar romance to claiming, "I am but dust and ashes; I revel in my creatureliness," and then escaping the true sense of demand that revelation imposes on us. We resist the idea and the imagery of command, and hence our need to respond in true commitment. Yet covenantal justice does proclaim His demand, just as it guarantees our right to principled defense. Mercy, in this sense, is within justice.

There is another dimension to our appeal to God's mercy. It is still from within the covenant. There are moments when sin overcomes us, when we feel despair at returning to God, when hope for our own self-correction fades. We know, in such times, that we deserve the punishment that He metes out. We admit our failures and we acknowledge the justness of His claims against us. We have no defense and we know it.

Those sins which are revealed, we have mentioned before You; and those which are not revealed to us are known and revealed to You . . . My God, before I was formed, I was not worthy and, now that I have been formed, it is as if I had not been formed. I am dust in my life, the more so in my death. I stand before You as a vessel filled with shame and remorse.[4]

Even at such moments, however, we recognize that God wants us to return. He wants us to live within His covenant. "And You, in Your great engaged love, have mercy upon us for You do not wish the destruction of the world . . . You want the return of the wicked and do not desire their death, as it says . . . 'Do I desire the death of the wicked person? Rather, that the wicked return from his or her ways and live.' "[5] And so we appeal to Him to suspend His justice; to have mercy on us, compulsive sinners though we are. We appeal from our grief and desolation to His trust. We appeal from our sinfulness and despair to His love. This is the appeal to merciful forgiveness. It is mercy beyond our due, but it is still within God's justice and His covenant.

As firm as we are in our faith in the covenant, in God's commitment to justice based upon His revelation, we cannot escape the fact that there is an unfathomable dimension to life. There is a realization that all of our deeds, no matter how righteous, are nothing, that all our efforts do not protect us from the harshness of reality. Deep inside us we know that part of our fate is simply not in our hands, that some aspects of life are seemingly not within the covenant. The irrational presses in upon us. Even pain and suffering close about us, sometimes in extremes, beyond our wildest terrors. It is then that we realize how truly helpless we are. It is then that we become aware of how severe our limits are in grasping His ways. In these moments, one casts oneself completely on God's mercy.

This is the way of pleading, propitiating, pacifying. "As the eyes of slaves are to their masters, as the eyes of a maidservant are to her mistress, so are our eyes to our God until He has mercy on us" (Psalm 123:2). "Please, Lord, save us, please; Please, Lord, secure us, please" (Psalm 118:25). "He Who is propitiated by mercy and He Who is pacified by pleading, be propitiated and be pacified toward us for there is no other help."[6] "Even if a sharpened sword is touching one's neck, one should not inhibit oneself from asking mercy, as it says, 'Yea, though He kill me, I shall yearn for Him' " (Talmud, Berakhot 10a, citing Job 13:15).

This total dependency on God's mercy is one of the most difficult aspects of religion for some modern people to accept. Our motto, after William Henley's "Invictus," is: "I am the master of my fate, I am the captain of my soul." To "beg for mercy" runs against our grain. It offends our sense of self-determination, of personal liberty. To "beg for mercy" is the furthest humans can get from that delicate web of secure human relations that defines our world. It is the lowest rung on the ladder of self-respect; perhaps it is worse than death itself.

Grudgingly, we concede that God has the right to make demands upon us and that, since we can also make demands upon Him, there is validity to the appeal to God's mercy from covenantal justice. But we resist the idea and the imagery of our utter helplessness, and hence our need to cast ourselves totally upon His mercy. Gladly, we accept God's unfettered grace. But we resist the logic that one cannot bind that grace to us when fate goes against us. We accept the possibility of our atheism but rebel against the possibility of God's disavowing His promises to us. Yet the power of our own experience of helplessness and the logic of the doctrine of grace impel us to recognize and to admit into our being that God does not have to have mercy on us and that there are moments when we can only beseech it upon us. Mercy, in this sense, is beyond justice.

Human existence confronts this interpretation of God's mercy and raises an important question. God does not always act in mercy. He does not always adhere to covenantal justice, nor does He always exercise merciful forgiveness. Sometimes He does not even act out of mercy rooted beyond justice. Logically and experientially these appeals contradict reality. One cannot logically assert both God's unbounded love for creation and His noncovenantal disregard thereof. One cannot logically assert both God's revelation-based judgment and His nonadherence to it. Experientially, one becomes aware of God's grace and feels that one can rely upon it. One experiences God's providence and is reassured that His power is circumscribed by it. God is our rock, our fortress, our refuge. And yet He acts in ways that deny this.

At no time in Jewish existence has this problem been more forcefully in our consciousness than in the aftermath of the holocaust. The reality of that event sears our psyche; it oppresses our souls and minds. For in it God did not grant covenantal justice, nor did He exercise merciful forgiveness to the sinners and the sinless. Nor was He propitiated by mercy or pacified by pleading. "But You deserted and shamed us . . . You made us retreat from our oppressors, and those who hate us tore us apart at their will. You made us as sheep that are eaten, and scattered us among the nations . . . You sold Your people for nothing . . . For You we have been murdered all the day, we have been considered sheep to be slaughtered" (Psalm 44:9–23). How can we hold within us the tension of God's mercy and His/our reality?

Denial is no answer; severing our tie with God is no response. Better to have a parent who abuses than no parent at all. Better to protest than to curse God and live. Better to remain loyal to our experience of His presence with all its depressing perplexity than to deny our own awareness of His being with us.

The answer of the tradition is complex. First, we do not shrink from stating the injustice of God's acts. We do not refrain from putting forth our case under His covenant.

All this happened to us and we did not forget You, nor did we deny Your covenant. Our hearts did not turn away, nor did our steps stray from Your path. Though You crushed us as a jackal and covered us with the shadow of death, did we forget the Name of our God, spreading our hands toward a strange deity? God Himself will surely search this out, for He knows the hidden ways of the heart. (Psalm 44:18–22)

Second, we pray. We turn yet again to God's mercy. We call upon His mercy which is rightfully ours under the terms of His own covenant. "Wake up! God, why do You sleep? Arise! Do not neglect forever! Why do You hide Your face, forgetting our oppression and affliction? For our souls are bowed down into the dust, and our bellies cling to the earth" (Psalm 44:24–26). And we invoke His act of merciful forgiveness. "Arise! Help us! Redeem us for the sake of Your grace" (Psalm 44:27). "We have sinned against You, Master; forgive us, according to the abundance of Your mercy, God."[7] And we plead, we propitiate, we pacify. "See our affliction, for our pain and the oppression in our hearts have become great. Have mercy upon us in the land of our captivity. Do not pour out Your anger against us . . . If not for our sake, act for Your own sake. Do not destroy the memory of our remnant."[8]

Finally, in this matter as in so many others in religion, God and the tradition intend us to think and to feel *seriatim,* that is, one after another. Anyone who has ever been on trial in a human court of justice knows that one is confident, frightened, reassured, and despairing in turn. So it is on the Day of Judgment, which is every day. We move to and fro in our relationship to God. Even the rationalists among us are cast about by the waves of life, though they appear to struggle a bit more to keep their balance. Faith in God's grace and His covenant sustains us. Awareness of His unbounded grace and His engaged love supports us. We must always return to our sense of His presence. With it, we may suffer in our souls; without it, we are nothing. We must know our helplessness, but we must also feel His might. His mercy encompasses all.

Returning to Levi Yitzhak's homily on chosenness with this insight on God's mercy and our proper response in the post-holocaust world, we note, first, that Levi Yitzhak sets aside the modern rejection of chosenness entirely. There is only one God. He created all that exists and He sustains it. He also, for reasons only He knows, chose certain parts of creation. He chose the holy land and He chose the Jewish people. The Jews, thus, are not a nation like other nations, or a people like other peoples. The Jews are the focus of God's creative energy as it expresses itself in human history. God is concerned with all humanity, but Israel are His special children and He acts for them and with them in mind. Whether we like it or not, there is the fact of our chosenness—

for joy and glory, and for suffering and pain. Second, Levi Yitzḥak teaches that faith is loyalty to God even when some of the evidence contradicts our expectations of Him; that faith is a continuing relatedness to God even when part of our personal or national lives shows us that God has failed us. There is something almost counterintuitive about Levi Yitzḥak's understanding of faith. It is rooted in reality but only partly so.

In the post-holocaust world, Levi Yitzḥak teaches that in spite of the horror, the humiliation, and the magnitude of the blow, we must be able to affirm with a clear mind and a whole heart that we are the center of history, though the price is enormous; that the Lord is the God Who pours all His energy into us, though the human cost to us is at times unbearable. In us, the nations are blessed and are judged. In the post-holocaust world, it is a frightening call to faith that Levi Yitzḥak issues when he asks us to assert in full faith, "Hear, oh Israel, the Lord is God Who directs the universe for the sake of Israel; that Lord is the absolutely simple one." And it is a shattering challenge he throws at us when he calls us, after the holocaust, to cast ourselves upon God's mercy, both upon that which is rooted in His covenant as well as upon that which is rooted in His grace.

True God-Fearingness

In this reading, all of the Torah seems to be summed up in one verse: "Now, Israel, what is it that the Lord your God requires of you? Only to fear the Lord your God, to walk in His ways, to love Him, and to worship the Lord your God with all your heart and with all your soul" (Deuteronomy 10:12). Each phrase in this verse requires a separate essay, perhaps a book. Levi Yitzhak comments on "fear the Lord your God."

It is known that there are two types of God-fearingness: upper fear and lower fear. Lower fear is the fear of sin which is not the fear of punishment alone . . . Fear of sin is the fear one experiences when one does something which is against the will of God for no one wishes to be set apart and isolated from God; rather, one's will and desire is to draw close to God. The root of this fear flows from contemplation of the greatness of the Creator, blessed be He, Who is the root and principle of all the worlds, surrounding and filling them . . . and everything is as nothing compared to Him; rather, their existence depends on the light and vitality that flows from Him . . . One sees one's unworthiness and insignificance . . . and a fear and trembling falls upon one not to defy His will, God forbid . . .

Upper fear is annihilation in reality because of the grandeur and exaltedness of God which one arrives at by contemplating and meditating on the being of the Creator, may He be blessed: He is infinite, absolutely simple, beyond comprehension . . . One is annihilated fully in reality and does not feel one's self at all, nor can it be said that one is aware even of one's insignificance . . . the utter lack of awareness of self . . .

There are, then, two types of God-fearingness, and one preliminary stage. The preliminary stage is the fear of punishment. It is not truly a form of fear of God; even animals, and humans lacking all sensitivity, fear punishment. It cannot be ignored or denied, but its spiritual potential is limited.

The first type of God-fearingness is the "fear of sin." This comes to us when we meditate on God's greatness; that is, on the variety and power of His deeds. We see the sky, or a flower, and we reflect that it is His work, that it derives from Him. We see a picture or read a poem, and we realize that it expresses His creative power which is infinite in its variety. Or we contemplate an event and we reflect that it speaks of His Presence, that it adumbrates a greater hand at work in our destiny. Or we think about thinking, or contemplate about contemplating, and we wonder, "How great are Your works, oh Lord." The more we move in our minds from reality to God, the more we realize that everything flows from Him. Were He to sever His contact with creation for an instant, all being would cease to exist. Were He to shower upon us more of His blessing, we would faint away. We are the objects of the flow of His goodness and being. Sin, in this perspective, is separation from Him, "being cut off." It is alienation from awe, isolation from joy. It results from the fact that the more we realize God's presence, the more we become aware of our own insignificance and unworthiness, of our separatedness. The more real God is to us, the more we sense our incompatibility with Him, our alienness in His world. We fear this type of sin because we do not want to cut ourselves off from God Who is our source. This is "the lower fear of God."

The second type of God-fearingness is the "utter loss of self." This comes upon us when we meditate, not on God's creation and greatness, but on God's essence, on His very being. God is without border, without definition. He, in His essence, cannot be grasped by any mode of thought or awareness. He is beyond oneness, beyond existence, outside of being. One cannot contemplate that which is uncontemplatable. One can only make the truest statement possible about God and then realize that, at its best, the statement was untrue and false to His ultimateness. The more we ponder the imponderability of God, the more we realize that all our efforts are vanity and wind. The more we think that which cannot be encompassed by thought, the more we have to surrender our self-being—until nothing of our selves is left. The more we reach out with our consciousness toward that which is not within consciousness, the closer we get to God. Eventually even our insignificance has no meaning any longer. It is like the seed which must decay and dissolve before it can grow into something new. This is "the higher fear of God."

These two types of God-fearingness—"fear of sin," that is, fear of alienation from the wondrousness of God's action; and "utter loss of self," that is, the silence from all self-motivated attempts to make God a part of our world—are what is required of us by the verse, according to Levi Yitzḥak.

Both of these types of fear of God are alien to modern people. We are too scarcely aware of God's presence in reality to be afraid of being separated from Him. We are too remote from the world as creation to be worried about ontological alienation from its source. We have no "fear of sin." Modern people are also supremely confident about their ability to put things into intellectual, emotional, and social pigeonholes. Our culture teaches faith in our ability to know—if not now, then eventually; if not I, then another. We define our selfhood by our ability to construct these pigeonholes. We do not stand, lost and incompetent, before that which eludes consciousness. We have no "utter loss of self." Yet exactly these, Levi Yitzḥak teaches, are what God requires of us.*

---

*Note: There is also a God-fearingness which is a fear and trembling before the presence of God; see Thematic Index, "fear of God."

True Blessing

The reading of this week begins with the words: "See, I set before you, this day, blessing and curse" (Deuteronomy 11:26). What is "blessing" and what is "curse"? The answer, as it stands in the biblical text, begins only in chapter 27, verse 11, and continues through the end of chapter 28. There the rewards and punishments are stated in terms of personal and national physical security. Levi Yitzhak, who lived in a world where physical security was not an index of piety or sinfulness, proposed other terms by which to understand "blessing" and "curse." His teaching has several levels.

The sages say [Pirke Avot 4:2], "The reward of a mitsva is a mitsva." They mean to teach that the reward of doing a mitsva is the mitsva which was done, and that no further reward is required. Rather, this is the reward itself—that one has merited to do a command of God and to give pleasure to the Creator. There is no reward greater than this.

At this level, Levi Yitzhak teaches that "blessing" is the awareness of having done the will of God. It is the consciousness of having fulfilled a command of the Creator; of having been able, of having merited, to do something one has been asked to do—not for the sake of any reward of physical security, nor for any reward of emotional reinforcement, and not because one might feel bad, or guilty, if one did not do the act asked. Rather "blessing" is simply the knowing, the joy of having done that which is required, and it is available to us "this day," in the present.

Levi Yitzhak, however, knew that there was a certain danger in relying upon our subjective sense of having fulfilled God's will as the criterion of spirituality and so he taught:

One should not let one's heart swell such that one seems to oneself as if one were truly serving God by one's Torah-study, mitsvot, and with the love and fear of God that one experiences. For, in that which one feels in one's soul during service to God one can, God forbid, fall spiritually from level to level until one comes to a desire for physical rewards.

Here Levi Yitzḥak means to say that even service to God for its own sake can grow into a trap, into a self-reinforcing piety, and even into an unmerited pride. How much more so can the fulfilling of religious obligations for social, historical, or lesser emotional rewards run the danger of leading us into "curse"—into false pride and pseudo-piety.

What, then, is genuine "blessing"? Levi Yitzḥak teaches:

One should consider one's worship of God as if it were nothing and one should not have any feeling [of accomplishment] in one's worship. Rather, one's heart should be empty and broken because one has not yet even begun to worship the Creator at all. For, when one meditates well on the greatness of the Creator, may He be blessed—that He is the root and principle of all worlds, that He encompasses and fills all reality, that no thought can grasp Him at all, and that all the worlds, souls, and angels are all annihilated and as nothing and emptiness before Him—then one's soul is awakened to yearn and to be consumed in the flame of sweetness, bliss, and love. Then, one desires and has a passion to worship God at all times and one's [usual] worship is not recognized as valuable at all. The more one steeps one's mind in meditation on the greatness of the Creator, blessed be He, the more one's heart is enflamed to worship God . . .

At this level, then, Levi Yitzḥak teaches that "blessing" is a bliss attained by reflecting on the greatness of God's deeds and the inadequacy of our response, even that of intense service. We come to realize that, no matter what we have done, it is as if we had not yet begun.

Levi Yitzḥak uses two sources to illustrate this. The first is an interpretation reported in the name of Israel Baal Shem Tov, the founder of the hasidic movement: " 'He will lead us to childhood' [Psalm 48:15] can be understood metaphysically in the matter of how one teaches an infant to walk. Just as when one distances oneself from an infant it slowly learns to walk, so when we learn of the great distance between us and the awesome ineffable God we realize that we too are infants and have just barely begun to walk." The other is a saying from the Talmud [Ketubot 110b]: "One who lives in the land is as one who has a God, while one who lives outside the land is as one who has no

God." The talmudic rabbis speak of the land of Israel and their meaning is clear. Levi Yitzhak reverses the meaning and interprets:

- "One who lives in the land"—that is, one who lives in spiritually coarse terms and esteems himself or herself to be something;
- "is as one who has a God"—that is, is as one who thinks she or he worships God;
- "while one who lives outside the land"—that is, one who lives outside spiritual coarseness and sees himself or herself as lowly, rejected, not occupying any importance at all, and who considers his or her worship as nothing;
- "is as one who has no God"—that is, feels as if she or he has not begun worshiping God at all.

Levi Yitzhak's best advice, then, is to rid oneself of all pretension of having "achieved" spirituality, to rid oneself of all claim to "being religious." Rather, he counsels, "insofar as one sees oneself as excess and does not allow oneself to become concrete and substantial in one's own eyes, perhaps by this one may become a vessel prepared to receive the flow of God's continuous presence, for only an empty vessel is capable of being filled."

True "blessing" is an emptying of ourselves of our pious vanities and, in that emptiness, perhaps being worthy of being filled with the eternal presence of God.

Setting an Example
in Judgment

Perhaps in anticipation of Rosh ha-Shana, the Day of Judgment, Levi Yitzhak teaches:

The Holy One, blessed be He, will judge the community of Israel on the Day of Judgment with the greatness of His merciful love and grace. But there must be an action below which arouses this quality of merciful love above. We arouse that quality of merciful love when we, here below, act in grace, defending the merits of every Jew and judging him or her positively. By these acts, that quality of merciful love is aroused on high and, then, the merits of whoever so acted and indeed of all the seed of Israel are defended and grace granted . . . This is the meaning of [the first verse of this reading], "Judges and police shall you set for yourself in all your gates" [Deuteronomy 16:18]; to wit, that you, yourself, must set in order and prepare the judgment on high by the gates which you make and which you open with your deeds.

This very beautiful meditation is timeless. As the high holidays approach, even the most skeptical among us has reason to pause and to wonder what the future holds. The approaching days of awe are the time for reflection, even for those of us who do not give too much thought to it, on the precariousness of our lives, on the razor thin edge between life and death. This time of the year is a time to reconsider the underlying moral balance in which life and sanity hang so delicately, to measure ourselves against such words as "purity of heart," "true forgiveness," "sin," and "judgment."

Levi Yitzhak, following the Jewish mystical tradition, teaches that it is up to each Jew to set the example for God, so to speak; that it is up to each Jew to so live that God, in His interrelatedness with us, will be moved to act in merciful love and in grace.

Now, it is usually possible to sweep an offense against oneself under the carpet; but to reach a socially acceptable truce which restores surface relations, forgiveness, true and deep, coming from the heart, is very difficult to achieve. Most of us believe in our own righteousness, and hence in the wrongness of the other. Most of us see interpersonal incidents as injustice committed against ourselves. And our very righteousness makes it difficult, indeed unnecessary, for us to forgive: Why forgive when she or he is wrong and I am right? But imagine, Levi Yitzhak suggests, if God thought that. Who would ever be forgiven? Why should God forgive us even our petty sins, much less our serious ones? We cannot preach forgiveness to God if we do not practice it ourselves. We cannot urge Him to do that which we will not do. And, if this is true for us as individuals, how much more so is it true for Israel as a people?

The way out of the circle of self-righteousness begins with "defending the merits" of the other, with "judging [the other] positively." Why did she or he do what was done? What suffering—and we all are subject to inner suffering—motivated him or her to do that? What merit does she or he have that outweighs the evil done to me? To tell the truth: Why can't I forgive? Why don't I forgive? Why do I resist exercising the same compassion against him or her that I would have others, and indeed God, exercise toward me?

I have seen many interpersonal disputes where such questions as Levi Yitzhak might have asked were never posed, where only hostile statements overflowing with self-righteousness were heard. Is that what being Jewish means? Is that the judgment we all wish to see? And I have seen many community fights where such questions as flow from Levi Yitzhak's teaching were never posed, where only hostile statements invoking even God, Torah, and Jewishness in a totally self-contained, self-righteous manner were all that was heard. Is that what being Jewish means? Is that to be the tone of the judgment of the days of awe? Do we really intend to set the example of mean self-righteousness for God? Do we really intend to so live that God, in His interrelatedness with us, will be moved to act in self-justified anger? No, says Levi Yitzhak. Rather, "let each person teach himself or herself to become accustomed to 'judging the people by a judgment of charity and merit' [Deuteronomy 16:18] so that she or he and all Israel be judged innocent in the judgment on high."

Assuming Responsibility for Our Relationship to God

This reading contains the strange commandment concerning bird- and egg-hunting: "You shall not take the mother-bird and the baby-birds; you shall drive off the mother-bird and then take the chicks for yourself, so that it be well with you and you enjoy length of days" (Deuteronomy 22:6–7). The commandment itself, while poignant, is strange: Why chase the mother-bird away first? Is cruelty to animals the point here? Also, very few commandments end with the phrase "so that it be well with you and you enjoy length of days." Why was this particular commandment singled out for this? The tradition gives many answers; Levi Yitzhak proposes his own.

"It is known," he teaches, "that there are two ways in which God's action towards humankind is motivated: one which comes from within God and one which comes in response to the effort of human beings. It is, however, not permitted to rely totally on God's acting from His own will. Rather, a person must try to arouse himself or herself to act in a way that will stimulate a gracious and just response from God." This is a profound teaching because it places the responsibility for the relationship between God and humanity squarely on our shoulders, at least for half that relationship. Humanity cannot take God's grace for granted.

The commandment of the mother-bird is a paradigm for this spiritual principle. "For as, when a child is young, the mother must bend over it so that it can suck, so it is with God, may He be blessed. When one has no intellectual and moral training such that one cannot arouse oneself to act in the proper way, God acts unilaterally and sends one inspiration and blessing . . . This is the meaning of 'and the mother-bird is sitting on her chicks.' " However, Levi Yitzhak teaches, one should not rely on this one-sided relationship, as Scripture says,

"You shall not take the mother-bird and the baby-birds." Rather, the mature person must "drive off the mother-bird and then take the chicks for oneself." By this, Levi Yitzhak means to teach that, at some point in every person's life, he or she must assume responsibility for his or her relationship with God. At some point, one must say, "I will no longer rely solely upon the grace of God, but I will work hard to build an ongoing relationship with God." At some point, one must say, "I can no longer take God for granted."

This, too, is a very strange thought to modern minds for, if we think of God at all, it is as a background figure, as a benevolent shadow in our lives. We do not take God seriously and we certainly do not assume that our relationship with God is our responsibility. But that is the lesson of driving off the mother-bird in order to get to the chicks, Levi Yitzhak teaches.

The understanding of the text is not complete without the phrase "so that it be well with you and you enjoy length of days." Which gives more joy to a parent, asks Levi Yitzhak, that the child respond to a parental kindness or that the child initiate an act of love, especially if one talks of an older, mature child? Clearly, the act which flows freely from a person who has assumed at least partial responsibility for the relationship generates greater joy—and so it is with humankind and God, as it says, "so that it be well with you." And which type of act has consequences that endure, that last? Again, clearly the act that flows from mutual responsibility—and so it is with God and humanity, as it says, "and you enjoy length of days." By this Levi Yitzhak means to teach that, as we come to think of God as an ongoing Presence in our lives to Whom we have responsibilities as well as from Whom we have blessings, we can develop an extended, fuller awareness of God's presence. As we come to recognize our interrelatedness with God, we can reject the usual path of taking Him for granted and, by doing that, we can develop a deeper appreciation of our selves, of God, and of the interconnectedness of His reality and ours. That is blessing, well-being, and length of days.

Sin and Despair

As the high holidays approach, a Jew's thoughts turn to judgment. What remains in my mind, in my heart, and of my deeds from this past year? What accomplishments can I count? Where have I truly failed?

When I was a child, my world was laden with the unfulfilled expectations others had of me, and I knew what sin was. When I was an adolescent, I read the confessions in the liturgy, was amazed at the sinful world of adults, and did not know what sin was. But, as I have grown older, my world has again become laden with unfulfilled expectations—for myself, for my children, for my people, and for my God. Again, I know what sin is, and now I know how deep it runs. I know how set we are in our ways, how shrewd our self-defenses are, and how much easier it is to relinquish the standards against which we measure ourselves, or at least to modify them. Now I know much better than before how simple it is to befuddle the meaning of such words as "spiritual," "pure," "religious," "Jewish," "holy," and so on. Jewish tradition sets a high standard for us in learning, in observance, in loyalty, and in piety. And we fail; every day, every year.

Our accomplishments, when we count them, are of this world; our failures are of the other world. To have only accomplishments and failures in this world is to have really failed. To have accomplishments and failures in the other world is to have done something, to have tried. To be sinless is to have been insensitive. Spirituality is real, and therefore so is sin. Torah is real, and therefore so is transgression.

For those with spiritual aspirations—and everyone should, must, have them—there is always the danger of despair. To confront the reality of the intransigence of one's failures is depressing. To realize that one has compromised one's standards is crushing. To compare one's performance in life, and even one's aspirations, to God's expectations of us is heartbreaking—more so if we have tried, or at least yearned, to be spiritually close to Him. Encouraging clarification of standards and self-evaluation is a part of the season of judgment; countering despair is also a part. Levi Yitzhak addresses the latter in this week's reading.

There are two kinds of servant: the one who has regular contact with the king and who serves him, and the one who almost never sees the king but who arouses him or herself to serve him, not asking for his or her own needs but requesting only that she or he be able to serve the king . . . that is, that he or she be able to be in God's presence always and to worship [serve] Him for, although such a person has the worry of sustaining a family, she or he nonetheless submits him or herself to God. From such a person, the Holy One, blessed be He, has great pleasure and He says to His ministering angels, "Look at that person, filled with sin, yet whose heart is filled with the aspiration to serve Me and still, she or he is happy in that service." Of such a person, the rabbis said, "In the place where one who returns to God stands, not even the completely righteous can stand" [Talmud, Sanhedrin 99a]. From one who returns, the Holy One, blessed be He, has great pleasure since such a person has been ignorant and has walked in the way of fools but now he or she is enflamed in the service of God.

Levi Yitzhak's typology is simple: There are those who are privileged to serve God with a minimum of worry about the matters of this world: money, professional advancement, household management, family worries, and so on. These are, so to speak, "the righteous." They have the opportunity for living the life of the other world. They have been rewarded already for the good they have done. And there are those who, because they bear the worries of this world, can serve God only intermittently, incompletely, though they yearn to serve Him more fully. These are "those who return to God," who, burdened with having to live the life of this world, nonetheless turn again and again to Him in deep desire for wholeness of service. The service of the latter, Levi Yitzhak explains, gives great pleasure to God for He knows their longing for Him and recognizes the modest accomplishment of their service.

This insight also lends meaning to the verse which is repeated in the penitential prayers of this season: "He will turn to us and have mercy on us; He will subdue our sins; He will cast their iniquities in the depths of the sea" (Micah 7:19). Levi Yitzhak understands the phrase "He will subdue our sins" to mean, "God will take our sins [that which is hidden] and turn them into a source of pride for Himself [a garment of glory]." God, says Levi Yitzhak, is proud of His people who want to serve Him, they are His glory; and His pride in them includes even their sins. Were it not for the one, the other would not be. God, thus, wears the garment of the glory of His people, together with their sins.

Sin then, Levi Yitzhak teaches, is a part of life. It is normal. One should not therefore fall into despair on account of sin. Disappointment, yes; despair, no. Rather one must know that God wears our sins together with our accomplishments; that He derives pleasure precisely from the person who, though overwhelmed by the burdens of daily living and sin, nonetheless yearns to be His servant. God desires the returning of the sinner, not his or her death, as the prophet says (Ezekiel 18:23; 33:11). For this reason, one must always aspire to spiritual closeness to Him, in spite of sin.

The capacity God has given us to return to Him negates despair. Knowledge and practice of this is the counter to the black night of the desolation of the soul. As the days of judgment approach and our awareness of our sinfulness and failures becomes more acute, we need Levi Yitzhak's word of encouragement.

God Is Judged with Us

The reading of this week contains a strange verse: "And the Lord your God will grant you an excess in all the work of your hands, in the fruit of your body, in the fruit of your animals, in the fruit of your earth—for goodness; for the Lord will again rejoice over you for good, as He rejoiced over your ancestors" (Deuteronomy 30:9). What is the "excess"? Why the repetition of "for good"? And, what do we mean when we say that God will "again rejoice" over us? Levi Yitzhak, bearing in mind the approaching New Year, offers the following comment:

There are two ways in which [God responds] to humankind's requests: In the first way, a person asks of the Creator, may He be blessed, that He grant her or him [whatever He wishes] because the Creator, blessed be He, has joy and gladness in pouring His blessings on His chosen ones, His beloved children. Just as when a parent loves a child and pours out blessing upon it, the parent experiences joy and gladness, so it is with the Creator, blessed be He. In the second way, God forbid, the Creator is not able to pour forth His blessing because there are no fitting receptacles. In this case, God, may He be blessed, is ill at ease, so to speak, as the rabbis have said, "More than the calf wishes to suck, the cow wishes to nurse" [Talmud, Sanhedrin 112a] . . . Judgment, then, touches God Himself, so to speak for, since God receives pleasure from granting us His blessing, judgment touches Him Himself. This is the reason why God is called "unfortunate" in Sefer Raziel . . .

This can also be explained by a parable: A wise man asked advice on whether he should do such-and-such a thing or not and he was advised not to do it. The wise man, however, paid no attention to the words of his advisors and did it anyway. When it was done, it turned out, God forbid, as the advisors had said and the wise man was, then, deeply embarrassed. So it is with God, may He be blessed: When He thought to create humanity, He said "Let *us* make humankind in *our* image, according to *our* form" [Genesis 1:26], meaning, He asked the angels on high whether to create humanity and they counseled Him against it [Bereshit Rabba, 8:5]. But God, in His great mercies, did not listen to them and He created humankind anyway. Now, when people act against His will, God forbid, and it is better if they had not been created, then He, may He be blessed, is called "unfortunate," so to speak . . .

This too is the meaning of the verse [used liturgically on the New Year], "It is a decree for Israel, a judgment for the God of Jacob" [Psalm 81:5] . . . that, for Israel, His holy people, there is a "decree" of sustenance . . . and "the judgment is for the God of Jacob" . . . that the matter touches the Creator Himself, blessed be He . . . [This, too, the meaning of the liturgical poem], "fear and trembling seize them [the angels]" for they fear to open their mouths [against humankind] because then He will also judge them. Even though they are holy angels, they will not be acquitted in judgment . . . for God Himself is judged with us and no living thing will be acquitted, as it says, "Do not enter into judgment with us for no living thing would be justified before You" [Psalm 143:2] . . .

And this is the meaning of "And the Lord your God will grant you an excess . . . for goodness" [here]—that He will pour upon you goodness and blessing in excess of your deeds and merits, that He will pour them upon you because of His will for goodness. On this, the verse continues and explains, why will God, may He be blessed, do this? Because "the Lord will again rejoice over you for good, as He rejoiced over your ancestors," meaning, that He will receive joy and gladness from our receiving goodness and blessing from Him, Amen.

Weaving many strands into a whole in a fine example of rabbinic art, Levi Yitzḥak has made the point that, in creating humanity, God put Himself on the line. In the language of the midrash, He defied the advice of the angels, making Himself vulnerable to their reproach. In the language of Jewish spirituality, He exposed Himself to being judged, even to being condemned, as the one responsible for us. And, in the language of Jewish mysticism, He opened Himself to the possibility that humanity would reject Him and then He would be a solipsism, a being contemplating only itself, isolated and alone, unfortunate. How does one minimize this risk? How does God hedge His bet on humanity?

The solution is deceptively simple. Each of us has experienced the joy of giving of oneself to another. But giving of oneself cannot be done to everyone. Not everyone is a worthy recipient. One of the sorriest moments in a person's life is realizing that one may love another deeply, that one may feel the deepest empathy for another and desire greatly to aid the other, and not be able to do so. How often do spouses get into this situation of wanting to give and not being able to do so because the other has backed himself or herself into a corner? How often do parents find themselves yearning to reach out to a child and find the doors closed? Contemporary psychology has a tendency to say that such closedness is usually two-sided, that both parties are to blame. Sometimes this is true, but not always. People are very stubborn and will often follow their own paths even if the cost may be the expressibility of affection and love from intimates.

Here Levi Yitzhak urges us to remember that God stands in the same relationship with us as we stand with others: He wants to love us and we do not always want to be loved. He wants to relate to us and we are not always worthy receivers. The New Year is the time to "grant an excess," to judge others not on their deeds and merits but on our need to love, to give. The days of judgment are a time to act out of the joy and gladness of pouring forth blessing. Rosh ha-Shana is a good time for asking the question: Am I a worthy receiver?

The Words of Prayer

Jewish worship provides that one person "go before the lectern" and act as the leader of the service. The only real quality required of this leader is piety; there are no formal institutional requirements, such as being a rabbi or a cantor. There are, however, two terms used in the literature to describe this function: "to go down before the lectern" and "to pass before the lectern." Scholars do not know the exact nuance intended by this differentiation. Levi Yitzḥak, commenting on the verse, "And Moses went and spoke . . ." (Deuteronomy 31:1), offers his own interpretation drawn from the realities of the hasidic prayer life:

Sometimes the sages, may their memory be a blessing say, "one goes down before the lectern" and sometimes they say, "one passes before the lectern." There are righteous persons, who when they pray before God, may He be blessed, must attach themselves to the words of the prayers and the holy words themselves lead them. And there are very great righteous persons who are beyond this level and they lead the words. This is the level of Moses . . . This is the meaning of "one goes down before the lectern" [Hebrew, tevah], for the word [Hebrew, tevah] leads one and one is "down below" it. As to the righteous person who leads the word and is therefore of greater rank, such a person is one who "passes before the lectern." Here, when Moses was at the end of his days and when, according to the midrash, the fountain of wisdom was sealed for him, he was of the rank in which the words led him. This is the meaning of "and Moses went and spoke"—that he went to the word, which was above him.

Levi Yitzḥak has, here, set forth another of his wonderful typologies of the prayer life: There are those who, when they pray, are led by the words and there are those who lead the words they pray. Levi Yitzḥak does not make clear what he means. He may have reference to the hasidic doctrine that the saint has enormous intercessory power, as the talmudic saying adopted by hasidic thinkers, put it, "The righteous man decrees and God fulfills" (Talmud, Mo'ed Katan 16b). In this sense, the saint of the highest order "leads [directs] the words." One intercedes with the full power of one's saintliness and God must obey. The lesser saint, however, "is led [directed] by the words," that is, follows the liturgy and prays fervently, but it is the liturgy which informs the prayers, shapes them, and gives them substance. Such a person's intercessory abilities are limited to the words of the prayers.

Levi Yitzhak may, however, have reference here to a more general typology of prayer experience. There are moments when, being very upset or joyful or confused, we approach God but do not have the right words. Our own power of expression fails us. In that situation, we turn to words written by those who have preceded us along the way—the Psalms or the liturgy. And, through those words, made holy by the spirit which inspired them and the powerful use of the many who have prayed them, we find our own voice. In the words themselves, we find expression of our deepest feelings. In this instance, we are "led by the words."

But there are other moments when, being deeply moved by fear or love or anger or joy, we approach God and know that we are already close to Him; that He is there for us, with us. And still we pray. In this situation, our words flow freely from us and are directed to Him, without the effort of searching for the right word. In such moments, our words are an offering to Him, a gift given prayerfully even when they are petitionary. Not that we make up the words, not that we extemporize; but that our closeness to God precedes our awareness of the words and their meaning. In this instance, our sense of God's presence dominates the liturgy, we "lead the words."

Both are methods of true prayer. Furthermore, both of these types of prayer are also modes of leadership in prayer, as Levi Yitzhak indicates in his play on words. Sometimes, as leaders of prayer, we allow the liturgy to speak for us, through us. In such moments, we "go down before the lectern," as the rabbinic phrase would have it. And sometimes, as leaders of prayer, we know what we need to say to God, we feel close to Him and confident in Him, and we use the liturgy to say what needs to be said. In such moments, we "pass before the lectern."

The moment of being so close to God that the words are an offering is the highest rank of spirituality. It is the rank of Moses. The moment of using the holy words to approach Him, though it is a lesser spiritual achievement, is also a great prayer moment. Even Moses, Levi Yitzḥak teaches, had such lower moments as his career drew to a close. Religiously serious modern people ought to strive for both.

The Non-Jew, Conversion, and the Messianic Song

This week's reading is Moses' song, his prophetic summary of history. It includes verses which the tradition understands as alluding to God's choosing of the people in the desert, to their sojourn in the exile, and to their ultimate redemption. The song is introduced by the sentence: "And Moses spoke the words of this song into the ears of the whole community of Israel, even unto their end" (Deuteronomy 31:30). Levi Yitzhak, sensing the ambiguity of the word "their," offered the following comment:

The sages, may their memory be a blessing, have said [Talmud, Pesahim 87b]: "Rabbi Eliezer said, 'The Holy One, blessed be He, exiled Israel among the nations only so that converts be added to them, as it says, "I shall plant them for Myself in the land, and I shall have mercy on those upon whom no mercy falls, and I shall say to those who are not My people 'you are My people,' and they shall say, 'You are my God'" [Hosea 2:20]. Does one plant a measure unless it be to take in a larger measure?!'" For Israel raises the holy sparks which are among the nations of the world and, by this, they take all the sparks from them. Therefore, the words of Moses in this reading are called a "song" because they hint at joy. For, even though it is written that Israel will be in exile, nonetheless the exile itself is a joy because Israel will take the holy sparks from the nations of the world and, when the [reservoir of] holy sparks is exhausted and finished among the gentiles, they too will be exhausted and finished. This is the meaning of "And Moses spoke the words of this song," that is, that it is a song which points toward joy even though exile is written in it. Therefore, he also said, "even unto their end," meaning, that the exile will bring about the destruction of the nations of the world because Israel raises the sparks of holiness from their midst.

This is a motif which recurs in the thinking of Levi Yitzhak (see "sparks" in the Thematic Index): that, in the process of creation, sparks of holiness were scattered; that it is the task of Israel to meditatively redeem these sparks; and that, insofar as these sparks are scattered among non-Jews, Israel must "take" them from such persons and return them to God. Here, Levi Yitzhak adds three elements.

First, Levi Yitzhak roots his vision in a talmudic saying. The saying itself attempts to make sense of the exile and, interpreting the verse from Hosea, indicates that the purpose of the exile is to enable Jews to gather converts. The purpose of God's planting the Jews in the exile is to gather an even greater harvest of true believers and practitioners. It is to enable those who are not God's people to become His people, to include those who are beyond His active mercy among those who are already objects thereof.

Second, in making the connection between the talmudic text on conversion as the purpose of the exile and the Lurianic theme of the redemption of the sparks as the purpose of the exile, Levi Yitzhak suggests the possibility that "taking the holy sparks from the non-Jew" can best be done by the actual conversion of the non-Jew to Judaism. He advocates, then, not only a meditative process of redeeming the sparks but also a conversionist effort, perhaps even a missionary program. I am not aware, however, that he or his hasidim ever engaged in such a program.

Third, Levi Yitzhak links the meditation-conversion effort with the ultimate redemption. It is only when the non-Jews will have been deprived, by meditation as well as by conversion, of the holy sparks which are the source of their vitality that the full redemption will come.

Most modern Jews and non-Jews will be offended by this position, and I have expressed my own reserve elsewhere. Also, as indicated, I don't think that Levi Yitzhak himself took this position to its full conclusion in action. What, however, is the modern view toward conversion?

The Jewish community and the individual Jew are not of one mind on the subject of how to regard conversion. Generally, Jews are distrustful of converts for at least four reasons: (1) There are many examples of converts who later turned against the Jewish people. Jews learn about them, formally or informally. This generates a suspicion of converts and conversion which is deeply rooted in history. (2) There is also a semilogical question in the mind of the Jew: Jewish existence is full of Jew-hatred and persecution, as well as enormous responsibilities. This is especially true in the aftermath of the holocaust, in which there was no escape from Jewishness and of the establishment of the State of Israel which, as the focus of Jew-hatred, has become the major source of Jewish anxiety, though mixed with pride. Why, then, would anyone choose such an existence freely? This question generates a suspicion of converts and conversion which is rooted in common sense. (3) Since most non-Jews convert in order to marry Jews, Jewish parents want to make sure that their own children are married before they approve of a stranger taking the marital place that might otherwise be available to a Jew. This generates a suspicion rooted in social reality. And (4) theologically, the non-Jew is in no way bound to the covenant of Torah and Judaism. This realization generates a religious-intellectual suspicion of converts and conversion. It also discharges the Jew from any responsibility for the conversion of the non-Jew.

As a result of these considerations, most traditional Jews are reluctant to accept converts and surely do not encourage them. Most liberal Jews, however, reject these suspicions and theologically assert the equal truth of all religions. This leads them to a more receptive attitude toward converts and conversion, and there has even been a suggestion to create a mission to the gentiles to encourage conversion to Judaism.

I recognize, understand, and share the historical, common-sense, social, and theological suspicions of the Jewish community on the subject of converts. Hence, I do not encourage conversion. I also think that other faiths share in the universal holiness of creation and in the universal morality of the covenants of Adam and Noah. My own faith, however, contains theological and spiritual truths that are simply not taught elsewhere. In this sense, it is better, truer, simpler than other faiths. Conversion, therefore, must be a very serious matter—a matter of deep conviction and commitment, of ultimate truth and loyalty. In a sense, Levi Yitzhak is right: the ultimate redemption of humankind depends on others accepting the theological and spiritual truths which my tradition has evolved, preserved, and taught for so long.

There is a story told that Levi Yitzhak offered the following prayer: "Lord in heaven, if You cannot redeem Your people, at least redeem the nations of the world." Levi Yitzhak would have espoused meditation as well as conversion. I am prepared to advocate an increased awareness and acceptance of the deepest truths of Judaism among all peoples as the definition of the beginning of the redemption, as the point when the song of the messiah begins.

The Virtue of Pride

Jewish spirituality has a long tradition of quietist piety which emphasizes modesty and humility. In Psalm 131:1, King David says, "My heart
has not been proud, my eyes have not been lifted up, and I have not
associated with that which is greater and more exalted than I." The
Talmud (Sotah 5a) also stresses that coarseness of spirit and haughtiness
are vices which are sure to bring disaster upon those who live them.
Hasidism, in particular, made the motif of humility central to religious
consciousness partly because of its recurring theological emphasis on
God as the source of all vitality and action. But where is the limit to
humility? Life requires a certain toughness, and one should not be
humble and self-effacing all the time. Where is the point when one
must view pride as a virtue? And exactly what kind of pride is virtuous?
Levi Yitzhak addresses this issue in his comments to this reading.

It is forbidden to be prideful. Only this is permitted—to be afraid of no thing
and to have pride that one has a Father in heaven. This may be the meaning
of the saying of the sages, may their memory be a blessing [Talmud, Sotah
5a], "Rav said, 'A sage-scholar must have one eighth of an eighth.' " [To this
Rashi comments: "that is, that one must have a little pride so that those who
are less serious will not take advantage of one and so that one's words will
be accepted even unwillingly."] . . . This is the meaning of the verse [in this
reading, Deuteronomy 33:29], "Happy are you, Israel! Who is like you, a
nation saved by God, Who is the shield of your help and the sword of your
pride? Your enemies will be defeated before you and you will trample on their
high places." The phrase "the sword of your pride . . . high places" means:
"this pride—that you know that God, may He be blessed, is the shield of your
help—will be your sword and, with it, you will kill them and trample on
their high places"; that is, that, by your pride, the shells which are called "high
places" and "haughtiness" will be trampled and killed, for they take pride in
themselves and not in God, may He be blessed.

True pride, Levi Yitzhak teaches, is the pride of knowing that one is chosen, that one is the object of God's special care. True pride, which is a virtue, is the absolute confidence that God will right all wrongs, in this world or in the other; that the haughty will be brought low; that the evil will be punished; that the shells, those fragments of evil and limitedness in the universe left over from the first incomplete act of creation, will be ultimately annihilated. False pride, sinful pride, is pride in anything other than God.

A true story is told by witnesses to the massacre of the Jews of Lublin, a great hasidic center before the second world war. The local Nazi commander, known for his brutality, had assembled the Jews outside the city limits and had beaten them and assaulted them with his dogs. In the midst of his cruelty, he ordered them to sing a hasidic song. No one could sing under those conditions, so he increased his attacks. Finally, one voice rose in an old hasidic melody, *"Lomir zich iberbeiten, iberbeiten, ovinu shebashomayim:* Let us be reconciled, be reconciled, our Father in heaven." But the song died as soon as it began. Suddenly, someone else picked up the melody but with new words, *"Mir velen zey iberleben, iberleben, ovinu shebashomayim:* We will outlive them, outlive them, our Father in heaven." The song caught on quickly and the hasidim danced and sang with an enthusiasm that came from above. The Nazi commander ordered them to stop but they did not. They paid a heavy price, but the singing and dancing did not stop.[1]

From the point of view of this world, the singing and dancing of the hasidim of Lublin did not help; they were, after all, exterminated. Their pride in their Father in heaven and in His justice was a genuine virtue, but it did not help them. It is also true, however that, from the point of view of this world, the fighting and courage of those Jews who joined the resistance did not help either; they, too, died in great numbers. In truth, physical survival was, in preponderant measure, not really dependent upon one's own means. But resistance, military and spiritual, was necessary; pride was a virtue.

It is from the point of view of the other world that the singing and dancing of the hasidim of Lublin helped, for the story of their faith survived. The story of their pride in their Father in heaven persisted, long after they and their Nazi oppressors had died. Other stories of human heroism beyond imagination persisted. They express the same pride, but once removed to God's people and their Jewishness. These stories, too, make sense only in the perspective of the other world.

Jewish history, the story of God and His people, is very long and, in the end, Levi Yitzḥak is right—there is only the pride of knowing that we are chosen, that we are the object of the special concern of our Father in heaven. That is the limit of modesty. That is the line which one draws at all times between humility and pride.

THE HOLIDAYS

Four Types of Love

When Moses ascended Mt. Sinai to pray for the children of Israel after the sin of the golden calf, God Himself came down, wrapped Himself in a prayershawl, and taught Moses a prayer to say. It reads: "Lord, Lord—God Who loves compassionately and cherishes, Who is patient and overflows with grace and truth. He stores up grace for thousands of generations. He forgives rebellious sin, purposeful sin, and inadvertent sin. He cleanses" (Exodus 34:5–7). Because God taught it to Moses and, because it was used at the moment of greatest sin in Jewish history, this prayer became central to Jewish liturgy. Significantly, the penitential prayers of the high holiday season are composed of a confession of sins preceded by verses from Scripture and liturgical poems. This ultimate invocation of God's mercy is set between each group of verses and between each of the poems; it is the refrain of the penitential liturgy. But what does it mean? What is the difference among loving, cherishing, being patient, and granting grace?

Levi Yitzḥak addresses these questions as follows. To say that God "overflows with grace" is to say that God loves us, irrespective of our merits. This is a love that comes from Him because He is God. It is a one-way flow from Him to us. It is a sustaining of us in our existence. It is a powerful, unconditional love that He has for us. However, Levi Yitzḥak points out, there is nothing in grace that compels God. There is nothing in grace that is a product of anguish, pain, and suffering.

To say that God is "compassionately loving," however, is to say that God feels for us, that He is internally affected, that He cannot stand to see us suffer, and that He has a deep desire to do good to us. Love implies empathy, and empathy compels. God, then, is not only "overflowing with grace" but also "compassionately loving."

To say that God "cherishes" also implies a degree of relatedness. It implies that we have "found favor" in God's eyes, that He likes us, that He is attached to us—as a child "finds favor" in the eyes of its parent.

We see the face, the body, the person—and we just like it, as a whole. This is not compassionate loving, nor is it grace; it is cherishing, and God cherishes us.

Finally, to say that God is "patient" is to say that He knows us, that He studies our ways and our patterns of behavior and thought. He does not choose to judge us only on the basis of our manifest being. On the contrary, He chooses to blind Himself and to see us and accept us for what we are, in spite of ourselves.

In this analysis, Levi Yitzhak teaches us of four kinds of love: unconditional one-way love (grace), compassionate empathetic compelling love, love which cherishes being for its own sake, and love which purposely blinds itself to the faults of the other. It is a very profound analysis.

First, think of the people we know. Some of them we love because they are part of humanity. We need not even know them—the unknown children starving and abused, the poor and oppressed, Jews we don't know in Russia, the sick. These are all part of the broad family of humanity and the entire Jewish people. We love them even if they do not know of it. Sometimes we even love family members and friends, even if they don't know it, because they are fellow living creatures.

Some of the people we know we love because we have empathy with them. We know them, we feel their specific pain, we sense their specific distress. We cannot stand to see them suffer and we long to help them in any way. Their concrete being compels us. Our empathy binds us.

Some of the people we know we simply like. We may not even know why. It's chemistry, or instinct, or very finely tuned training, or the subconscious. But we know we like them. We cherish their presence.

And for some people, we know we have a great deal of patience. We know their faults yet we accept them. We know their shortcomings yet we love them.

Second, think of ourselves. We all want to be loved unconditionally; to be loved compassionately; to be cherished for ourselves; and to have others ultimately be patient with us, accepting us in spite of our faults.

As a matter of reflection, each of us really should ask, Which type of love do I need most? And which type of love can I give best?

So it is with God, says Levi Yitzhak. God loves each one of us in grace, in compassion, in cherishing, and in patience. But which is the most important, the most powerful? We need only consult God's own prayer to see the order in which He put them: it is compassionate love. Why is compassionate love first? Precisely because it is *engagé*, involved, bonded; it is covenantal. We have a moral claim on God's compassionate love. We have a right to His empathy, as a child has the right to the bonded love of a parent. And the reverse is true too: God has a moral claim on our compassionate love, a right to our empathy; as a parent has a claim on the compassionate love of a child. As it is with God, so it is with humanity. Each of us has a moral claim on the compassionate love of the other, a right to the empathy of the other. And others have a claim on our compassionate love and empathy. Compassionate love is not the easiest kind of love; indeed, it may be the most difficult, the most demanding. But it is the most profound, the most spiritually resilient. This is a very powerful lesson for the Day of Judgment.

Complete and true love encompasses all four types. It belongs to God, though it can be ours fleetingly. This is the love for which we can only pray. This, too, is a powerful lesson for the Day of Judgment.

Two Types of Repentance

This Shabbat, which comes between Rosh ha-Shana and Yom Kippur, is called Shabbat Shuva, "the sabbath of repentance." The liturgy for the day contains special prayers for a good new year as well as modifications of the text to emphasize God's kingship over all creation. The *haftara* (reading from the prophets) sets the tone with the verse: "Who is a God like You Who lifts up sin and passes over transgression for the remnant of His inheritance? He will not hold on to His anger forever because He desires grace. He will have compassionate love for us again and will subdue our sins. You will cast their iniquities into the depths of the sea" (Micah 7:18–19). Levi Yitzḥak, following the Talmud (Rosh ha-Shana 17a), notes that two different metaphors for God's forgiveness of sins are used: "lifts up" and "subdue." What can the difference be?

It is truly the case that, from Rosh ha-Shana to Yom Kippur, each person certainly has his or her eyes open to that which he or she is doing in order to repent and return to God—each one according to his or her intelligence and station—out of fear of God and the glory of His majesty when He arises to judge the earth. For the day of the Lord is near and who can be judged righteous before Him? Who, then, is the person who is not afraid and which soul will not exert itself when it must come to be judged on its deeds before the Judge of all creation? Is it not true that one who is earnest about the word of God will do, in the heights of his or her mind, everything to straighten that which has been distorted? This is called "repentance motivated by fear."

But, after Yom Kippur, when one busies oneself with the commandments of *sukka,* of *lulav,* of the four kinds, and of charity—in generosity and in love according to the blessing of hand of God—in order to worship God in joy and in gladness of heart, then this type of repentance is called "repentance motivated by love."

Now, as the sages, may their memory be a blessing, have indicated [Talmud,

Yoma 86b], by "repentance motivated by fear" purposeful sins are transformed into inadvertent sins and, by "repentance motivated by love" purposeful sins are transformed into acts of merit.

In this text, Levi Yitzḥak has pointed to two types of repentance, one motivated by fear of God's judgment and one motivated by the love which we feel for Him when we perform His commandments. Each requires some explanation. Modern people are inclined to deny the realness and the validity of the fear of God's judgment. We tend to discount the metaphor of the "book of life." We usually trust our acts and feel secure in our existence. I can think of no greater illusion. Life, itself, is very precarious and, from one year to the next, we never know who will be with us and who will die, even among our intimates. In addition, the threat of nuclear war is never so far from us that we can rest secure in our existence.

It is also the case that each of us has some sense of the inextricably moral quality of existence. There really is right and wrong; there really is good and evil. Life is a constant struggle to do the right, to make life's chaos conform to a moral order. We all feel guilty for not having done enough good and for having, actively or passively, done evil. Jewish religion brings these two motifs together in the teaching of God's judgment. God, we are taught, takes our moral measure and He links it with our security. We really are judged and, according to our evaluation, we are blessed. Sometimes His judgment may seem wrong; but He does judge. Hence Levi Yitzḥak is right: we all have reason to be afraid, or else we are just thick-skinned and stiff-necked.

The same holds true for our love of God. Moderns tend to dismiss the idea that "God loves you" and that He is glad when we do certain things. But, says Levi Yitzḥak, God does love us, He does want us to do certain things, and He does tell us about it. And, when we do these things "in generosity and love," we too experience joy. As a matter of fact, that is what joy is—doing, in love, that which one who loves us wants us to do; responding, in fullness of heart, to a fullness that has been extended to us. Both paths, Levi Yitzḥak teaches, lead to God; they are ways of "return" to Him.

Because there are two ways of repentance, God does not complete His judgment of us until we have had the opportunity to experience and walk both paths. He does not finish counting up our sins until they can be transformed into merits. When He sees our "repentance motivated by fear" and realizes that we really don't mean to sin, he "lifts the sin" and, in so doing, our merits outweigh our sins and we are vindicated before Him. And then, when He sees our "repentance motivated by love" and realizes how much we want to be fully His children, He "subdues our sins" and casts them away from Him into the depths of the sea. Both ways, followed with a serious heart and effort, lead to Him and bring favorable judgment.

Who Am "I"?

There are many stories about Levi Yitzḥak and Yom Kippur, the prayers he said, the fervor with which he prayed. But his book *Kedushat Levi* does not include any word of Torah for this holiday. Why the silence? Was it, perhaps, because the time had come for more action and fewer words? Was it because the season of judgment swept him up? I do not know. Perhaps his other books contain the secret.

I would like to share, however, a meditation which I think is in the spirit of Levi Yitzḥak. There is a story told about a hasidic rebbe who came into synagogue and sat down to pray. The hasidim noticed that he did not move and they went on with their prayers. By late afternoon the rebbe still had not moved from his chair. Finally, the hasidim dared to interrupt him and ask if something was wrong. "No," he said, "nothing is wrong. I opened my mouth to say 'I give thanks before You' and suddenly I began to think, 'Who is this "I" that is about to give thanks? Who am "I"? What am "I" '? And I have been meditating on that all day long."

The story is a very profound one. Who am "I"? What is the "self"? It is strange; we use the word "I" all the time, but what do we mean by it?

One way to look at the "I" is in terms of the roles one fills in life. I am a father; that takes energy and inner strength. I am a husband; that too takes time and effort. I am a teacher; it demands vigor and intensity. I am a scholar; it demands concentration and stamina. I am a member of several communities, serving in various official and unofficial capacities. I am an active Jew, giving time and energy to my people. I am a friend, searching and supporting. I am a rabbi, a faculty member, a citizen, a consumer, an author and editor, a colleague, a student, a son, and much more. Some of these roles are more important to me than others. Am "I" those important roles? Am "I" the sum of all these social roles? The contemporary literary critic Northrop Frye has commented that the older we get, the harder it becomes to shed our social masks. That's true, but are we our social masks?

Let us entertain for a minute the possibility that "I" am not my social roles, that I am not everything that I must be to be a functioning, effective human being. What, then, am "I"? Perhaps, "I" am my personal history. Perhaps, "I" am my life and everything that has gone into it. It is true: I am my fears, my loves, my aspirations, my body, my passions, my guilt, my spiritual and aesthetic sensitivities. I am the complex person that I was born, was brought up to be, and have made myself into. In modern culture, we call this the "self" or the "person." But is it true? Am "I" the sum of my feelings, concepts, and actions? Is my "self" defined by the range of emotions and thoughts of which I am capable? Freud has shown us that we all have inner masks by which we talk to our selves, even lie to our selves; and that we have masks within the inner masks, unconscious motives and feelings of which we are unaware. This is true. But am "I" my conscious feelings and thoughts? Am "I" my unconscious feelings and thoughts? What, or who, am "I"?

Let us entertain for a minute the possibility that "I" am neither the sum of my social roles nor the sum of my conscious and unconscious feelings and thoughts, that "I" am neither my social masks nor my inner masks. What, then, am "I"? To say that "I" am my "soul" does not help. For if I mean that I am an observant Jew, then I am defining myself in a sociocultural role. If I mean that I strive spiritually, I am defining myself in a psychological role. Even if I say that my soul is divine and, hence, I am a part of God, what does that *mean,* aside from being a theologically acceptable answer? Am "I" a theological proposition? Am "I" an intellectual second thought?

Let us start again. If "I" am not the sum of my social roles or my psychological functions, and if "I" am not a theologically acceptable hypothesis, what am "I"? What is the "I" of which I speak when I talk? Who is the "I" that is capable of returning thanks to God? Or doing anything? Perhaps, "I" am truly no-thing, utter void, undefinableness. Not some-thing ethereal, like a fine spray of water or isolated atoms in interstellar space; but no-role, no-feeling, no-thought. Not even the absence of these definitions; just no-thing. At first, this is very frightening. Nature abhors a vacuum and the mind abhors lack of definition. The "I" shies away from lack of location. That's why we have culture. But, if culture is secondary, what is primary? If formulation and articulation are secondary, what is pre- or non-, formulated?

Jewish spirituality teaches that there are three levels of being: thought, speech, and action. First, we think; then, we put what we think into words; and then we act upon what we think and speak. But what precedes thinking? What is prearticulate, preconceptual? Whatever enters our consciousness, even if it is chaotic, has some form; and we give it more form by thought, speech, and deed. But what is before consciousnes? What am "I" at this level of before-thinking, before-words, before-action?

After the fear comes joy. But even the joy is secondary; it is a response. It is an echo, a realization that "I" am no-thing but God is; that "I" am because He is; that "I" am nothing but He; that my no-thing-ness is true but it too is a mask for His being-ness. Everything I think, speak, and do is secondary and tertiary. From the innermost, "I-He" radiates through what my "I" thinks, speaks, and does. My psychological functions and my social roles are clothes, decoration. The "I" behind them is not mine or "me"; it is He. Perhaps, not even "He" in the sense of the God described in the words of the tradition but "He" as the because of my "I". Joy is allowing oneself to be aware of this. Joy is being open to this.

The rebbe was right; it takes all day, even many days, to meditate on such matters.

Kavvana: The Art of Jewish Prayer

Again for the holiday of Sukkot, we have many stories about Levi Yitzhak but, in his *Kedushat Levi,* no direct teaching. I do not know why. Perhaps, it was the intensity of the season. Perhaps, it was, as with Yom Kippur, the time for action not for words.

I have always found the Sukkot season difficult. One is supposed to be joyful. There is pleasure in making the sukka and in eating and studying in it. There is also pleasure in taking the *lulav* and *etrog* and blessing them. But pleasure is not joy. Joy is the feeling of serving God in the way He wants because He wants it that way. In this sense, there is also joy on Sukkot, but I find that it flickers like a flame. It is present, powerfully, during parts of the prayers—particularly the *hallel* and the *hoshanot,* if they are done slowly and with *kavvana.* But it is absent in the inbetween-times. Life, its chores and its tasks, calls us. The desire to control our time and to use it "productively" calls us. Society pulls at us and causes us to lose the sense of servanthood, and hence the joy. As a result, one must work at servanthood, and at joy. How does one do this?

Levi Yitzhak offers a comment to two verses from hallel that may be instructive. They read, "Open for me the gates of righteousness so that I enter them. This is the gate to God; the righteous [zaddikim] enter through it" (Psalm 118:19–20).

The rule is that the zaddik is always insignificant in his own eyes for, in his own eyes, it is always as if he had not started serving Him, may He be blessed. This is a general principle in the service of God—that one always be humble in one's own eyes. The result is that the zaddik is always praying to God to open the gate through which he can enter to serve Him and this is the essential principle of servanthood. This, too, is the meaning of the verses, "Open for me the gates of righteousness . . . the righteous enter through it."

Servanthood for the zaddik—and indeed for everyone, Levi Yitzḥak teaches—is a returning again and again to the basic prayer: that God enable us to be His servants.

Prayer, in Jewish tradition, is a form of work. It requires mental and spiritual effort. In the spirit of trying to convey how one opens the gates of traditional Jewish prayer, I offer the following meditation on *kavvana,* the art of Jewish spiritual consciousness-raising:[1]

Can you hum a melody and think a thought? Can you dislike a person yet be polite? Can you knowingly do something wrong? If you can do any of these things (and all of us can do them), then you know what "multiple consciousness" means. It means that we, in the course of our normal lives, can sustain several levels of awareness at the same time.

What do you have in mind when you "recite" prayers? What do you think of when you "participate" in a religious service? What do you have in your consciousness when you "pray"? These questions, too, reflect our ability to sustain multiple consciousness—in particular, the multiple consciousness which we call "religious" or "spiritual." To pray is more than to "say one's prayers." It is to raise one's religious consciousness. It is to focus one's spiritual senses.

The traditional Jewish term for spiritual consciousness-raising is *kavvana.* *Kavvana* is a set of consciousness-raising techniques; that is, it is a set of techniques for broadening one's awareness of what one is doing. The technique is accomplished by directing one's thoughts and one's awareness to the various aspects of what one is doing. In Hebrew, there is a verb, *le-khavven et ha-lev,* which literally means "to direct the heart" but which can also be translated as "to do (something) with attentiveness." The result of the use of *kavvana,* as is the case with all consciousness-raising techniques, is to change an act from a routine, or semiconscious, act into an experience in which one is more fully present and more fully aware of all the realities touched.

One way to elucidate the nature of *kavvana* is by example and I present here an example of the various modes of *kavvana* and the levels internal to each mode as an indication of the range of living religious reality within traditional rabbinic Judaism.

On certain holidays, the liturgy prescribes the recitation of Psalms

113 through 118, which together are called hallel ("praise"). Toward the end of Psalm 118 (verse 25), the psalmist writes: "Please, Lord, save, please; Please, Lord, grant success, please." This verse can be recited with varying levels of awareness. At the lowest level, it is recited as a matter of routine, in a semiconscious manner, with the person reciting it being vaguely aware of doing what she or he is supposed to do. This is called *keva'* or *she-lo lishma,* that is, mindless prayer. It is prayer without *kavvana.*

In one mode of *kavvana,* the rabbinic Jew reciting this verse must become aware of the various meanings of the words. One must first become aware of their simple, direct meaning. Then one must become aware of their context within this very beautiful Psalm, which itself speaks of "crying from the straits" and of God's response. On a broader level, such a person would have to become aware of the rabbinic regulations regarding the recitation of this verse: that it is recited by the leader first and then the congregation; that on Sukkot there are prescribed movements of the lulav (palm branch) and etrog (citron) which accompany the recitation of this verse, and that all movements cease when the word "Lord" is said; and so on. On still a broader level, such a person would have to become aware of the report in the Mishna (Sukka 4:5) concerning the circumambulation of the altar during which this verse was recited, and that according to another sage, a strange metamorphosis of this verse was recited: "I and 'ho,' save, please," and that this metamorphosed version occurs in the later liturgy and is reputed to have magical properties. At the outer limits of this mode of *kavvana,* the praying rabbinic Jew would be aware of the kabbalistic "unifications" attendant upon recitation of this verse and one would "make" them.

In a different mode of *kavvana,* the rabbinic Jew reciting this verse must become aware of what it is one is praying for, of that from which one wishes to be "saved," of what kind of "success" one wishes to have. One must begin with simple personal needs: health, sustenance, strength, love, and insight. One then must broaden one's awareness to include the needs of one's family, immediate and more remote. More broadly, one must make oneself aware of the needs of Jews elsewhere: their need for peace, for security, for freedom. And more broadly still, such a person must make him or herself aware of the need of human-kind for peace, for sustenance, and for life. At the outer limits of this mode of *kavvana*, the praying rabbinic Jew would have to become aware of him or herself and, indeed, of all people, as truly, existentially alone, separated from one another by the silence that separates all being, and realize that one's prayer is a primal cry into eternity for oneself, for one's children, and for all people everywhere.

In a different mode of *kavvana*, the rabbinic Jew reciting this verse must become aware of him or herself. He or she must first become aware of his or her own physical presence; then of his or her presence in the greater congregation of worshiping Jews the world over; then of his or her presence in the greater congregation of worshiping Jews through time; and so on. On a broader level, such a person would have to become aware of those brothers and sisters of the flesh and spirit who cannot pray, whose lives were cut off in the crematoria; that they, too, deserve to have their prayers recited; and that through this mode of *kavvana*, the praying rabbinic Jew becomes more than him or herself. Our consciousness becomes the instantiation of theirs. Our presentness becomes their presentness, and we speak, or rather cry out, for them too.

In a different mode of *kavvana*, the rabbinic Jew reciting this verse must become aware of God. One must become aware of God's absolute transcendence, of the utter power of God, which knows no limits but those which are self-imposed. And one must become aware of God's absolute love of humankind, of the inalienable bond to which God has committed Himself. More broadly, one must contemplate the types of fear of God and the types of love of God. One must meditate on the essential contingency of all reality upon God—that nothing exceeds God's knowledge, power, and providence. And one must ponder the acts and the Person of God as reflected in the traditional texts. More broadly still, such a person must confront his or her own real fear of God and his or her own real love of God. One must confront the reality of one's relatedness to God. And then one must consciously broaden one's awareness to let the Presence of God into one's mind and heart. One must knowingly broaden one's consciousness to permit oneself to stand in the Presence of God—person to Person, presence to Presence.

At the outer limits of this mode of *kavvana,* the praying rabbinic Jew must, in his or her own awareness, be ready to die, in that moment. She or he must be ready to immediately cast him or herself into the abyss. He or she must be completely ready to give up his or her soul for God, for His Truth, for His Torah, for His people. And then one must say what one has to say, for whom one has to say it. Then, and only then, the rabbinic Jew may, and indeed must, pray.

Not everyone can achieve or sustain such a broad spectrum of consciousness—in all its modes and levels—but in its full scope (and there is undoubtedly much that I, in my ignorance, have omitted), *kavvana* is the key to the range of traditional religious reality, to Jewish piety and spirituality.

The Torah and the Messiah

The appearance of the new moon thirty days before Rosh ha-Shana signals the beginning of the high holiday season. On the second day of that month (Elul), we begin blowing the shofar, which calls us to repent of our deeds and to rededicate our lives to God. During this time, we consider our lives. If we seem sinless, it is only our insensitivity. If we seem righteous, it is only our false pride. We must penetrate ever deeper into ourselves, criticizing ethically and spiritually. As we approach Rosh ha-Shana, the work intensifies and we begin reciting penitential prayers.

On the new moon of the month of Tishri, we celebrate Rosh ha-Shana. It is the Day of Judgment. On that day, God proclaims Himself King over creation. He opens His books of judgment in earnest. On that day, we begin the ten days of repentance. We examine ourselves even more carefully. We strive for moral rectitude and repel despair. We meditate on His love and our sinfulness. We contemplate His power and our merits. We seek to resolve all interpersonal conflicts. We are more meticulous in observing the mitsvot. We give charity, study, and watch our tongues.

On the tenth of the month of Tishri, we enter Yom Kippur, the central Day of Judgment, the last of the days of repentance. We do not drink, eat, make love, wash, or dress lavishly for a little more than twenty-four hours. We pray all day. We recite confession. We recall the great sacrificial purification from sin in the temple. And we consider who "we" are and who He is. We come into His presence, individually and as a community. The day ends with the confession of faith and the sounding of the shofar, which has been silent since Rosh ha-Shana, to signal our belief in the coming of the messiah.

Having repented from fear, as Levi Yitzhak teaches, we now have four days to prepare for the holiday of Sukkot which is the time to repent from love. On the full moon of the month of Tishri, we begin the holiday of Sukkot. We live in the sukka. We recite the blessing over the lulav and etrog. We recite the hallel. We recite the sacrificial service. We circumambulate the synagogue with the lulav and etrog once each day, reciting the hoshanot. And we strive to be joyous, in the simple sense and in the spiritual sense of serving God. We seek to serve God out of love, out of a sense of doing His will because we love Him and want to do His will. On the seventh day of Sukkot, some of the high holiday motifs reappear. God judges a final time. We give charity. We circumambulate the synagogue seven times and thrash the extra willow branches.

On the eighth day of Sukkot, we have a holiday which is really a holiday unto itself, Shemini Atseret. The full range of the holiday laws returns, as on the first days of Sukkot. But the sukka, the lulav, and the etrog are no longer obligatory. We pray for rain—physical rain for the holy land and spiritual rain and renewal for all.

The twenty-third of the month of Tishri is not a holiday in the land of Israel. But, in the exile, for complicated calendrical reasons, it remains a holiday. Slowly, it has evolved into the holiday of the Torah. On this day of Simhat Torah, the annual lectionary cycle of the Torah is completed. Each week we have read a portion. On this day, we read the last portion of Deuteronomy and then we immediately begin again with Genesis. Before the reading, all the scrolls of the Torah are taken from the ark. We circumambulate the synagogue with them and then we dance with them, seven times. The dancing and rejoicing goes on for a long time.

Two stories, both true: In Soviet Russia, there are no Jewish calendars. There are no Jewish schools. Very few people have enough Jewish education to know what the holidays mean or what is in the Torah and the tradition. Very few younger people attend synagogue. Yet, on Simhat Torah, the streets around the great synagogues of Russia are filled with Jews. They come to celebrate, to be together. They rally around the Torah. Once, a friend of mine attended such a rally and found in his pocket a note, *"Am Yisrael hai,* the Jewish people lives." The second episode took place in the kingdom of night.

In one of the barracks, several hundred Jews gathered to celebrate Simhat Torah. In the shadow of shadows? Yes—even there. On the threshold of the death chambers? Yes—even there. But there was no Torah scroll. So how could they organize the ritual hakafot, the traditional procession with the sacred scrolls? As they were trying to solve the problem, an old man—old? . . . the word had no meaning there—an old man noticed a young boy—who was so old, so old—standing there looking on and dreaming. "Do you remember what you learned?" asked the old man. "Yes, I do," replied the young boy. "Really," said the old man, "you really remember 'Sh'ma Yisroel'?" "I remember much more," said the boy. " 'Sh'ma Yisroel' is enough," said the old man. And he lifted the boy from the ground and began dancing with him—as though *he* were the Torah. And all joined in, they all sang and danced and cried. They cried but they sang with fervor—never before had Jews celebrated Simhat Torah with such fervor.[1]

What is the power of the tradition and the holiday? Levi Yitzhak, here as on the other holidays of this season, is silent. He too was rejoicing, not writing. Yet a study of the liturgy reveals some of the depth of the spiritual tradition that lies behind Simhat Torah. There are two high points to the liturgy. I learned both from Rabbi Nahman Cohen who was, at the time, the head of a Jewish school in Providence, Rhode Island.

Normally, the circumambulation and the dancing precede the reading of the final section from Deuteronomy and the first section of Genesis. It was Rabbi Cohen's custom to reverse the procedure. The appropriate sections were read first and then the celebration began. The reason is, he explained, that we have been involved in the high holiday season for fifty-seven days. During that time, we have criticized ourselves, repented of our sins, and tried to fulfill God's commandments in love. All this time, we have striven to achieve a wholeness in our relationship to God. This striving reaches its climax in the reading for Simhat Torah for, on that day, we read only Genesis 1:1 to 2:4, that is, we read only the story of the creation before the fall. For those few moments, we attain the garden of Eden. For those few moments, we achieve that prelapsarian purity of relationship to God for which we have been morally and spiritually striving for fifty-seven days.

It was also Rabbi Cohen's custom to read the creation story with the melody of the high holidays. And, before each occurrence of the verse "and there was evening and there was morning . . . ," he would sing a tune, the same tune he had used to introduce the section on God's kingship in the Rosh ha-Shana liturgy. Each "day" of creation thus became a crowning of God and a step toward the Sabbath of creation. Each "day" thus became a step closer to Eden and to the Sabbath which was then, and will be again in the end of time. I have followed Rabbi Cohen's custom for many years in the synagogues I attend and have read the section from Genesis as he would. The reading of each "day" is a recreation and the days accumulate His glory and power until the peace of the great Sabbath overwhelms all.

By putting the dancing after the reading, Rabbi Cohen enabled us to celebrate this moment of Eden. The celebration went on for a long time. And, as it ended, he called us all into one circle. We repeated the final confession of faith of Yom Kippur, and then we burst into the songs of the messiah: "David, king of Israel, lives and abides," "Next year in rebuilt Jerusalem," and so on. God's Torah, our relationship to Him, and His messiah were one.

Which Is the True Spiritual Joy? A Sermon

We begin this week the holiday of Ḥanuka. It is the first real holiday we have had since the end of the high holiday season several months ago. And it is a festival of joy, of triumph over our enemies, and of rededication to God.

There is an interesting difference of opinion in the Talmud (Shabbat 21a) between the followers of Shammai and the followers of Hillel. Bet Shammai says, "On the first day we light eight candles and on the following days we *diminish* the number of candles we light." Bet Hillel teaches, "On the first day we light one candle and on the following days we *increase* the number of candles we light." The custom today is to follow Bet Hillel; we light first one candle, then two, then three, and so on until the last night when we light all eight candles. In the early years of rabbinic Judaism, however, both practices were followed and the Talmud reports the case of two learned men in one city, each of whom followed one of these opinions.

As is the custom of the Talmud, the question is posed, why do the followers of Shammai and Hillel hold their respective opinions? The text answers that Bet Shammai believed one should follow the precedent of the sacrifices in the temple on Sukkot, there being an analogy between Sukkot and Ḥanuka, because Solomon dedicated the first temple on Sukkot while the Maccabees rededicated the second temple on Ḥanuka. On Sukkot, the Torah tells us explicitly, the priests offered thirteen bulls on the first day, twelve on the next, eleven on the next, and so on, until the seventh and last day on which seven bulls were offered. As the number of sacrifices diminished on Sukkot, so the number of candles should diminish on Ḥanuka. This was the reasoning of Bet Shammai.

And what was the reasoning of Bet Hillel? The Talmud answers that the followers of Hillel believed that one must apply the general principle that one always *increases* in holy matters and one never decreases in such matters. There are many examples. Perhaps the clearest example is drawn from the provisions for the high priest on Yom Kippur. If the high priest becomes ritually impure right before Yom Kippur, the elders may appoint an ordinary priest to take his place and perform the Yom Kippur sacrifices. Afterward, when the original high priest is no longer impure, he may of course resume his duties. But what is to become of his Yom Kippur replacement? He cannot continue as a high priest because he is not one. But he cannot return to his status as an ordinary priest because of the principle that one increases in holy matters and never decreases. Using this principle, Bet Hillel reasons, we should increase, and not decrease, the number of Hanuka candles. These are the words of the Talmud and, as I noted, the custom today is to follow the advice and reasoning of Bet Hillel. Levi Yitzhak, too, pondered this difference of opinion.

A person who is in serious trouble has two deep needs, Levi Yitzhak teaches. The first is the need to *figure out* how to alleviate one's trouble, how to resolve one's crisis. The second is the need actually to *do something* about one's trouble. Take the example of the person who is starving. Such a person has a deep need to find a way out of his or her dilemma, to figure out how to help herself or himself out of trouble. But he or she also has the need to take action to relieve the specific need, hunger. Or, take the example of the person in an emotional crisis. Such a person has a need to see a way out of his or her dilemma but she or he also has the need to take concrete steps to solve the specific problem at hand.

Levi Yitzhak illustrates this two-sided need of the person in trouble by reference to a verse from Psalms that is used by the sephardim at the end of their version of the grace after meals, "God fills the need of the yearning soul *and* He fills the hungry soul with goodness" (Psalm 107:8). "The yearning soul," says Levi Yitzhak, is the need a person in trouble has to see a way out, while "the hungry soul" is the need a person has to resolve his or her actual, concrete problem. God, in His great mercy, fulfills both needs of the troubled person.

Having come this far in his remarkable analysis of human nature in

blessing is the one in response to the concrete deed. We are, he seems to be saying, to fill ourselves, each day, with more light until we achieve a fullness of joy in God and Torah. May this holiday of Ḥanuka be one of increasing joy, blessing, and life for us and for all Israel; Amen.

A Kabbalistic Half-Shekel

Six weeks before the holiday of Passover, word was sent out to Jewish communities all over the world that the time had come for each male Jew to pay his half-shekel to the temple treasury. Money changers were set up to change the coin of the realm into the sacred shekels used only in the temple precincts. Anyone who sought to shirk this duty was subject to court action. The purpose of this collection was to generate funds to cover all temple public expenditures. Thus the cost of the two daily communal offerings (the morning and afternoon lambs of the perpetual offering), the communal holiday offerings, the wood for the altar, the scapegoat for Yom Kippur, and so forth, were all paid for out of the half-shekel levy. According to Maimonides, judges who dealt with money crimes were paid from this source too. Finally, the upkeep of the temple precincts, of the walls and towers of Jerusalem, and of the roads leading to the city and the aqueducts were paid for from this tax.

When the temple was destroyed, the obligation to give the half-shekel formally ceased but the custom continued. The section from Exodus (30:11–15) which deals with the giving of the half-shekel is still read in the synagogue six weeks before Passover and the "half-shekel," which is now used for charity, is usually given just before the holiday of Purim. The Sabbath of that reading is known as Shabbat Shekalim and it is the first of five special Sabbaths which precede the holidays of Purim and Passover. The second of these Sabbaths is the one just before Purim. On it, the section dealing with Amalek (Deuteronomy 25:17–19), the archenemy of the Jews, is read. It is called Shabbat Zakhor. The third Sabbath is the one right after Purim. On it, the section dealing with the red heifer (Numbers 19:1–22), from whose ashes the waters of purification which allowed persons who were impure to be cleansed so that they could partake of the sacrifices, is read. It is called Shabbat Para. The fourth Sabbath is the one just before the beginning of the month of Nisan, the month in which Passover occurs. On it, the section consecrating that month as special (Exodus 12:1–20) is read. It is called Shabbat ha-Ḥodesh. The final Sabbath, called Shabbat ha-Gadol (the Great Sabbath), comes just before the Passover holiday.

Shabbat Shekalim, then, is the first of the special Sabbaths. Levi Yitzḥak used the occasion to provide a kabbalistic interpretation of the first four Sabbaths which he, then, tied into the theme of the half-shekel:

First, I will explain to you the secret meaning of the four Sabbaths: Shekalim, Zakhor, Para, and ha-Ḥodesh. They are hinted at in the Tetragrammaton [YHVH] and in four aspects: female, male, mother, and father. Shekalim is the last H [of the Tetragrammaton; it is also female]. Zakhor is the V [of the Tetragrammaton]; it is male. Para is the sefira Bina which is the supernal mother and the first H [of the Tetragrammaton]. And ha-Ḥodesh is the Y [of the Tetragrammaton]. It is the sefira Ḥokhma. From it, the world is generated and therefore Ḥokhma is called "father" for it gives birth to the worlds . . . The four cups [of the Passover Seder] are parallel to the four Sabbaths. . . . Up to these four aspects, we have comprehension for, by them, God may He be exalted directs His world. But above them, there is an aspect called "Arikh Anpin" which is only the point of the letter yod . . . It is absolute zero; no thought can grasp it at all. However, thought floats there, moving up and down without rest . . . when thought reaches above, it is called "healing." . . . What results for us from this is that the thought which floats above is called "half-shekel" and that half-shekel protects the thought below so that abundance and life flow forth from it. This is the secret meaning of "This shall they give, everyone who has passed muster—a half-shekel of the sacred shekels." [Exodus 30:13]

At first reading, this may seem incomprehensible; but the symbolism can easily be deciphered (see figure on page xix): Shekalim is Malkhut, the lowest of the sefirot. In the name symbolism, it is the final H of the Tetragrammaton. In the sexual symbolism, it is female. And in the thought symbolism, it is the lower thought, the means by which God directs creation. Zakhor is Tiferet, the sefira in the middle of the sefirotic realm. In the realm of symbolism, it is V and male; (no thought symbolism here). Para is Bina, the third from the highest sefira. It is the first H and mother; (again, no thought symbolism). And ha-Ḥodesh is Ḥokhma, the second sefira, the one where the preconscious becomes articulate. It is Y, father, and upper thought. Beyond them is Keter, the ineffable aspect of God, about which nothing can be known or said. Thought is present in Ḥokhma and Malkhut; it is also depicted as a restless energy that moves between them, that is, through the whole realm of the sefirot.

Since Ḥokhma is the sefira closest to the ultimate source and since it shares thought-energy with Malkhut, it is the "half-shekel of the sacred shekels." The act of giving the half-shekel, then, is not simply paying a communal tax so that the city of Jerusalem can be repaired after the rainy season before the great Passover pilgrimage. Nor is it the collection of money to properly pay for communal sacrifices. Giving the half-shekel is, Levi Yitzḥak teaches, the beginning of a meditation on the divine energy which will last over several weeks. It has two purposes: first, to ponder the nature of God—to be attentive to the restless thought-energy that permeates God and to explore the many symbolisms by which we grasp the divine even though He is ultimately ungraspable—and, second, to see the thought-unity of that part of the divine which we can grasp and to return that thought-unity meditatively to its ineffable source. Levi Yitzḥak thus sets us spiritually on the path to Passover and the great redemption by asking us to begin the meditation, to give the half-shekel.

The Saintly Leader, Joy, and Meaning

The story of Purim as related in the Book of Esther is at once both an exciting story of court intrigue and an indication of just how irrational reality can be. On one level, everything happens as expected and the "good guys" win but, on another level, every key act is suspended over a void of what appears to be chance and whim.

Toward the end of the story, after Mordecai has become a powerful officer of the court and has sent out instructions allowing the Jews to defend themselves, there is the following report: "The city of Shushan was cheerful and joyous; the Jews had light and joy, gladness and felicity" (Esther 8:15–16). Levi Yitzhak calls attention to these verses, pointing out that both contain the word "joy" which is paired with "cheerfulness" in the first and "light" in the second. What caused the common "joy" and how was the "joy-cheerfulness" different from the "joy-light?"

"The rule is," teaches Levi Yitzhak,

that, when a saint worships God, even the simple people have joy because the pious, by performing their mitsvot, bring blessing and joy to all the worlds. Thus, it happened that the people of the city of Shushan who were not Jews also had joy even though they did not know its cause, for Mordecai's steward-ship brought blessing and joy on all the people. Therefore it says, "the city of Shushan"—that is, its people, the non-Jews—"was cheerful and joyous." But the Jews had good reason to be joyous because they had been saved from Haman. And the rule is that, when a person knows the reason why he or she is happy, then he or she experiences a joyous light, for reason enlightens them as to the purpose of things. Therefore it says, "the Jews had light and joy."

What a wonderful double insight. First, we learn that the sheer presence and stewardship of a saintly person brings blessing to all. The mere fact that our leaders are pious, saintly people assures blessing to us all. Their piety colors their this-worldly governance, and blessing flows from them. Levi Yitzhak does not mean that political leaders should be unworldly. After all, it is Mordecai who recognizes that the execution of Haman is not sufficient and that the Jews need to arm themselves and prepare to resist their enemies, and he spends ten months preparing them for the battle. Political leaders must be firmly rooted in social reality. But they must also be firmly rooted in spiritual reality. They must also be pious, saintly. And if they are both, blessing flows from their efforts to all and, with that blessing, joy.

Second, we learn that knowing why is a positive goal to be striven for. It is always better to know why we are happy (or unhappy). Reason brings us genuine enlightenment—not because we are rationalists and not because knowing why adds to our store of effectual knowledge, but because knowing why sets a framework of meaning for us. To be part of a meaningful framework is to experience enlightenment and the joy that comes with that enlightenment. It is not enough to know that one has been victorious; one must also know how that victory fits into the larger picture of meaning. True being is being a part of meaning, and it is the latter that brings true enlightenment and joy.

The Futility of
Knowledge of God

In order to offer the Passover sacrifice, the worshiper had to be in a
state of ritual purity. So the Bible commands that, several weeks before
Passover, a red heifer be sacrificed. Its ashes, when mixed with water,
became the formal means of ritual purification. In memory of this
procedure, the section dealing with the red heifer is still read in the
synagogue several weeks before Passover. The law of the red heifer
(Numbers 19), however, contains a strange provision which is repeated
in the Talmud (Nidda 9a): the priest who sprinkles the ashes-water and
the person upon whom the ashes-water are sprinkled become (or remain) ritually pure, but the priests involved in preparing the ashes and
anyone else who touches the ashes become ritually impure. This seeming irrationality—that the officiant and the recipient are pure, while
he who touches or prepares is impure—has puzzled Jews and non-Jews
alike for centuries. Levi Yitzhak evolved a spiritual interpretation of
this conundrum.

It is the foundation of foundations and the pillar of those who serve God to
enlighten and arouse the hearts of human beings to seek God with all one's
heart and soul. This is done in two ways: First, by contemplating the revelation
of His divinity, may He be blessed, in all the details of the existence of the
created and formed beings, for everything that happens in the world is from
Him . . . In this respect, one addresses Him in the "present" mode and calls
Him "You," as if one had achieved some knowledge of Him from studying
the details of reality. However, when a person contemplates how extraordi-
nary and wondrous all this is, then one realizes that it is not within the power
of the human being to achieve any knowledge of Him. This is the second way
and, in this respect, one addresses Him in the "hidden" mode and calls Him
"He." This is the usual custom of people, to speak in the "present" mode using
"you" to indicate that one has comprehended the other and to speak in the

"hidden" mode using "she" or "he" to indicate that the other is beyond one's understanding . . .

It follows from the above that the essence of our worship of God is worship of the Infinite, which we do not comprehend, combined with a knowledge that there exists such a Being Who brings all things into being and sustains them because of His goodness . . . The secret meaning of the law of the red heifer according to which the officiant and the recipient are pure while he who touches it is impure is, then, as follows: The officiant is pure because he is the conduit for the divine energy from the Infinite to this world; the recipient is pure because his service is according to the hidden; the one who touches, however, is impure because he is trying to reach up and touch the divine energy; that is, the officiant and the recipient worship without having comprehended God or His ways but the one who touches worships by his claim to have "touched," to have knowledge of, God and His ways . . .

Levi Yitzhak's basic insight is twofold. It is also very clear and profound: First, we do have knowledge of God. In this sense, He is "You," a knowable entity. However, in spite of all our striving for knowledge of God—whether it is based in rational contemplation or rooted in emotional or conscious experience—there simply is a dimension of God that is unknown and unknowable. In this sense, God is "He." Because of this "hidden" dimension, all our knowledge, all our experience, all our spiritual awareness is, ultimately, futile.

Second, Levi Yitzhak teaches, there is something sinful in claiming that one has achieved knowledge of God. To "touch" God is wrong. To move the divine energy without comprehending God is sin. Levi Yitzhak puts it very delicately: "This is what is meant by the teaching that the red heifer atones for the sin of the golden calf. The essence of the latter was that the people wanted to see their God. Their error was in claiming that they had achieved knowledge of Him . . . For this reason, the Holy One, blessed be He, had to command them to take the red heifer." To build the golden calf, to touch the red heifer, is to claim more than we can properly know. It is sin; it renders one impure. To be the officiant or recipient, the conduit or the vessel, is to act in the presence of God's hiddenness. It is good; it purifies us of sin.

There is something depressing about this insight. We are commanded to worship God with our minds, in knowledge and in consciousness. We are commanded to contemplate His world and to meditate upon His ways as evidence of Him. Yet, at the same time, we are taught that such effort is useless; even worse, that it is sinful to claim success for our struggle. What is the purpose of the discipline of thought, consciousness, and act if, in the end, one can claim nothing from it?

Everything in life follows the pattern of the officiant-recipient and the one who touches. We reach out and try to achieve in all areas—professionally, in our families, in our intimate lives—and we usually like to claim at least partial success in these efforts. But it is not so. Most of what happens to us is beyond our control. Life plays tricks on us; it shifts. Our own psyches set up barriers that impede our achieving what we aim for. We huff and puff, and sometimes we do blow the house down; but, in the end, we do not. In the end, life acts upon us and we muddle through as best we can. For moderns, who are success-oriented, this is very frustrating. For those who believe that we are the masters of our fate, this is very difficult to support. But it is true nonetheless.

As it is with our secular life, so is it with our spiritual life. We try to "touch" God—ritually, socially, intellectually, spiritually—but, in the end, we are only officiants and recipients, conduits and vessels. Life is given to us; God is hidden from us. The answer, Levi Yitzhak teaches, is that knowledge must lead to unknowledge, that doing must lead to receiving.

Two Types of Faith

At the beginning of the liturgy of the Passover Seder, the leader points to the *mazzah,* the flat, tasteless bread which is eaten during the whole Passover holiday, and says, "This is the bread of affliction which our ancestors ate in land of Egypt." Some manuscripts, however, prescribe that the following be said: "This [the mazzah] is *like* the bread of affliction . . ." The variation in wording prompted Levi Yitzḥak to pose the question, what is *like* the mazzah? What, in our existence, is like the bread of affliction? What renders our lives slavelike?

"This can be explained," Levi Yitzḥak teaches,

by recalling the words of the sages (Talmud, Bava Batra 10a): "When the Jews do the will of their Father in heaven, they are called 'children'; and when they do not do His will, they are called 'slaves.' " On the surface, this saying seems strange for, when they do not, God forbid, do the will of God, they should be called, God forbid, "wicked." The true meaning, however, is that, when a person believes in whole faith that the Holy One, blessed be He, is our Father and that He has pleasure when He causes His blessing to flow upon His people Israel, then such a person is whole, lacking nothing. She or he is "doing the will of the Father in heaven" and is called "child." . . . But when a person does not believe in these matters, he or she is incomplete and is preventing the flow of blessing upon Israel and indeed upon the whole world. Such a person is "not doing the will of the Father in heaven" and is called "slave." For this reason, we say "This is *like* the bread of affliction which our ancestors ate in the land of Egypt," for they were in a state of imperfect faith there.

Levi Yitzḥak's point is simple. No Jew would consciously not do the will of the Father in heaven. Hence no Jew could be truly "wicked." However, it does happen that we waver in the completeness of our faith. We doubt God. And when that happens, we are ourselves incomplete and we render God incomplete. Then we are like "slaves," following God and tradition blindly, giving no *kavvana* to our observance, no attentiveness to our mode of being. We are servants without raison d'être. The mazzah, then, is *like* the bread of affliction, representing the flat tasteless religiosity that orthopraxis without faith brings, the dullness of a life unenlightened by faith.

But what is faith? And what is whole faith? To answer this question, Levi Yitzhak has recourse to another section of the Haggadah.

The Haggadah presents four sons, each of whom poses a question to the leader. The wise son's question is, "What are the testimonies, statutes, and laws . . ." The answer given to him is, "One does not eat anything after the last bit of mazzah." The meaning of this question and answer in the context of the Passover liturgy need not distract us. Levi Yitzhak's interpretation of it is fascinating:

All the mitsvot of this night are a remembrance of the miracles that God wrought for us. This is for the person whose intellect is in a reduced state (Hebrew, *qatnut*) and who grasps the Creator through miracles. But, when a person is in a state of expanded intellect (Hebrew, *gadlut*) and grasps the Creator, may He be blessed, by virtue of his intellect, then he is called "a wise man." Such a person asks, "What are the testimonies . . . ?" To this the leader replies, "One can fall easily into a lower state of intellectuality. Therefore, one must believe in the miracles and wonders which the Holy One, blessed be He, did for us. This taste will remain always. Hence, "One does not eat anything after the last bit of mazzah."

What is Levi Yitzhak saying in this terse exegesis of the Haggadah? There are two kinds of faith, Levi Yitzhak teaches. The one flows from a systematic intellectual meditation on God and His creation. We ponder His works. We contemplate His mysterious ways in history. We reflect on His presence in our lives. We even meditate on the very fact that we can ponder Him at all. And we come to the conclusion that He is and that He is active in His creation and in our lives as a people and as individuals. This is the intellectual grasping of God. It is a faith rooted in the expansion and exercise of the mind. It is the higher form of faith and one is called "a wise person" because of it. And then there is the faith that flows from being overwhelmed by God's miracles. We simply stand in awe of what He has done. We do not understand it; we cannot. We accept it, in wonder and in awe. We simply confront the facticity of His acts and admit them into ourselves as such. This is the experiential grasping of God. It is a faith rooted in the awareness of the holy. It is the more basic type of faith. It leaves a "taste" in the soul.

A wise son, Levi Yitzḥak teaches, may ask, Why, if one has reached the higher realm of intellectual faith, must one rehearse the story of the miracles? To this one must reply that, since one can fall from intellectual faith, one must retell the story and strive to achieve experiential faith, for the latter leaves a "taste," an experience that sustains one in moments of intellectual doubt.

Moderns have trouble with both kinds of faith. We do not tend to think about God. We do not see Him as an active force in our world. We actually suppress the God-hypothesis in order to use scientific analysis in the whole range of human intellectual endeavor, from the psychoanalytic to the astrophysical. Most of us do not hold ourselves open to the experiential kind of faith either. Our sense for the holy is atrophied by our intellectual training and by our secularism.

Even those of us who do hold ourselves open to the facticity of God's miracles have trouble finding a place for this faith in our total view of ourselves. We feel a little schizoid because we know we are admitting an awareness that doesn't quite fit with our general intellectual worldview or with our view of ourselves in the world. And so we compartmentalize: God and His presence in one area, and we and our world in the other.

This state of affairs is mazzah. It is *like* the bread of affliction that our forefathers ate. It is the staple of slavery; not wickedness, but slavery. It is not freedom. Faith—intellectual held in dialectic tension with experiential, sophisticated supplemented by direct—is freedom. Fullness of faith is redemption, for us and for God. Passover is the holiday of striving for direct faith, for receiving God's miracles into our being, for becoming "children" of God.

A Song About Singing

The Jewish liturgical calendar calls for the reading of the Song of Songs on the Sabbath which falls during the week of Passover. This celebration of love and spring fits appropriately with the time of year. As a song, it parallels the song which Moses and the Jews sang after the crossing of the Red Sea. And, as an extended metaphor of God's love for Israel, it embodies in poetry the miracle of His love in redeeming us from Egypt. But what is a "song of songs?" Is it the best of all songs? Or, a song about songs? Or, a song about singing? What "songs" are intended? Surely not songs of physical love.

Levi Yitzḥak bases his homily on the words of a great medieval commentator to the prayerbook:

We will explain, with the help of Heaven, the meaning of "Song of Songs" on the basis of the comment of the Al-Sheikh, may his memory be a blessing, to the words of the prayerbook, "God, great King, Who is lauded by praises." [To this, he commented], "We ought to laud God for the very fact that we have merited to praise His great Name. This is the meaning of 'Who is lauded by praises'—that we laud Him, may He be blessed, for being worthy to praise Him." This [Levi Yitzḥak continues] is also the meaning of the phrase, "Song of Songs,"—we sing to Him that we have merited to sing to Him songs of love . . . It is a "song about songs."

This is a very beautiful thought, mentioned repeatedly by our teacher, Abraham Joshua Heschel: the very fact that we *can* sing songs to God is itself a song; the very fact that we can praise God is itself a source of praise. We wonder at the capacity we have to wonder. We are amazed that we can be amazed.

For moderns this thought is particularly poignant. We live in a society that forces us into a state of isolation; sociologists and existentialists call it "alienation." Our lives are largely removed from nature by clothing, heating and air-conditioning, year-round availability of even luxury foods, and so on. The press of career and of just keeping up with the details of living make us remote from a sense of rootedness in life. It seems as if life is a fast stream rushing past us and we must simply try to stay afloat. None of us ponders life. None of us leans on our pitchfork watching the birds or contemplating the growing crops. Almost none of us just sits and looks at a child, wondering without talking, being amazed at the other's being. There are too many things to do. Even prayer fits into our schedule of things to do. Modern people have lost, in large measure, the capacity for wonder, and hence the ability to praise. One way to recover the ability to sing praises is to remember that one has such a capacity; just to say, "I have the capacity to wonder, I have the power to praise."

But where does this power to praise come from? Why do we have it? What good is it? The capacity to be amazed and the power to sing come from God, Levi Yitzhak teaches. He gave us this ability. He didn't have to; after all, He has myriads of angels who do nothing else but sing His praises and they do not even sleep. Yet He desired to create human beings and He wants to have their praise. So He implanted within us this strange capacity—to wonder and to sing. That fact itself is a wonder. God could have left us isolated (as the deists claimed several centuries ago) or He could have left us to ourselves (as Bertrand Russell and the secularists of our time claim). Yet He did not. We do have these capacities; we can be amazed and we can sing. We are not alone no matter how terrifying existence in a nuclear world may seem. We are not deserted no matter how cramped and pressured our lives make us feel. We are not abandoned no matter how schizoid the conflicts within ourselves. The power to praise is itself a wonder. The power to sing is itself a matter for amazement. Hence the ultimate praise is praise about praise, a hymn about lauding. And the ultimate song is a song about songs, a song about singing.

The Non-Jew and the Law

The holiday of Shavu'ot celebrates the bringing of the first fruits to the temple. It also commemorates the revelation of the Torah to the Jewish people. It is "the time of the giving of our Torah." The rabbis put much thought into this moment. One source, *Pirkei de Rabbi Eliezer* (chapter 41), relates that, when God wanted to give the Torah to humankind, He took it to the various nations of the world. The people of Esau studied it and saw that it contained a law against murder, and they rejected it because of this. The people of Ishmael studied it and saw that it contained a law against adultery, and they rejected it because of that. The children of Israel, however, accepted the Torah, saying "We will do and we will obey" (Exodus 24:7). Levi Yitzḥak, in pondering this text, notes the following:

The people of Esau did not want to accept the commandment "You shall not murder" but they did want to accept the rest of the Torah in order to be servants of God. Esau, thus, had a little bit of yearning to be a servant of God. The people of Ishmael, too, did not want to accept the commandment "You shall not commit adultery" but they did want to accept the rest of the Torah in order to be servants of God. Now it is known that everything that happened at the time of the giving of the Torah left a trace which remains to this day. There is, therefore, a trace among the nations of the world of the little bit of yearning they had to receive the Torah. The action that results from this is that, when a Jew speaks to a non-Jew, she or he draws [Hebrew, *mamshikh*] this trace of the little bit of yearning from the non-Jew and takes [Hebrew, *notel*] it to himself or herself. For this reason, Rabbi Isaac Luria, may his memory be a blessing said, "The Jews were exiled among the nations for the purpose of redeeming the holy sparks that have been lost there," that is, that every Jew, when he or she speaks with a non-Jew, should draw the holiness from the non-Jew. Even though the Jew is holy without that, it is good that one do so. This is like a rich person who has hundreds of thousands of gold coins; when one acquires another, that too is good.

It is also the case that, at the time when Israel accepted the Torah, the yearning of the whole world, even the little bit of yearning felt by each of the nations of the world to accept the Torah, descended upon Israel. The Jews had, then, their own desire plus that of the nations of the world ... Similarly, the sages, may their memory be a blessing, indicated [Talmud, Shabbat 89a] that the angels wanted to accept the Torah but the Holy One, blessed be He, replied to them, "Do you have a father or mother ... ?" For God, may He be blessed, purposely aroused the desire of the angels to accept the Torah so that their desire would later descend on Israel. Hence, the sages, may their memory be a blessing, said that, when the Holy One, blessed be He, said "I am," the very throne of glory trembled, for all the awe and love which was in the upper and lower worlds descended on Israel when they accepted the Torah.

Levi Yitzhak has three profound teachings here: First, that the nations of the world had, and still have, a partial desire to live the life of Torah, a limited yearning to accept the divine command. Second, that the failure of the nations of the world to accept the Torah increased the responsibility of the Jews because they had to bear the yearning, love, and awe of all reality. And third, that the Jew has as his or her purpose to talk to the non-Jew, to surface that divine spark, and to redeem it by taking it to himself or herself. This is Levi Yitzhak's teaching (see "non-Jew" in the Thematic Index) and, while some Jews and Christians will take offense at his attitude toward the non-Jew, Levi Yitzhak does firmly assert that sensitivity to the divine, particularly to the divine law, is a universal human capacity, that the desire to accept and to live by Torah is definitive of humanity.

As a modern person, I am prepared to agree to most of Levi Yitzhak's points: I agree that non-Jews have a yearning for the holy. I think they also have a certain yearning for Torah; that is, for the law, for the legal and binding aspect of God's covenant, for the divine command. Law has its disadvantages as a religious category but it also has some advantages. It is firm. It is absolute. Embodied in a scholarly tradition, it cannot be twisted too easily to fit the vagaries of society and human whim. Non-Jews have a residual need for the divine law and that need, in turn, defines one of the basic qualities of universal human existence.

I agree too that Jews have a special responsibility to the divine, especially to the Torah, exactly because the non-Jewish world rejects it. The Torah is God's law, not ours, or theirs. The firmness of our commitment to the Torah is a measure of our commitment to God. We are a people alone, separated exactly by our attachment to the law. The further the world gets from the law, the more we must cling to it.

Finally, I agree that the Jew has a special task to surface the residual Torah-consciousness of the non-Jew. We must speak of Torah and help non-Jews to understand themselves in that category. We must teach the spirituality that is peculiarly ours, for through it non-Jews gain perspective on themselves and on us as within the full range of God's creative action and revealed will. And yes, there is a messianic undertone to this task. I disagree with Levi Yitzhak's Lurianism, that we must redeem or take away that spark from the non-Jew in order to save it. It is better for the non-Jew to keep his or her spark and to use it in a way consistent with the presence and law of God. The giving of the Torah evoked yearning by all and the continued presence of Torah in human history must do so too.

Reacting Properly to Tragedy

Tish'a b'Av is the day of mourning which commemorates the destruction of the first and second temples. It has been extended to encompass later tragedies too, including the holocaust of our own time. On Tish'a b'Av we fast, we read Lamentations, and we mourn the martyrs of our people and the brokenness of our national and religious existence. Tish'a b'Av raises forcefully the question: What does one do in the face of national tragedy?

Not since the days of the destruction of the second temple has this question so oppressed a generation as it does ours. To read Lamentations is to conjure up the pictures of the destruction of our people in Europe. To read the dirges and the elegies written in the Middle Ages is to hear the story of our people in our own time. Was the holocaust "worse," or was it part of the genre of Tish'a b'Av? Many ask this question but I think that it is useless, even disrespectful. The humiliation and murder of our people is one. We cannot hear of one moment without listening to all the others. What, then, does one do? What, then, does one affirm and believe? Levi Yitzḥak offers four counsels on how to respond to national tragedy.

First, Levi Yitzḥak teaches:

When a person really cries, then his or her tears leave an impression; God forbid [that one should need to cry so]. In truth, it is so with the destruction of the temples. When a person cries over this, then she or he makes an impression with his or her tears, as it says, "She surely cries at night and her tears are on her cheek." [Lamentations 1:2]

In normal human relations, Levi Yitzḥak teaches, when one cries it makes an impression. To express grief and to know that someone has listened attentively is part of the substance of human living. To cry and to be heard is of the essence of our existence. Interpreting the pronouns in the verse from Lamentations with great subtlety (they all refer to Jerusalem in the original context), Levi Yitzhak understands the subject to be the Jewish people and the person on whose cheeks the tears make an impression to be the Shekhina, God. Deeply felt tears, Levi Yitzhak then teaches, leave a mark on the cheek of God, they leave an impression on Him. Our pain touches God. He hears us, is hurt, and is present to us. Crying is a proper way of responding to national (and personal) tragedy.

Second, Levi Yitzhak teaches:

The fact that God, may He be blessed, destroyed our glorious sanctuary and that we, Israel, are in the exile, all is undoubtedly for the good of Israel. For surely He will have even greater mercy on us and will rebuild our sanctuary with greater strength and more power . . . This is as it says, "He is as a bear waiting for me, but He is also a lion [of mercy] in hiding" [Lamentations 3:10] . . . There are parts of the earth that are meant to be settled and there are parts that are meant to be desolate. As to the land of Israel, when Israel dwells securely there, it is settled but, when Israel is in exile even if other nations dwell there, the land is desolate. For the land of Israel is ours and it accepts no settlement other than ours, as it says, "You, Lord, have settled there forever." [Lamentations 5:18]

No matter how severe national tragedy may be, it is not grounds for despair. On the contrary, Levi Yitzhak teaches, the terrors of the exile and the destruction of the land are signs and witnesses to the greater promise of national restoration and return. The vicious attack of the bear is a portent of the protective action of the lion. Renewed faith in God's ultimate promises is a proper way of responding to national tragedy.

Third, Levi Yitzhak teaches:

By the greatness of our sins, the bellies of the haters of our people roar against us. But, from the very fact that we "remember our misfortune and oppression and that our souls are trampled down" [Lamentations 3:19–20], it is clear that "the eternal in us is not lost" [Lamentations 3:21]. It is decreed for the dead that they be forgotten because that which is eternal in them has risen on high without hope of an immediate return here. It is not so with the living who are not forgotten . . .

For the time being, Levi Yitzhak teaches, the dead are beyond the salvation of this world, but the living are part of the immediate ongoing process of redemption. Hence the living must remember. They must call to mind the suffering and the humiliation. They must remember the faces and recount the stories of the dead and of the survivors. For from memory comes yearning; from recalling comes longing for redemption. Pain remembered evokes the pain of hope. Humiliation recalled evokes the agony of expectation. Remembering, recalling, is a proper way of responding to national tragedy.

Finally, Levi Yitzhak teaches:

Zion is called an orphan and the kingdom of the house of David is called a widow. He who is merciful to the orphan and the widow will merit seeing the comfort of Zion and the reestablishment of the kingdom of the house of David.

Caring for others, renewed human bonding—these are the proper responses in action required by national tragedy.

In recent years, I have taken to dedicating the day of Tish'a b'Av to reading holocaust survivor literature. Each year, I think I have read the worst in horror and the best in courage. Yet each year brings more of both. Perhaps, because of the inhumanity of it all; perhaps because of the terrifying doubt about God's goodness that the holocaust raises, I find these lessons of Levi Yitzhak—tears, faith, remembering, and caring for the oppressed—more poignant than ever.

Afterthoughts

All reflection on Jewish spirituality must begin with God's presence. To be spiritual is to be sensitive to that presence. To use words like "holy," "sacred," "sanctified," and so forth is to be pointed toward an awareness of God's presence. But we sense God in different ways: in prayer, in moments of personal anguish or joy, in historical events, in the call to justice, and in messianic faithfulness. Furthermore, our relationship with God is not uniform: He comforts, He demands, He loves, He is angry, He is simply present, and sometimes He is hidden, veiled, distant. Nor is it one-sided: we, too, are present to Him, but in various modes and intensities; yet always it is God's presence that haunts us and that we seek. As Abraham Joshua Heschel noted, God is in search of us as we are in search of Him.[1]

All of Jewish spirituality takes place within Jewish tradition. The tradition—its stories, its laws, its practice—forms the intellectual structure within which we experience God's presence. It instructs us how to attain awareness of God's presence. It gives us a language with which to approach and relate to Him. It teaches us what to expect. Furthermore, the tradition limits our experience by excluding certain thoughts and patterns of awareness. One cannot be Jewishly spiritual in a context which is idolatrous, polytheistic, or antinomian (anti-Torah).

While tradition molds our experience, our experience of God's presence also affects the tradition. Our awareness of God confirms, or verifies, the teachings of the tradition. It reinforces and lends experiential meaning to the images, the metaphors, and the spiritual insights. Our experience of God's presence also enables us to sharpen, to critique, indeed to purify the teachings of the tradition. After being in relationship with God, a particular teaching may seem lackluster while another may seem in error. We measure the tradition by our experience, even as the tradition measures our experience by its teachings. Life and tradition are intertextual.

Jewish spirituality is not a straight road. Nor is it a spiral, moving ever upward. It is, rather, a meandering path filled with obstacles and blind alleys which only slowly moves toward its end. To walk this path is to stumble. To be spiritual, in Jewish tradition, is to grope in the darkness between the flashes of light.

Yet Jewish spirituality is not just stumbling and groping. It is determined marching. When one way fails to bring us close to God, we try another. When the obstacles on one path overwhelm us, we try another. I have called this impulse of seeking first one way and then another the *seriatim* dimension of Jewish spirituality. It is a moving in series, as a sailboat tacks in the wind in order to move forward. In a practical sense, this means that when we cannot experience God's presence by meditating on His goodness, we observe His commandments. When we cannot experience God's closeness through prayer, we try study. When we cannot experience His grace, we activate ourselves in the community of His chosen people. When we get too involved with the community, we withdraw to contemplate His being. When liturgy fails, we try personal prayer. When personal prayer fails, we try liturgy. And so on. One is supposed to alternate the patterns of one's life so that, and because, all patterns lead to God's presence.

Interpretation is of the essence for, through it, the tradition continues to live and, through it, the tradition continues to shape our expectations of the divine. Because our awareness of God is so varied, our interpretation is multiform. Because our experience of God is seriatim, our interpretation is multilayered, flexible, even at times contradictory. At one moment, we read the tradition in the light of our experience of God as remote; at another, in the illumination of His closeness. At one moment, we read the tradition depressed at our failure to live in consonance with His will. At another, we read it joyous at being the objects of His concern. The text is alternately concrete in the humanness of His insight and incomprehensible in the mystery of His will. Always, though, the interpretation is bounded, for Him and for us, by the holy and the moral. Neither He nor we can be permitted to do that which is unholy or immoral. We both are bound by Torah.[2]

Jewish spirituality is also a matter of law, not a matter of personal preference or inclination. All deeds are commandments and one must do all commandments with *kavvana*. But *kavvana,* as we have seen, has many levels. How does one put this into law? The classic of Jewish law, the *Shulkhan Arukh,* citing earlier sources, subtly formulates the laws of *kavvana* as they apply to liturgical prayer as follows. Note the proposing of thought motifs, the recommendations for the external setting, and the shading of emphasis from concentrating upon the words and their meanings to the more intense stripping away of materiality followed by intellectual meditation (Orah Hayyim, section 98, "Laws of Prayer: That one must have *kavvana* in one's prayer"):

1. One who prays must direct his or her heart to the meaning of the words which one brings out of one's mouth. One should think that it is as if the divine Presence is opposite one. One should remove all distracting thoughts until one's thought and *kavvana* are pure when one prays. One should think that, if one were talking to a king of flesh and blood, one would order one's words and have them properly in mind so that one not stumble. How much more so would one do this before the King of the king of kings, the Holy One, blessed be He, Who probes every thought.

   Thus would the saints and people of deeds do: They would set themselves apart and have *kavvana* in their praying until they would reach the stage of stripping away all materiality and of strengthening the intellectual faculty such that they attained almost to the rank of the prophets.

   If another thought comes to one in prayer, one should be quiet until that thought has been annihilated.

   One must think of things which bring humility to the heart and which direct one to one's Father in heaven; one should not think of things which bring one to lightheadedness.

2. One should not pray in a place where there is something that destroys one's *kavvana*. Nor should one pray at a time which destroys one's *kavvana*. Now, however, we are not so careful in this matter because we do not pray with so much *kavvana*.

3. One should pray in a pleading manner as a poor person who begs at the door.

One should pray in calmness so that prayer not seem like a burden which one seeks to put down.

4. Prayer takes the place of the sacrifices. Therefore, one must take care that the model of the sacrificial service in *kavvana* be observed such that no other thought mix in with the act, for a stray thought rendered a sacrifice invalid. Prayer must be said standing like the sacrifices. It must also be done regularly, as they were. . . . It is appropriate that one have special pleasing clothes for prayer as the clothes of the priest were special, though not every person can spend money lavishly on this. In any case, it is best that one have special pants for prayer because of the matter of cleanliness.

5. One should not think that one is so worthy that "the Holy One, blessed be He, will fulfill my request for I have had *kavvana* in my prayers." It is the opposite of this. Such a thought calls one's sins to mind. Rather, one should think that God will act in His graciousness and one should say to oneself, "Who am I, poor and despised, to come and to petition the King of the king of kings, the Holy One, blessed be He, were it not for His great kindnesses with which He directs His creatures."

Tradition, experience, interpretation, and law are the warp and woof of all Jewish spirituality. They are the elements of its multi-intertextuality. Jewish "mysticism," however, is a subset of Jewish spirituality. It is a special set of experiences within a broader range of the awareness of God's presence. Jewish spirituality becomes properly "mystical," in my opinion, when it conforms to the following characteristics: First, the intellectual framework in which we reach out for God is hierarchical. There is a distance between us and God which is bridged by a clearly defined set of beings (angels, spheres, hypostases, sefirot, and so forth). Second, attaining an awareness of God is a function of climbing up the hierarchy of being. Experience of God is achieved by a clearly defined technique for scaling the distance between us and Him along the hierarchy. Third, after scaling the hierarchy (after passing through the palaces of Merkaba mysticism, after attaining contact with the Agent Intelligence in philosophic mysticism, after returning the divine energy to the sefirot in zoharic-Lurianic mysticism, or after achieving annihilation of the self in hasidic mysticism), the various types[3] of mystical experience of God's presence are very abstract. They are presence without attribute, being without predicate, non-self, no-thing, negation of negation. Fourth, these experiences are totally beyond the control of the mystic. He or she can neither force them to come nor adequately shape them or determine what will become of them. Mystical experiences themselves are thus passive, though the way to them is very active.

In all these four ways, Jewish mysticism differs from the mainstream of Jewish spirituality which is based upon the experience of the personal presence of God. God's presence, in Jewish spirituality, is most often experienced as distinctly anthropopathic. "It" is a He—alternately loving, demanding, gracious, angry, comforting. God's presence is personal, bound by His covenant with us, creative, active, interfering in our lives, responding to our needs and even to our requests. We portray Him in images and metaphors; He gives us concrete laws. Our relationship is interpersonal. Jewish spirituality is broader; Jewish mysticism a subset of it.[4]

Jewish spirituality exists in the interstices between obedient servanthood, personal commandedness, and God's law. Each creates its own tension and each creates its own temptation.

The first tension is that of obedient servanthood, for being Jewishly spiritual means many things. It is not just a feeling or an awareness. It is not just a following of one's spiritual instincts. It is a sense of being drawn, of being compelled. Being Jewishly spiritual is also the anger at not being free to desist, of not being at liberty to live out one's fantasies. To be a servant, "slave" is the Hebrew word, is just that—to be bonded, bound, with all the anger that that brings, especially in the modern world. Being Jewishly spiritual is also to be different, to stand outside the security of a community which does not question its own righteousness. It is rather to question, to wonder; indeed to ask different questions. Others will observe the political and social implications of an act; to be a servant in God's presence is to ask about the spiritual implications. It is to question and hence to be friendless; lonely, yet in the haunting presence of God. Finally, being Jewishly spiritual is to be frustrated. When God sends the tempter to distract with other tasks, with doubts, and with social, administrative, and intellectual problems, it is to be angry and frustrated that the center has moved out of focus, that the core insight has faded, that He is veiled, that He is hiding His face. A person who loses sight of his or her direction is an angry animal, lost in temptation and irrational in frustration. One who does not know this is not spiritual. Yet, despite anger, loneliness, and frustration, one *is* bound; one can only be an obedient servant. Jonah must return to prophesy, Abraham must wander, Ḥanania must continue mending the broken vessels. The first temptation, then, is flight from obedient servanthood. Anger at not being free, social isolation, and frustration at not being able to achieve full spirituality tempt us to flee God.

The second tension is the subjectivity of personal commandedness. There is only one judge of whether God is present to us, ourselves. Only we, each one of us, know if we are commanded, haunted by His presence. Others can see it in us, and we in them, because we see it in ourselves. Were there no voice, there would be no echo. Or perhaps, were there no echo, there would be no voice. Yet, how do we know? How can we be sure? And, as we carry the Presence with us into the world, how do we know that we do Him honor, as the liturgy for the Grace After Meals puts it: "May the all-merciful One be praised from generation to generation, be glorified in us forever and forever, and be proud of us always and in all worlds"? How do we differentiate our awareness of His presence from our fantasy?

The question has no simple answer, only traces of guidelines: The experience of the Presence must be felt. It must also show a direction. It must conform to the spiritual and moral norms of the tradition. And it must return, again and again, in spite of our sinfulness. If the experience lacks one of these four qualities, it is false: If our awareness of God leads us into sin, it is spurious. If it leads us away from the community and its Torah, it is faithless. If it leads us to solipsism, it is untrue. We cannot avoid saying, "I feel God's presence; He demands this of me." But these very words are also a temptation and we must be very wary of the crookedness of our hearts and the deceivingness of our tongues.

The third tension is the law. The King has His law and this law circumscribes our existence with the divine; it embodies the divine in our world. It forces us to confront the concreteness of the divine will in the everyday. It gives form and shape to His presence. Soloveitchik has put it most clearly:

When halakhic man approaches reality, he comes with his Torah, given to him from Sinai, in hand. He orients himself to the world by means of fixed statutes and firm principles. An entire corpus of precepts and laws guides him along the path leading to existence. Halakhic man, well furnished with rules, judgements, and fundamental principles, draws near the world with an a priori relation. . . . When halakhic man comes across a spring bubbling quietly, he already possesses a fixed, a priori relationship with this real phenomenon: the complex laws regarding the halakhic construct of a spring. The spring is fit for the immersion of a "zav" [a man with discharge]; it may serve as "mei ḥatat" [waters of expiation]; it purifies with flowing water; it does not require a fixed quantity of forty se'ahs; etc. . . . When halakhic man approaches a real spring, he gazes at it and carefully examines its nature. He possesses, a priori, ideal principles and precepts which establish the character of the spring as a halakhic construct, and he uses the statutes for the purpose of determining normative law: does the real spring correspond to the requirements of the ideal Halakha or not? . . . When halakhic man looks to the western horizon and sees the fading rays of the setting sun, . . . When halakhic man chances upon mighty mountains, . . . of all the animal functions of man—eating, sex, and all the bodily necessities . . . Halakha has a fixed a priori relationship to the whole of reality in all of its fine and detailed particulars . . ."[5]

This is spirituality embodied and its very embodiedness is its temptation, its idolatry. The law with its sureness, with its very decisiveness, with its ability to encompass the holy, seduces even as it gives form, depth, and concreteness. The temptation is to submit totally to the authority of the law; to become God's judges and policemen, not his prophets and saints.

The way of Jewish spirituality is a narrow bridge over the abyss of obedient servanthood, personal commandedness, and God's law. As I respond to Levi Yitzḥak, I see, preach, and try to live this precarious balance of the spiritual, the personal, and the ritual; of the holy, the human, and the learned; of the sacred, the individual, and the social.

God's presence, however, is no oracle. I do not have direct or simple solutions to the problems of nuclear disarmament, structural poverty, terrorism, Jewish and Palestinian nationalism, Jewish sectarianism, and the host of other problems that plague human existence. I only know that there is a direction, a responsibility that goes beyond the social and the political, and that our solutions to these problems must be consistent with God's presence or they will not be true, no matter who agrees with us or how many texts and arguments are advanced in their favor. It is not enough to say, "I think, therefore I am" or, "I feel, therefore I am" or, "I observe the law, therefore I am." God's presence requires all our capacities in interaction with one another. One must always strive to be able to respond, *"Hinéni;* here I am, present to You."

Notes

INTRODUCTION

1. There are many books on the modernization of the Jewish community. The difference between the modernization of the sephardi and ashkenazi communities of France is very instructive. Cf. A. Hertzberg, *The French Enlightenment and the Jews* (New York: Schocken Books, 1968/1970). On the modern dimensions of hasidism, see the preliminary statement in D. Blumenthal, *Understanding Jewish Mysticism*, vol. 1, (New York: Ktav Publishing, 1982), 193–196.

2. The basic work in English on Levi Yitzhak is by Samuel Dresner, *The World of a Hasidic Master: Levi Yitzhak of Berditchev*, updated edition (New York: Shapolsky, 1986, paperback). Short descriptive notes can also be found in the *Encyclopaedia Judaica*, "Levi Isaac ben Meir of Berditchev," 11:102–103, and in E. Wiesel, *Souls on Fire* (New York: Summit Books, 1982), chapter 5. The *Encyclopaedia Judaica* and Dresner disagree on the year of Levi Yitzhak's death; I have adopted the date given by the former.

   Throughout this book the word "rabbinic" does not mean "pertaining only to rabbis." Rather, it means "characterized by the type of Judaism formulated and practiced by traditional Jews in the centuries since the turn of the era" (see glossary). Since this type of Judaism was formed and taught by rabbis, we call it "rabbinic."

3. Dresner, *The World of a Hasidic Master*, 128.

4. Ibid., 107. Dresner gives both the original and his translation. Here I give my own translation. The original has both Hebrew and Yiddish, and I have indicated Hebrew by use of quotation marks. Cf. also Blumenthal, *Understanding Jewish Mysticism*, vol. 2, 153.

5. Dresner, *The World of a Hasidic Master*, 64–65, 80.

6. The pairs of references are as follows: Isaiah 40:25 with Jeremiah 9:23; "An'im Zemirot," in *The Authorized Daily Prayerbook*, edited and commentary by J. H. Hertz (New York: Bloch Publishing, 1960), 214; Maimonides, *Guide of the Perplexed*, I:58, edited by Shlomo Pines (Chicago: University of Chicago Press, 1963), 134, with *Mishne Torah*, "Hilkhot Yesode ha-Torah," 1:1, *A Maimonides Reader*, translated by I. Twersky, (New York: Behrman House, 1972), 43; and the section of this book entitled, "Being and Nothing in Spirituality" (pages 7–9) with Zohar, I:243b–244a cited and explained in Blumenthal, *Understanding Jewish Mysticism*, vol. 1, 151.

7. Cf. H. A. Wolfson, *Religious Philosophy* (New York: Atheneum, 1965), 1–68 and H. A. Wolfton, *Studies in the History of Philosophy and Religion*, edited by I. Twersky (Cambridge: Harvard University Press, 1973), vol. 1, 98–114. For a less technical presentation, cf. D. Blumenthal, "Lovejoy's *Great Chain of Being* and the Medieval Jewish Tradition," in *Jacob's Ladder and the Tree of Life*, edited by M. L. and P. G. Kuntz (Bern and New York: Peter Lang, 1986), 179–90.

8. On Jewish mysticism as a subset of Jewish spirituality, cf. Blumenthal, *Understanding Jewish Mysticism*, vol. 1, xv–xviii, 185–91, and vol. 2, 197–9.

9. On zoharic thought, cf. ibid., vol. 1, unit 2, with special reference to the diagrams (116–18) and the deciphering method of interpretation (113–19); G. Scholem, *Major Trends in Jewish Mysticism* (New York: Schocken, 1961) chapters 5 and 6; and *Encyclopaedia Judaica*, 16:1193 ff.

10. See the Thematic Index for further references to this term.

11. On Lurianic thought, cf. Blumenthal, *Understanding Jewish Mysticism*, vol. 1, 159–76; Scholem, *Major Trends*, chapter 7; *Encyclopaedia Judaica*, 11:572 ff.; and the section of this book entitled, "Mystical Creation," pages 3–4.

12. On hasidism, cf. Blumenthal, *Understanding Jewish Mysticism*, vol. 2, unit 2; Scholem, *Major Trends*, chapter 8; *Encyclopaedia Judaica*, 7:1390 ff.; and J. Dan, *The Teachings of Hasidism* (New York: Behrman House, 1983).

13. Shemuel Yosef Agnon was one of the outstanding Hebrew writers of the century. He won the Nobel Prize for Literature in 1966. This story appears in English in Agnon, *In the Heart of Seas*, translated by I. M. Lask (New York: Schocken Books, 1980).

14. Heschel's bibliography is considerable. One can start with *Man Is Not Alone* (New York: Farrar, Straus, and Giroux, 1976), or with *God in Search of Man* (New York: Farrar, Straus, and Giroux, 1976), or with the anthology of his works edited by Fritz A. Rothschild, *Between God and Man* (New York: Free Press, 1959). The last contains a full bibliography.

15. André Neher, *The Exile of the Word*, translated by D. Maisel (Philadelphia: Jewish Publication Society, 1980); French original reviewed by me in *Association for Jewish Studies Newsletter 31* (1982):6.

16. See, for instance: G. Lindbeck, *The Nature of Doctrine* (Philadelphia: Westminster Press, 1984); W. Lowe, *Evil and the Unconscious* (Chico: Scholars Press, 1983); and the works of C. Geertz, D. Tracy, and others.

17. See, for instance: D. Saliers, *The Soul in Paraphrase* (New York: Seabury, 1980); D. Saliers, *Worship and Spirituality* (Philadelphia: Westminster Press, 1984); L. Dupré, *The Deeper Life* (New York: Crossroad Press, 1981); and the works of M. Basil Pennington, especially *O Holy Mountain* (New York: Doubleday, 1978).

18. See, for instance, the works of James Cone, José Miguez Bonino, Nancy Hardesty, and others.

19. Translated by S. Pines (Chicago: University of Chicago Press, 1963), 7. On Maimonides's philosophic mysticism, cf. D. Blumenthal, "Maimonides: Prayer, Worship, and Mysticism," in *Approaches to the Study of Judaism in Medieval Times* (Decatur: Scholars Press, 1987) 1–16.

20. Cf. D. Blumenthal, "Religion and the Religious Intellectuals," in *Take Judaism for Example*, edited by J. Neusner (Chicago: University of Chicago Press, 1983), 117–142.

21. M. Wyschogrod, *The Body of Faith* (New York: Seabury Press, 1983) 173–74, reviewed by me in *Association for Jewish Studies Review*, 11:116–21.

22. The word "presence" is capitalized when it stands alone, as in "the Presence," but not when it is modified by a noun or pronoun which refers directly to God, as in "God's/His presence."

ON SPIRITUAL COUNSELING (YITRO)

1. Maimonides, *Guide of the Perplexed*, III:51, edited by Shlomo Pines (Chicago: University of Chicago Press, 1963).

ON BUILDING A SANCTUARY (VAYAKHEL)

1. On this, cf. the *Sefer Yetsira* tradition in D. Blumenthal, *Understanding Jewish Mysticism*, vol. 1 (New York: Ktav Publishing, 1982).

JEW-HATRED (BALAK)

1. For a similar analysis, see Jacques Maritain, *Antisemitism* (London: G. Bles, Centennary Press, 1939).

ON WAR AND WANDERING: AN INITIAL MEDITATION (MATOT-MAS'EI)

1. Maimonides, *Code of Law* (Book of Judges, Laws of Kings, chapter 5, paragraphs 1–5).
2. Maimonides, *The Book of the Commandments*, Positive Commandment 187.
3. Drawing upon Maimonides *Code*, ibid, chapter 6, paragraph 1.

LAND, LANGUAGE, AND STATE: AN EXCURSUS INTO ZIONISM (DEVARIM)

1. H. Fisch, *The Zionist Revolution* (New York: St. Martin's Press, 1978), 17–18.

ON BEING CHOSEN: A POST-HOLOCAUST REFLECTION (VA'ETHANAN)

1. "Amidah," J. H. Hertz, editor, *The Authorized Daily Prayerbook*, rev. ed. (New York: Bloch Publishing, 1960), 143.
2. C. S. Lewis, *Reflections on Psalms* (New York and London: Harcourt Brace Jovanovich, 1964), 9–19.
3. Daily liturgy, "Avinu Malkenu," Hertz, *Daily Prayerbook*, 166; ibid., "Taḥanun," 178; ibid., New Year Liturgy, "Amidah," 854.

4. Hertz, *Daily Prayerbook*, Day of Atonement Litergy, "Amidah," 920.
5. Ibid., Day of Atonement Liturgy, "Ne'ilah," 932–934, quoting Ezekiel 33:11.
6. Ibid., "Taḥanun," 184.
7. Ibid., 186.
8. Ibid., 186.

THE VIRTUE OF PRIDE (VEZOT HA-BERAKHA)

1. M. Prager, *Sparks of Glory*, 9–13, cited in D. Blumenthal, *Understanding Jewish Mysticism*, vol. 2 (New York: Ktav Publishing, 1982), 104–107.

KAVVANA: THE ART OF JEWISH PRAYER (SUKKOT)

1. Taken from D. Blumenthal, *Understanding Jewish Mysticism*, vol. 2 (New York: Ktav Publishing, 1982), 112–114.

THE TORAH AND THE MESSIAH (SIMḤAT TORAH)

1. E. Wiesel, "Against Despair," Pincus Memorial Lecture, 1973.

AFTERTHOUGHTS

1. Two of Heschel's books contrast this nicely: *God in Search of Man* and *Man's Quest for God.*
2. I have called the circumscribing of mysticism by the rabbis, "the rabbinization of mysticism." It is what makes Jewish mysticism "Jewish." Cf. D. Blumenthal *Understanding Jewish Mysticism*, vol. 1 (New York: Ktav Publishing, 1982), 189–91. Rudolph Otto in *The Idea of the Holy* tries to isolate the numinous from the moral. That cannot be done within the Jewish understanding of the holy.
3. On these types of Jewish mysticism, cf. D. Blumenthal, *Understanding Jewish Mysticism*, vols. 1 and 2. I am not convinced that there is only one type of mystical experience precisely because of the variety of paths that lead to the ultimate point(s). I disagree, then, with Louis Dupré (*The Deeper Life*, New York: Crossroad Press, 1981) and others who understand mystical experience only to be unitive and who then define that experience to be the vitalizing core of all other spirituality. The reverse seems to me to be true.
4. On this, cf. also Blumenthal, *Understanding Jewish Mysticism*, vol 1, 185–187 and vol. 2, 197–199 where the formulation is not as clearly put forth as here. Cf. also the

distinction of "prophetic prayer" from "mystical prayer" in Friedrich Heiler, *Prayer* (London: Oxford University Press, 1932/1938), chapters 7–9.

As I indicated in the Introduction, I recognize that the masculine language I use may inhibit women coreligionists from experiencing the fullness of the spiritual dimension of the tradition. I repeat my urging that those who feel this way create a language of their own which will embody their own understanding of the spiritual depth of Judaism.

5. J. Soloveitchik, *Halakhic Man* (Philadelphia: Jewish Publication Society, 1983), 19–22.

Suggestions for Further Reading

In the area of Jewish spirituality, the works of Abraham Joshua Heschel are central: *God in Search of Man* (New York: Farrar, Straus, and Giroux, 1976); *Man is Not Alone* (New York: Farrar, Straus, and Giroux, 1976); *Who is Man?* (Stanford, California: Stanford University Press, 1965); *The Insecurity of Freedom* (New York: Schocken Books, 1972). All these books and others have appeared in several editions. An anthology of Heschel's writings was prepared by Fritz Rothschild, *Between God and Man* (New York: Free Press, 1959) which, in its later editions, has a complete bibliography of Heschel's work.

In two essays, *The Place of Faith and Grace in Judaism* (Austin, Texas: Center for Judaic-Christian Studies, 1985) and "Mercy," in *Contemporary Jewish Religious Thought*, edited by A. Cohen and P. Mendes-Flohr (New York: Scribners, 1987), 589–596, I have tried to make a modest contribution to the elucidation of two central concepts of Jewish spirituality in the modern context.

In the area of Jewish mysticism, the two volumes of texts with commentary and explication which I published still remain a good place to begin: *Understanding Jewish Mysticism* (New York: Ktav Publishing, 1978 and 1982). Frankly, I think it is easier to begin with volume 2. Each of those volumes has a section entitled Suggestions for Further Reading. The other anthologies in the field do not have commentaries. For those interested in the Zohar, the new selected translation by Daniel Matt, *Zohar: The Book of Enlightenment* (New York: Paulist Press, 1983) is very fine.

In the area of hasidism, E. Wiesel, *Souls on Fire* (New York: Summit Books, 1982) remains the most accessible to the lay reader. Arthur Green and Barry Holtz, *Your Word is Fire* (New York: Paulist Press, 1977) is short but very intense. And Louis Jacobs, *Hasidic Prayer* (New York: Schocken Books, 1972) is very scholarly.

For both Jewish mysticism and hasidism, the *Encyclopaedia Judaica* is an excellent place to begin scholarly research.

On Levi Yitzḥak, the basic work is Samuel Dresner, *The World of a Hasidic Master: Levi Yitzḥak of Berditchev*, 2d ed. (New York: Shapolsky, 1986). See also the article in the *Encyclopaedia Judaica* and the chapter in Wiesel's *Souls on Fire*.

Works on contemporary Jewish spirituality are harder to find. Jewish energy is largely devoted to Jewish communal concerns on the local, national, and international scenes. A search of the *Index to Jewish Periodicals* under "Ḥavurah" (Hebrew for fellowship group) might be useful. Similarly, occasional articles in such current periodicals as *Response* and *Sh'ma* may yield some results. It would be helpful to have a journal for Jewish spirituality and Jewish creative theology.

There has been a renewal of theological work in orthodox Jewish circles. I call the reader's attention to Michael Wyschogrod, *The Body of Faith: Judaism as Corporeal Election* (New York: Seabury Press, 1983); Joseph Soloveitchik, *Halakhic Man*, translated by L. Kaplan (Philadelphia: Jewish Publication Society, 1983); Joseph Soloveitchik, *On Repentance*, translated by P. Peli (Paulist Press, New York: 1984); Joseph Soloveitchik, "The Lonely Man of Faith," *Tradition* 7:2 (Summer 1965): 5–67; and David Hartman, *A Living Covenant* (New York: Free Press, 1985).

It is my personal conviction that modern Jewish spirituality will be a matter of individual conviction and dedication. I welcome correspondence and suggestions from concerned persons. My address is: Department of Religion, Emory University, Atlanta, GA 30322.

Glossary

The reader is urged to consult also the Introduction and the various passages of the book which deal with these matters as indicated in the Thematic Index.

annihilation: see bittul.

anthropopathic: having human feelings; contrasted with "anthropomorphic," having human shape. Traditional Jewish theology teaches that God is anthropopathic but not anthropomorphic.

attention: see *kavvana*.

Ayin: nothingness; the ineffable, inexpressible dimension of of God; refers to the sefira Keter.

bittul: a mystical technique in hasidism in which one loses all sense of self and is aware only of God and His presence.

C.E.: the Common Era; contrasted with "A.D." (anno domini, the year of our Lord), the usual Christian designation of this era.

classical Judaism: see rabbinic Judaism.

contraction: see tsimtsum.

creation: the universe as a whole, including humankind and human history, guided by God; contrasted with "nature" which has connotations of impersonality and independence from God's guidance.

devekut: attachment or clinging to God; has different meanings at different levels of Jewish spirituality.

etrog: a citron or lemon-like fruit used ceremonially on the holiday of Sukkot.

exile: the state of not living in the holy land; also the state of not living in God's presence or of living in nonmessianic times.

experiential: having to do with experience; contrasted with having to do with intellectual or social patterns of understanding and acting.

grace: God's love to us independent of whether we deserve it or not; contrasted with "compassionate love," which is His love for us in covenant, that is, His love insofar as we have deserved, or are entitled to, it through our deeds and faith.

Haggada: the liturgy for the Passover meal.

halakha: traditional Jewish law; includes ethical and civil, as well as ritual, dimensions of life.

hallel: Psalms 113–119; recited liturgically as praise on certain holidays.

Ḥanuka: the holiday celebrating the victory of the Maccabees over the Seleucid Greeks, in which the temple was recaptured and purified, 176–174 B.C.E.

hasidism: the movement which began in eighteenth-century Poland and is still alive today, and which emphasizes immediate spirituality in Jewish life and practice; Levi Yitzḥak was one of the leading figures in the third generation.

holiness: the quality inherent in people, texts, places, and ceremonies which makes them distinctively religious or spiritual; not identical with "aesthetic" or "moral" although, in Judaism and Christianity, there is a certain overlap.

holocaust: the systematic extermination of six million Jews, including their humiliation and degradation, during the second world war.

hoshanot: a series of prayers recited on the holiday of Sukkot in which we circumambulate the synagogue carrying the lulav and etrog and ask God to have mercy upon us.

kabbala: the stream of Jewish mysticism which derives from the Zohar and its successors; its central feature is the ten sefirot (q.v.).

kavvana: the technique of directing one's consciousness to one's acts, including prayer, so that one can intend those acts as worship of God.

Luria, Rabbi Isaac: a sixteenth-century kabbalist who developed the theory of tsimtsum, shevira, and tikkun (q.v.).

lulav: a palm branch used on the holiday of Sukkot.

Maimonides: a twelfth-century scholar whose overwhelming authority in Jewish law and philosophy dominated the Jewish Middle Ages and continues into today.

mazzah: the unleavened bread eaten by Jews on Passover in commemoration of the unleavened bread eaten during the Exodus.

meaning: the dimension of life that makes sense and gives significance to our acts and thoughts; used also in the context of God's will and our service to it.

menorah: a candlelabra; the one in the sanctuary had seven holders and the one used during Hanuka has eight holders.

midrash: the process of interpreting Scripture; also an anthology of such interpretations.

mitsva (pl. **mitsvot**): a command of God; used to refer to ethical and civil, as well as ritual, commandments.

Nothing: see Ayin.

omer: the grain offering given on Shavu-'ot; the period during which one counts the fifty days between Passover and Shavu'ot.

rabbinic Judaism: the Judaism developed by the rabbis between the first century and current times; characterized by such institutions as the rabbinate, rabbinical schools, the development of Jewish law, the traditional liturgy, and so forth; contrasted with secular Judaism and certain forms of modern liberal Judaism; also called "traditional" or "classical" Judaism.

Rashi: an eleventh-century exegete of the Bible and Talmud whose commentaries are read by all rabbinic Jews.

rebbe: hasidic term used for the spiritual and political leader of the community; has spiritual authority which extends beyond that of the usual rabbi; see zaddik.

rehabilitation: see tikkun.

Rosh ha-Shana: the Jewish new year; characterized as the Day of Judgement and the beginning of the ten days of repentance.

saint: see zaddik.

Sefer Yetsira: a second-century book describing the creation of the world from letters.

sefira (pl. **sefirot**): In the kabbalistic stream of Jewish mysticism, there are ten sefirot internal to God. They represent aspects of His character, so to speak. They contain and channel the divine energy; they are interactive. The acts of humankind rechannel the divine energy back to God. This allows humankind a certain "influence" over the inner dynamic stability of God. The ten sefirot are: Keter, Ḥokhma, Bina, Ḥesed, Gevura, Tiferet, Nesaḥ, Hod, Yesod, and Malkhut. They can be represented symbolically in the form of a tree (see diagram, page xix), or in the form a person, or a sea, and so forth.

sephardim: Jews who lived in the culture sphere of Islam; refugees from Spain and Portugal after the Inquisition there (1492–1497 C.E.).

Shabbat: the Sabbath day; used interchangeably with "Sabbath."

Shavu'ot: the holiday of Pentecost; commemorates the bringing of the first fruits and the giving of the Torah.

shells: the remnants of the primordial vessels which shattered after the primordial light penetrated to them and they could not contain it.

shevira: the shattering of the primordial divine light and vessels as the former penetrated into the universe and proved to be too powerful for the latter to contain.

shofar: a ram's horn blown on Rosh ha-Shana to arouse God's mercy in judgment.

sparks: the fragments of the primordial divine light after the shattering.

sukka (pl. **sukkot**): the booth in which Jews lived in the desert and in which Jews observe the holiday of Sukkot.

Talmud: the written compilation of the previously oral law which includes legal as well as ethical and instructive material; has two parts, the Mishna (ed. 220 C.E.) and the Gemara (ed. 500 C.E.).

tikkun: the process of meditatively redeeming the sparks that, according to Lurianic kabbala, were scattered through creation after the first unsuccessful attempt at creation.

tsimtsum: the process by which God, Who occupied all space, contracted and created space for the universe to come into being.

Torah: the first five books of the Bible; a scroll containing those five books.

Yom Kippur: the Day of Atonement; characterized by fasting and confession of sin.

zaddik: a saint or righteous man; in hasidism, the rebbe; said to have special spiritual powers and hence special responsibilities.

zimzum: see tsimtsum.

Zohar: the central work of kabbalistic mysticism, probably written in the thirteenth century; contains the doctrine of the sefirot.

The Lectionary Cycle of Readings

GENESIS

Bereshit	1:1–6:8
Noaḥ	6:9–11:32
Lekh Lekha	12:1–17:27
Vayera	18:1–22:24
Ḥayye Sarah	23:1–25:18
Toldot	25:19–28:9
Vayetse	28:10–32:3
Vayishlaḥ	32:4–36:43
Vayeshev	37:1–40:23
Mikets	41:1–44:17
Vayigash	44:18–47:27
Vayeḥi	47:28–50:26

EXODUS

Shemot	1:1–6:1
Va'eira	6:2–9:35
Bo	10:1–13:16
Beshalaḥ	13:17–17:16
Yitro	18:1–20:23
Mishpatim	21:1–24:18
Teruma	25:1–27:19
Tetsave	27:20–30:10
Ki Tisa	30:11–34:35
Vayakhel	35:1–38:20
Pekude	38:21–40:38

LEVITICUS

Vayikra	1:1–5:26
Tsav	6:1–8:36
Shemini	9:1–11:47
Tazri'a	12:1–13:59

LEVITICUS

Metsora	14:1–15:33
Aḥare Mot	16:1–17:30
Kedoshim	18:1–20:27
Emor	21:1–24:23
Behar	25:1–26:2
Beḥukotai	26:3–27:34

NUMBERS

Bamidbar	1:1–4:20
Naso	4:21–7:89
Beha'alotkha	8:1–12:16
Shelaḥ Lekha	13:1–15:41
Koraḥ	16:1–18:32
Ḥukat	19:1–22:1
Balak	22:2–25:9
Pinḥas	25:10–30:1
Matot-Mas'ei	30:2–36:13

DEUTERONOMY

Devarim	1:1–3:22
Va'etḥanan	3:23–7:11
Eiqev	7:12–11:25
Re'eh	11:26–16:17
Shoftim	16:18–21:9
Ki Tetse	21:10–25:19
Ki Tavo	26:1–29:8
Nitsavim	29:9–30:20
Vayelekh	31:1–31:30
Ha'azinu	32:1–32:52
Vezot ha-Berakha	33:1–34:12

Thematic Index

This is a thematic index, not a word index. Hence, the references are to each meditation. Furthermore, reference is made to the appropriate meditation even if the specific word indexed is not found there. To locate and trace ideas, the reader should also make use of the Introduction, Contents, and Glossary.

Source Index